THE MANAGEMENT OF NORMALITY

Critical Essays in Health and Welfare

ABRAM DE SWAAN

ROUTLEDGE
London and New York

FOR ELLEN, MY WIFE, AND MEIK, OUR SON

First published 1990
by Routledge
11 New Fetter Lane, London EC4P 4EE

Simultaneously published in the USA and Canada
by Routledge
a division of Routledge, Chapman and Hall, Inc.
29 West 35th Street, New York, NY 10001

Laserset by LaserScript Limited, Mitcham, Surrey
Printed and bound in Great Britain by
Biddles Ltd, Guildford and King's Lynn

British Library Cataloguing in Publication Data

Swaan, Abram de
The management of normality.
1. Social control
I. Title
303.3'3

Library of Congress Cataloging in Publication Data

Swaan, A. de.
The management of normality / Abram de Swaan.
p. cm.
Bibliography: p. .
Includes index.
1. Social norms. 2. Conformity. 3. Helping behavior – Case studies. 4.
Social adjustment – Case studies. 5. Dependency (Psychology) – Case
studies. 6. Medical care – Sociological aspects – Case studies. I. Title.
HM73.S89 1990
303.3'2 – dc20
89-10352
CIP

ISBN 0-415-03200-8

CONTENTS

INTRODUCTION

Maintaining normality is hard work: a body must be rested, cleaned, groomed, and clothed every day; it must be fed properly and decorously at the correct time and it must be made to walk the right tracks and talk the right things. Such normality presupposes that everyone else behaves more or less as expected, and that the entire society pursues its appointed course, so that for any one person the preconditions of achieving his or her individual normality are fulfilled. Society thus enables its members to pursue their business as usual, and at the same time it compels them to do so. Whatever becomes a possibility for many turns into a necessity for everyone. If some physical defect or affliction can be cured, it must be. If a majority can read, the others thereby become illiterates who must also be taught to read and write. If running water becomes generally available, it puts everybody under constant pressure to wash.

The conditions for achieving normality having been realized for everyone, its canons having become widely accepted, deviance is attributed solely to personal failure, to an individual handicap that should be corrected by the proper specialist. What once was the sole province of priests has now become the task of policemen and teachers, doctors and psychotherapists, and other normalizers. But they could never accomplish this task without some complicity on the part of their clients, patients, students, and charges and without subtle pressures from the wider environment.

Complicity, however, already implies dissimulation and latent conflict. There is indeed a shifting balance between manifest collaboration and tacit opposition in the relations between those who come for help and those who profess to provide it. This goes

1

together with a manifest dependence of these help-seekers upon the providers of the services, but also with a much less apparent, latent dependency of the latter upon the former, a changing balance of dependencies between the two sides. This study sets out to analyse what goes on at the intersections between personal lives and the professional or institutional sphere, focusing on latent dependencies and latent conflict.

However, there is in this book a third and broader interest. It is tempting to confine the research and the analysis to these personal–professional encounters: patients obligingly stay in their wards; doctors and therapists are always to be found in their offices; and, moreover, the helping professions publish a flood of self-justifying (and thus incriminating) material for sociological study. Since the professional circle seems to have the upper hand, nothing is more obvious than to explain everything in terms of the professionals' design (more or less selfish or selfless depending on the author's *parti pris*). But, as mentioned, there are latent dependencies and latent resistances that work the other way. There is, however, another consideration: the rise of the professions is itself to be explained and so is the change in sensibilities, in *mentalités*, in the wider society, which is not solely the result of professional intervention and discourse. The encompassing social transformations that form the context from which the professions have emerged also altered the relations between people in general, and with these relations their modes of conduct and experience also changed, and the kinds of troubles they made for themselves and with others. Therefore, a study of modern sentiment, of contemporary psychic problems, cannot be limited to the professions and their impact alone, but must take into account other, broader transitions in society, changes in the actual dependency relations that tie people to and against one another.

None of this is particularly original or profound. On the contrary, it seems all quite obvious, almost a truism. Most people would agree – quite a few sociologists, even – but in the abstract, in general. When confronted with actual episodes of seeking and providing help, people generally find themselves drawn into an entirely different discourse, recommending some course of action as beneficial, advising against another as damaging to the treatment, or justifying one party and blaming the other. In short, even when they are not directly involved personally in the episode, they cannot resist adopting the perspective of some participant in it for the simple reason that in actual life that seems the more interesting, the more pressing consideration: after all, there is a real problem waiting to be solved then and there. Sociologists, on the other hand, also rarely adopt in their work the approach sketched above. It may be that they have placed themselves in the service of the parties involved, advocating clients' interests or decrying institutional abuse, or, more frequently, carrying out applied social research for hospitals or government agencies. And even if they take a more detached approach, their particular method of research may impose other terms upon them, which appear more precise and more systematic, but at the cost of being less realistic.

Most, maybe all, of the basic tenets of social science are truisms. Almost everybody agrees at first sight, almost everyone knew it all along – except that most people all along have also held the opposite to be true, without being much bothered by the contradiction. Thus everyone agrees that human beings in society are interdependent, and yet, in daily life people tend to think of healthy adults as persons who can take care of themselves, who are literally 'independent'. But of course, the best that people can ever hope to do is to make sure that others take care of them; the more resources they have at their disposal to achieve this, the more they are said to be of 'independent means'. Truisms all, but not all of them true. Social science is based upon platitudes, good social science is based on true platitudes, and what is difficult is to abandon the equally familiar false ones. Because social science starts out so commonplace, there is an unquenchable thirst for profundity. 'There must be more to it than that.' No, there is less to it than most pretend. Sociologists are not much better at explaining social processes than well-informed, detached, and judicious lay persons, but that is already quite good and sociologists might still do somewhat better. And as soon as sociologists come up with new and interesting findings, these are absorbed right away by the public and their origin in sociology is soon forgotten. Sociologists are somewhat ahead of most in understanding the way society works, but it is only a small lead. It is this slight edge, this uneasy margin that makes sociologists uncomfortable about their professional position and prompts them to seek a safer place in society.

A general *sauve qui peut* is going on in social science in every direction, and sociologists especially are in a continual panic. One year finds them as rebels and reformers, demanding and recommending social transformation; the next they have become language interpreters, declaring society to be really a text; and another year later they have turned into computer analysts modelling society as an information flow. There is a flight forward into contract research for subsidizing agencies and a flight backward to the idolization of natural science; a flight outward into pop sociology or public posturing and a flight inward into jargon, method, or exegesis; there is a flight upward into grand but groundless theory and a flight downward into asking, counting, adding, and factoring; and finally, there is the flight rightward into resentful conservatism and the flight leftward into gratuitous progressivism.

However, some social scientists, and certainly many sociologists among them, should stay with the main task, to explain how societies and the human beings that make them up have developed. That is the great tradition of social science, and among the classical predecessors my allegiance is most of all to Marx and Freud (but not with all that they wrote). I never felt much torn between them, but that is mostly on account of Norbert Elias whose sociogenic approach and concept of figuration have helped much to conceptualize individual human beings and their emotions as part of an ongoing, encompassing societal process. Much of what has been discussed so far can be found in his writings, and much else in addition. Elias is often considered somewhat of an eccentric among social scientists, deserving, if not of being read and quoted, at least of the highest praise, but wholly outside of the mainstream of academic social science. This is a fundamental error. Elias has confronted the central task of social science in the tradition of the classical authors, and his historical, sociological investigations into state formation and the civilizing process have pointed to a new course for mainstream social science to follow.

Most questions of method and theory remain implicit in the essays in this collection, which were written to clarify substantive problems in the sociology of the emotions and of the helping professions. Nevertheless, a common approach underlies these studies.

4

First of all, the explanation of social processes must be both dynamic and historical. Social reality is to be explained in terms of structured processes; the more phenomena are considered as changing, the fewer aspects are held constant, the more dynamic the approach. The more events from the actual past are taken into consideration in the explanation, the more historical it is. But the two need not coincide. A historical but static approach to classical Greek society is perfectly conceivable; and a dynamic approach, say, to the conjunctural cycle, may hardly refer to prior actual events.

Although transitions may occur in dramatic spurts, history does not proceed in discrete stages. Foucault and others have presented a contrary concept: as in a kaleidoscope, with a sudden twist one complex and fascinating pattern, after a brief moment of chaos, turns into a different structure. But this begs the question of who or what does the twisting. The present approach is in many senses evolutionary: subsequent phenomena are explained from those that preceded them; these changes have a pattern or structure; society is a process and it continues to change. But these transformations do not have a single cause, nor a single direction; their course cannot be predicted, and they do not necessarily proceed from a 'lower' to a 'higher' stage in any ethical sense.

Three simple metaphors may help to clarify some of the difficulties of 'sociogenetic' and 'psychogenetic' argument in sociology. First, the notion of a clock with wheels which turn at different speeds; some cogs, moving so slowly that the observer hardly notices any movement, nevertheless drive other, faster wheels, which finally connect to a balance wheel, which by its frenetic oscillation controls the movement of the entire machine. In the description of social processes, short-term changes must be both distinguished from and connected to transformations on a larger time scale and to underlying developments in the long and very long run. Thus, within the very slow clock of biological time turn the wheels of human history and within it again, much faster, the cogs of succeeding generations. There is the rhythm of the species, the rhythm of societies and of individual lives. But that is where the metaphor stops, since clocks are cyclical and periodical, while biological evolution and human history within it occur only once.

The second metaphor is that of scale. Each scale has special rules of description and verification, just as a cartographer will apply particular rules of simplification and abstraction, or elaboration and concretization, depending on the scale being used. The analysis must move from single persons and face-to-face relations to larger figurations and even nations or global society, and move back again to institutions or groups and intimate relationships.

Finally, there is the image of the web, of patterned connections. Although people appear to be enclosed in a crust of skin and clothes, in truth they are connected. And although each one perceives himself, and equally herself, as a *Homo clausus* (a term much used by Elias), a person can only be understood by considering his or her relations to others. The metaphor of the web also encompasses the observers, as intricately entangled in the pattern of relationships as the objects of their scientific attention. 'Studying human beings' is one way of relating to them, 'studying society' one way of being part of it. There is no vantage point outside the human community, no privileged position from which to observe it; one may at best disentangle oneself, but one can never be disconnected. An observer may be a bit more detached, but even that stance in itself is not sufficient for understanding. Insight requires at one level reflexive detachment, and at other levels involvement. In order to understand how people relate to one another and themselves, empathic involvement is required. In order to explain these relations as part of a wider figuration, one needs analytic detachment. And finally, the enterprise of sociology as such presupposes a commitment to human society in general. Thus there is an immediate involvement for the sake of sociological detachment, and an analytic detachment for the sake of intellectual commitment. The greater the awareness of the ways in which people are tied together, the observer included, and the greater the capacity to adopt the various sociological stances as they are required, the more reflexive the sociological enterprise.

Human beings must be seen as intersections in a network and these networks again as part of a wider figuration of relations: society as a whole. But people cannot be understood from this actual network alone. They have developed in earlier networks, from the pristine mother–child dyad on. These preceding relations have shaped them and still continue to affect them, through memories invoked and repressed, through inner dialogues and recurrent scenes. People are also involved in relations that are neither actual nor past, but imagined: anticipated or expected, feared or hoped for, existing as an interior colloquy or tableau, and, once more, they may not allow themselves these fantasies with so many words or images, and yet they live with them.

Just as in the theories of conics and optics, the actual figure or focus is completed with a 'virtual' counterpart, which is necessary to explain its actual complement, so in order to understand the conduct and experience of human beings in society their actual relations may be complemented with their virtual relations, those from the past, remembered and repressed, and those from fantasy, imagined or also repressed. This brings psychoanalysis into the field of sociology, or at least the psychoanalytic conception of repression and unconscious fantasy. Freud's psychoanalysis may indeed be read as a radically relational approach to human development.

The conceptual pair of 'psychical' and 'social' usually refers to what goes on 'inside' persons and 'between' them. But in this radically relational approach a person is conceived of as an intersection in a network, and 'psychical' refers to the 'virtual' and more 'intimate' relations in this network, 'social' to the 'actual' and more 'distant' relations.

Human beings may not be aware of the figuration of which they are a part, of the nature of the prevailing interdependencies, and therefore they may ignore or misunderstand the results of their actions. It is because of these unintended consequences of human actions that developments may occur as a 'blind process'. With the hindsight of later generations and with the overview of more detached observers, social scientists may reconstruct the figuration, identify the interdependencies, and explain the process as one that is unintended, and yet the aggregate result of actions with an intent partly or wholly different.

Human beings may not allow themselves to articulate their fantasies with so many words. They may have repressed them, the strivings having literally become 'unthinkable' to them. And even if they allow themselves to think of their strivings in so many words, they may still not express them in any given social episode: such strivings remain 'unspeakable' to them. When people can afford to think and express their strivings, they may nevertheless find them completely impracticable in a given episode and they will not even try to act upon the strivings and consider them 'infeasible'. Finally, they may feel that their strivings can be realized, but that they lack legitimacy in some vocabulary of justification that is relevant in the episode and they find their strivings 'unacceptable'. Thus, in any episode people may repress their strivings in various modes and degrees of concealment.

Again, as a relatively detached outsider, the observer may try to extricate him- or herself from the situation, reflect upon it, and try to find the virtual relations, to find what is in any situation unthinkable, unspeakable, infeasible, and unacceptable.

To reconstruct the figuration of interdependency and to reconstruct what cannot be thought, said, done, or condoned requires an act of the imagination – the sociological imagination; it requires interpretation. Such interpretation is by no means arbitrary; on the contrary, it sometimes may be compelling in the way in which some riddles or crossword puzzles have an immediately convincing solution no matter how difficult it was to find. At other times, when the context is more ambiguous, the interpretation remains more open to doubt.

Since individuals are not completely aware of the figuration of interdependency they form with others, and ignore part of their own strivings and those of others, their own statements are not the last word, the society they constitute is more than the texts they produce. The surplus in understanding comes from sociological interpretation. Sociologists have no monopoly on such understanding, but their profession is the only one which has as its sole calling the understanding of society and does not also have another task, in the management of normality.

THREE THEMES

The first part of this collection deals with doctors and patients. At its core is a study of a cancer ward. At the time the psychoanalyst Andries van Dantzig initiated a project to study the management of anxiety among cancer patients, and his ideas on the 'system of hope' guided much of the research, which was undertaken by a team of two psychoanalysts, two sociologists, and a psychologist. The administrators of the hospital refused to allow publication of the research report, but many of the findings could be corroborated from other sources, and that is how the Dutch version of this text was rewritten.[1]

By that time I was a candidate of the Netherlands Psychoanalytic

Institute, taking a training analysis and receiving patients for short-term psychotherapy and full psychoanalysis. And the challenge was to apply some techniques I had learnt in the consulting room to a wider social setting.

The central concept in the study of the cancer ward is repression, both in its social and its psychical sense. I tried to look at it with a sociological and a psychoanalytic eye: in the cancer ward anxiety, and with it anger and jealousy, had to be controlled, in part by conjuring them away with the might of medicine. The social order of the hospital could be interpreted as a defence mechanism and the repressed content might be traced back in somatizing displacements, professional rationalizations, and in the eccentric episodes of comedy, anxiety attacks, and loss of decorum.

Again with the support of Andries van Dantzig, a research project was initiated on the sociology of psychotherapy in the Netherlands with the collaboration of four young sociologists. One part was a historical sociology of Dutch psychotherapy, its contested professionalization and institutionalization; another part consisted of an analysis of initial interviews. Now that the object was psychotherapy, the perspective became more sociological (maybe for fear of competing with the psychoanalytic insight of the psychotherapeutic subjects themselves). The attempt was to find the hidden structure of the initial interview and to relate it to its social context.

The studies on the sociogenesis of the emotions, included in the third part of this collection, could not be based on observation or interviews, but had to rely on the literature. By then I was no longer so aware of either the psychoanalytic or the sociological viewpoint, but tried to look with both eyes, and see depth. The basic question in these pieces was whether changes in people's emotional expression, and by inference, their experience, could be related to transformations in the larger society of which they were a part. Could the spread of agoraphobia be connected to the disappearance of restrictions on the movement of women? Or can the rise of intimacy be related to the general prevalence of shielded homes with separate rooms for the parental couple and the children and special spaces for isolated bodily acts, for preparing food, and for joint domestic activities, such as eating, watching TV, and entertaining guests? Is there a special 'downward jealousy' that makes itself felt to a social stratum under increasing 'pressure from below', as Elias has called the competition from the next lower social grouping? And can private pathology be related to the absence of public elaboration of historical events?

Although most of it was written much earlier, in many respects this volume may be read as a sequel to my *In Care of the State* (1988). In that book my main concern was with the 'collectivizing process', a long-term development on an ever-expanding scale. The collectivizing process is the mostly unintended outcome of social conflicts in which powerful and wealthy strata of society have sought to ward off the threats emanating from the poor in their midst and to exploit the opportunities with which the same poor presented them. But in minimizing these dangers and maximizing the opportunities, the established strata in society had to engage in collective action among themselves. The dilemmas this created for the elites often paralysed all initiative, but sometimes were resolved by state intervention. It is this emergence of collective arrangements for coping with individual adversity and deficiency that forms the historical antecedent and the social context of the processes that are discussed in this volume over a briefer time-span and with a more limited scope. In the course of collectivization education, health care, and welfare have become the province of large, bureaucratic institutions, closely tied to the expanding state. Such institutions are staffed with professional experts each managing a specific clientele which is transformed in the process, as it comes to live more and more under a medical, an educational, or a welfare regime. These institutions form the environment within which doctors and their patients, psychotherapists and their clients operate.

One transformation in the societies people form with one another is the emergence of groups of specialists who claim special competence in dealing with specific categories of problems. They define the problems, and increasingly people articulate and experience their troubles in those terms and come to present them for treatment in a relatively new kind of relation, a client–expert relationship. This is, indeed, one of the unifying themes of the present collection.

On the whole these essays are being reprinted here as they appeared in the original, except for the translation.[2] I have made no attempt to update the references to the literature in systematic fashion, but whenever I have come across titles or quotes which I found especially interesting or pertinent, I have not hesitated to add them. In translating and re-editing these texts, I have of course made changes whenever they seemed improvements to me.

PLAN OF THE BOOK

Part One: The medical regime

A medical regime has established itself over the population of modern societies. In everyday life it exists in an extensive but not very intensive version: as a permanent and general alert for the early warning signs of ill-health: it operates through mass screenings, routine tests, physicals for insurance and job appointments, and school and company health check-ups. But it constitutes a total regime for institutionalized patients, controlling almost all aspects of their lives for a shorter or more extended period of time.

Chapter 1   Disease and dependency

A person may be seen as an intersection in a network of dependencies. The stages of human life may then be characterized by particular states of this network: a total dyad in the first month of life, gradually evolving into more numerous, more different-iated relations as an infant grows up, relates to siblings and other relatives, makes friends, enters school and, still later, the workplace, and so on. The child mainly depends on others, but as a person grows up others come to depend on him or her: in other words, the balance of dependencies shifts as the individual becomes more needed and less dependent. In old age the network shrinks again and, on balance, dependence increases.

This normal pattern may be disturbed by disease. The disease process involves loss of function, social and physical, and causes increasing dependence. The network contracts until only a few caring relatives are left and one bond of dependency becomes predominant: the 'medical nexus' with the doctor. A radical sociological theory of the disease process and of health care may be formulated in these terms of network contraction, increasing dependency, and progressive loss of social functions. This is the sociological complement of the medical interest in the loss of physical functions.

Chapter 2   Affect management in a cancer ward

The medical regime operates in its total form in the cancer ward. The disease takes over, the patient's network contracts, and as social functions are abandoned, almost complete dependency on the medical nexus and a few relatives results. The cancer ward is a community geared to the management of anxiety. The time schedule of the coming medical treatment divides up the future in small steps, granting some expectations until the next intervention. In the cancer ward the main consolation and every new hope come from the next medical treatment. In the hospital, too, a decorum must be maintained; a pseudo-medical notion that self-control helps the cure and that loss of control hampers it, serves to maintain discipline and a semblance of normality.

Information and support are the scarce values in the affective economy of the hospital. The patients exert their demands upon the nurses and interns, and the latter, in turn, pass it on to the specialists, who can never supply enough. The ward is organized to protect the staff against this overload.

Within the social context of the hospital order, staff and patients may employ coping strategies of their own. Patients may displace a tacit wish for support by an overt claim for treatment, and staff may overtly ask task guidance by superiors instead of emotional comfort. Patients may manoeuvre themselves into a state of exception, as the ward comedian, or as an anxiety psychotic, or find that the restrictions on expression are relaxed for patients losing their sense of decorum.

Chapter 3   Expansion and limitation of the medical regime

The medical regime operates in a light and extensive form throughout modern society. By now, whoever is not a patient is considered a not-yet patient: a permanent alert for the early warning signs of disease is in operation; mass screenings, routine check-ups, physicals for insurance clients, military recruits, and job applicants process the entire population. Entire categories of apparently healthy persons are declared, *a priori*, medical subjects: pregnant women, infants, senior citizens. Everyone is under constant pressure to stay fit and avoid harmful pleasures. Under the medical regime a growing range of everyday activities and events acquire a medical meaning and are managed according to doctors' instructions. But the doctors did not assume power like a clique of corporals. Rather, theirs was a 'reluctant imperialism'. Like others, individual doctors strove to maximize the chances of income, prestige, and the realization of professional ideals, time and again exploring new social niches for medical intervention. More often than not medical men succeeded in re-defining and encapsulating socially contested situations as medical-technical problems. But they did so with the complicity of the parties involved in the conflict, who stood to gain from this medical re-definition. The profession as a whole was more reluctant to claim controversial fields as its legitimate province of authority: the conflict might invade its ranks and undermine the professional consensus which constitutes the basis of its authority in society at large.

Part Two: The psychotherapy trade

Chapter 4   On the sociogenesis of the psychoanalytic situation

The psychotherapeutic setting, secluded and confined in space, limited in time, may well have been Freud's greatest sociological invention. A reading of Freud's writings on technique and of contemporary manuals for the general practitioner show that his procedure consisted in a consistent and radical application of the rules of modern medical practice as they emerged at the time to his new 'talking cure'. Freud's insistence on a contractual relationship, 'on complete candidness in exchange for absolute discretion', on punctuality in time and payment are related to the social circumstances in which he found himself in the early stages of his career.

Freud did indeed invent a new, dyadic social relationship in which one person, the client, articulates all his emotions according to the rule of association, while the other, the therapist, refrains from the expression of personal preference, judgement, or even advice, in accordance with the rule of abstention and is sworn to absolute confidentiality. As the confessions remain protected by the seclusion and confidentiality of the therapeutic setting and are not acted upon in any way, everything may be expressed without practical consequence. Someone who is allowed to say anything may allow himself to think anything.

Chapter 5 From troubles to problems

The internal process of professionalization creates external effects among ever-widening circles of laymen, who adopt the basic stances and fundamental concepts of the profession as means of orientation in their everyday life: it is a process of 'proto-professionalization', in which laymen learn to recognize some events as 'a case for the lawyer', others as 'a suitable case for treatment', and so on. A proto-professional lay person is an expert in re-defining everyday troubles as problems amenable to treatment by this or that profession; he or she organizes the everyday world according to the existing division of labour among the professions.

In the recent past, psychotherapy has gone a long way down the road towards professionalization without achieving the privileged status that medical doctors have acquired. The professionalizing process in psychotherapy has resulted in a re-definition of troubles among informed lay persons in 'proto-psychotherapeutic' terms. People who are socially close to professional circles are the first to be so proto-professionalized, but formal education – mostly by way of its hidden curriculum – also conveys such knowledge. More recently, mass media have organized their editorial format according to the same professional division of labour, always obligingly allowing the last word to the appropriate expert.

The establishment of a profession owes much to intellectual achievements – sometimes even to scientific accomplishments – but it is also the result of a struggle with adjacent professionalizing groups for the demarcation of competences between them, and accordingly for access to potential clienteles. Psychotherapists had to carve a niche for themselves in the midst of pastoral helpers, nurses, social workers, psychologists, general practitioners, and psychiatrists. They succeeded in doing so by using medical strategies of professional organization, by claiming medical privileges for the protection of their profession and for the financing of their services, and by pitching their version of the canons of scientific treatment against the religious and moral precepts of pastoral workers.

14

Chapter 6 The initial interview as a task

The structure of the initial interview which serves to select clients for one form of psychotherapeutic treatment or another reveals in its features many of the structural characteristics of the professional division of labour around the psychotherapy profession. Thus, in the first phase of the intake interview a sequential elimination occurs, of medical problems first, psychiatric symptoms next, until some troubles remain as a residual category, fit only for psychotherapeutic intervention. The problems that belong to the competence of the surrounding, competing professions are peeled away like onion skins, until a psychotherapeutic core problem remains.

As there are no external diagnostic means to verify the patients' complaints, the problem to be treated must be reconstructed from the clients' own account of their troubles. Within the brief and condensed episode of the office hour, the psychotherapist and the client together must construct a fragmented, negative autobiography of the client in which the latter appears as socially competent and accountable for what went wrong in his or her life. If the two succeed in this task, the client is considered fit for psychotherapeutic treatment. Clients who have been protoprofessionalized are much more likely to collaborate adequately in this biographic work than complete outsiders who have not yet picked up the basic notions and attitudes of professional psychotherapy.

Part Three: Emotions in their social matrix

Chapter 7 The politics of agoraphobia

Mental problems are not just 'out there', or rather 'in there', in the way most medical afflictions may have a cause that can be ascertained by external diagnostic means independently of the patient's foreknowledge and understanding. Such mental problems must be articulated, told and 'made' by the patient and his therapist. In that sense, they represent social constructions. Recent research has given much attention to the definition process with respect to mental problems within the helping professions themselves. But mental problems are not simply psychiatric inventions which are next compliantly reproduced by patients seeking a receptive ear for their complaints. They also reflect contested social relations; accordingly, an increase in their prevalence is revealing of transformations in wider society. 'The difficulties which people encounter with others and with themselves change as their relations with each other change. Within these relationships they develop a vocabulary and a conceptual system which allow them to verbalize their difficulties and thus to experience them in a specific manner' (see Chapter 7:139). Agoraphobia made its appearance in the literature around the time that the restrictions on the movement of women in public were being relaxed. The refusal to leave home alone which before was taken as proof of decent self-restraint now had to be explained in terms of an incomprehensible and overwhelming anxiety. Changing relations of dependency within the family may have caused domestic tensions which had to be resolved by the formation of an anxious–protective couple, one forever shielding the other, the other keeping close watch on her protector.

Literary and social historical accounts of women's behaviour at home and in public are used to reconstruct a sociogenesis of agoraphobia. The historical sociological premises of this approach are made explicit in a polemic with the modern moralists of the Frankfurt school (Adorno, Marcuse) and its contemporary American successors (Sennett, Lasch).

Chapter 8   Jealousy as a class phenomenon

Envy is directed 'upwards', towards those who have or are more, but there exists also a 'downward' jealousy towards those who may obtain or become what one is or has already. Between groups, too, jealous relations may prevail, one group envying another which it considers to be more privileged, or jealously protecting its own advantages against another group, even if the former does not stand to lose anything from the latter also acquiring them. Such jealous group relations characterized the conflict between the independently employed bourgeoisie and the organized working class over the introduction of compulsory social insurance in the period 1880–1940.

Chapter 9   Intimate relations and domestic arrangements

The material conditions of everyday life constitute the precon- ditions – that is, the historical antecedents and the functional requirements – for the modes of interaction and forms of experience of the people living them. Thus, the very possibility of intimacy is predicated on the availability of domestic spaces that may be shielded from outsiders, shared with chosen partners. Modern family homes are constructed as a stage for the enactment of such intimate scenes with an exclusive cast and for an audience on invitation only. The development of urban housing serves as the background for a discussion of bourgeois intimacy.

Chapter 10   The survivors' syndrome

The survivors of concentration camps are the victims of a man-made disaster. Increasingly, their fate has been defined under the technical heading of 'survivors' syndrome', and has become the subject of professional discourse and intervention. Yet the main problem of many former concentration camp inmates arises out of the impossibility of telling others in a meaningful way what they have been through. As a consequence, the task of listening to their tales became the province of professional helpers. In this manner, the testimony of the political history of mass murder was transformed into a succession of complaints in the consulting room. What are essentially public issues have been reduced to private troubles, for lack of a public and political elaboration of the war experience which might have granted the survivors a status as witnesses in a cause of concern to the entire political community.

Part One

THE MEDICAL REGIME

Chapter One

DISEASE AND DEPENDENCY

In striving to realize their objectives, human beings are for ever dependent on one another; everyone depends on other people and almost everyone is needed by some others. That is what conveys to people their significance for their fellow human beings and that is where they find the fulfilment of their existence.

Human beings are the nodes in a network of dependency relations, and for any person these dependencies may be more or less in balance. Someone upon whom many others depend but who does not need those others to the same degree occupies within the network a position with a power surplus. Yet, such a person will still depend on others, even if it is only to maintain and strengthen this power position. Although the terms are somewhat different, these are key thoughts from the sociology of Norbert Elias.[1]

The course of these dependency relations may be described for a specific case, but they are difficult to measure or even compare, and network positions are even harder to evaluate. A 'balance of dependencies' or a 'power surplus' has therefore only metaphorical meaning.

In most people's lives the network of dependencies develops in a roughly similar manner. Children are born in total dependency upon their mother, and only gradually do they develop attachments to other people around them – a father, siblings, grandparents, other relatives and friends, teachers, or class mates. Throughout childhood the network is small in size and the balance remains tilted towards dependency.

Step by step the network is extended and differentiated: in various relationships different objectives are realized and one single relationship does not remain total and all-encompassing. As a person becomes an adult, other people come to depend on him or her, the ties growing in number and becoming more specific, while the balance of dependencies may shift in the direction of a relative power surplus, at least with respect to the intimate network. At that point a person is 'in the prime of life'. Sometimes imperceptibly, but at times quite abruptly, the balance of dependencies may shift again; a person finds that those around him or her begin to detach themselves and seek others with whom to achieve their objectives: the children leave home, it is time to retire from one's job, the network shrinks back to a few close relatives and a couple of friends. That is ageing.[2]

This pattern of development is not a law of nature, even though physiological processes play their part in it. Women who have raised their children, for example, nowadays often find a job outside their home, making new acquaintances and in so doing extending their network while making themselves more needed in their new relationships, until in old age their network of dependency relations shrinks again.

It is possible to describe the course of a disease in terms of changes in this network of dependencies: in terms of a process of increasing dependency. Protracted diseases, especially diseases that get worse, make patients increasingly dependent upon the persons surrounding them, often more and more dependent on ever fewer people.

In a medical perspective, what matters is the loss of bodily functions; in this sociological perspective what counts is the loss of social functions, the contracting and condensing of the network of dependency. It is this notion of increasing dependency that is at the core of a radical sociological theory of disease and health care.

Even as the network of the patient contracts, new relations of dependency are formed: the 'medical nexus' with the doctor in the first place.

When, for whatever reason, someone abandons or loses the functions in society that go with his or her social position, it must be either from unwillingness or incapacity. 'Increasingly, it seems that deviance can be subsumed only under crime or sickness and that other possibilities – witchcraft, spiritual intervention, sin, bad taste, poor manners, and the like – are less and less available.'[3]

If it is not unwillingness, it must be incapacity. If someone cannot do what he or she is expected to be able to do, he or she must be sick and should see a doctor. If it is not unwillingness, the person must want to get better and co-operate in the treatment. This is how Talcott Parsons describes the 'sick role', the role in which those who allow themselves to be labelled sick by the people around them end up.[4]

Inappropriate and unwanted loss of functions in modern society is conceived of as disease and brings the sufferer under a medical regime. Sometimes the patient comes with complaints and the doctor 'can't find anything'. No connection can be found between the patient's complaints and the results of a physical examination that is independent of the patient's foreknowledge and intentions.[5] The doctor has only the patient's information to rely on. In such a case the complaints may be brushed aside as imagined or fabricated, but in recent times doctors have tended to relegate such cases to a 'residual category' in medicine, that of mental problems.[6] Then follows a referral to different kinds of doctors: psychiatrists, psychologists, and psychotherapists.

The point is that manifold conceptions percolate through society as to what a person of a specific age and gender and of a specific social position should want and what he or she should be capable of. If the person is willing but unable to function, the search for a disease begins.

> Medical definitions of disease constitute a special type of social deviance. The norms applied are socially defined with respect to biological functioning. Judgments are made as to whether or not the organic processes exceed permissible limits . . . if so, it is judged that a pathology is present, the individual in question is sick (i.e. deviant) and should be subjected to the controls of a therapeutic regimen.[7]

This socially recognized incapacity entails, next to loss of bodily functions, a loss of social functions. The sick become more dependent upon others for the achievement of their objectives and can provide less of whatever those others may need from them.

In this respect the medical and the sociological perspective run parallel: disease and ageing may be considered as processes of loss of function – too early in the case of disease, in due time with ageing. The notions of chronic and acute, and of progressivity or deterioration, are key concepts in both perspectives.[8]

What distinguishes the sociological from the medical vision is the doctors' interest in biological processes within the sick person against the sociologists' attention to developments in the network of relations around the sick person.

One cannot decide in general what comes first and what is worse, bodily or social loss of function. Such questions of primacy and priority are issues to be fought out in the confrontation between adherents of a 'medical model' and a 'social model', in the competition between a well-established medical professional circle and the more recent professional circles of medical sociologists, social psychologists, social workers, and so on. In every single case and for every individual sufferer deterioration and dependency are aspects of one and the same agony. The members of these professions are the ones to determine which complaints are to be dealt with in each particular instance. Bodily complaints tend to be treated with priority, since the helping services have been arranged so that doctors will usually be the first to be consulted, medical technique having evolved in a manner which allows them to do something concrete, and because physical complaints often are taken as a danger signal for a risk of further deterioration.

And yet most complaints refer to a 'feeling', precisely in the double meaning of physical sensation *and* of state of mind, of biological process *and* emotional experience: anxiety, stress, depression, aggression are only a few from a sequence of terms which suggest that people live in relations with other people that may actually make them sick, affect their bodily functions. Social processes such as exclusion and labelling may equally provoke sickness behaviour and induce physical deterioration.

People can make one another sick – actually, by contaminating one another; more inscrutably, by blaming and blackmailing one another, compelling and harassing, threatening and humiliating, by proclaiming others deviants and excluding them. All this may occur in small circles and in intimate relations, but broad social developments may also contribute to the spread of disease: harmful working conditions, pollution of the environment, malnutrition, and so forth. The exclusive medical attention for biological processes in a patient who has been identified is a quite recent development in medicine: eighteenth-century medical intervention also implied speculations and conversations about the overall life situation of the patient; and nineteenth-century medicine was dominated for a long time by a 'medical police', who investigated sanitation and nutrition, housing and working conditions, and strove to improve them. Only in recent times has the focus of attention in the medical profession broadened again beyond the strictly physical processes within the patient who reports for examination. If it cannot be decided what comes first and which approach should have precedence, it is equally impossible to determine in general what is worse for the sufferer, the bodily or the social loss of function.

A word like 'pain', which denotes first of all a physical sensation, acquires its social meaning in the context of a complaint that is meant for someone to do something about it, something medical or otherwise human. The physical decay that comes with sickness and old age is also experienced as a loss of independent functioning, as a need of help from others, as solitude, and sometimes even as expulsion. It never stands alone, just as no one stands on his own; it is bad in its entirety.

In matters of disease, the primacy and the priority of the physical aspects and the medical approach are not intrinsic in the nature of things, but are the result of a social solution that people have gradually developed in order to cope with a loss of function considered to be unwanted and inappropriate. This socially constituted solution is the medical regime: the totality of precepts that medical doctors prescribe to their fellow human beings, the domination of doctors over the means of orientation, the modes of experience and ways of conduct in matters of repair and maintenance of functions.

The conclusion that this regime is not for all time and that it has been much extended and intensified in recent years has an accusatory ring to it – as if a cabal of doctors had grabbed power like a sergeants' junta. Studies of the relationship between 'doctor' and 'patient' often attribute such a dominating and initiating role to the physician. Only in more recent research is the patient portrayed as someone who, albeit from a lesser, more dependent, position, nevertheless intervenes actively in the interaction – for example, by presenting his or her complaints selectively, ordering them, and bargaining implicitly or with so many words about diagnosis and treatment, by exacting information or ignoring it, by shopping around or playing off the medical personnel one against the other, and by complying or not with the doctor's precepts.[9] That does not refute the vision of medical dominance, but corrects and confirms the notion of asymmetric dependency relations between doctors and patients, in which the balance veers towards the doctors, who nevertheless remain dependent on their clientele in its entirety and therefore must show their individual patients a certain degree of courtesy.[10] In a more encompassing social context, equally, the establishment of a medical regime was not the achievement of a determined iron cohort of medical men, but on the contrary, the unintended effect of social conflicts in which doctors became involved, apparently had solutions to offer, and time and again were allotted new managerial functions.

As this medical regime was being established, in society at large people began to orient themselves to medical instructions for more and more aspects and phases of their lives, in the process becoming increasingly dependent on doctors. In the course of every individual disease dependency increases, offset in part by establishing a nexus with the medical regime – in part, because patients also remain embedded in relations with 'lay people', with relatives and friends, and, in the hospital, with their fellow patients.

Such dependency relations have received little attention in medical sociological studies: family and work relations are usually mentioned in a perfunctory manner and that settles the matter.[11] If any attention is paid at all to this 'natural' or 'informal' network,[12] it usually remains limited to the relations with a life companion, the salutary 'affective spouse'.[13] No studies exist of the changes in the patient's network of dependencies in its entirety as a consequence of the disease process.

It has been reported in the literature that the nature of the relations in which a person lives helps to determine his or her tendency to notice complaints, discuss them, and present them to a physician as a problem that may be suitable for treatment.[14] The familiarity with the various helping agencies is also a function of network characteristics: in tightly closed networks, in which everyone knows everyone else, lay persons will not be referred as quickly to professional helpers as in an open network in which most contacts in their turn know others who may not know the sufferer but who may well be familiar with the helping professions.[15] The compliance with medical precepts may be facilitated or opposed by people in the environment, and the surrounding network determines to a high degree the kind of support and care which a patient may receive during illness.[16]

Nevertheless all these studies are mainly concerned with problems of health care; what occurs between the sufferer and those around him or her is usually ignored. Yet the first thing that happens when people fall ill is that they can no longer do their work; they no longer have to, because disease is an acceptable reason for absence, and they are no longer able to because their bodily functions diminish. In the short term sometimes that may be a welcome interruption, in a longer perspective it implies that the sick will lose significance for those around them, who depended on them at first but now can no longer achieve their objectives through them and so gradually begin to establish dependency relations with others and finally need the patients no more. That applies in work situations, and, of course, also in the family context. Loss of function affects all other relations, in sports and leisure activities, in the circle of friends, and in the community. Those who fall sick can no longer do what once they could; the sicker they are, the less they accomplish.

As the disease progresses, sick people can do less and less for others and less and less for themselves. When it is said of people that they can take care of themselves, what is usually meant is that such persons can make sure that others will take care of them, that they can return every favour with a counter-favour which is considered its equivalent. Such people buy what they need and pay with money that they themselves have earned (or inherited, or won, because in such ways too, one acquires 'independent means'), and if they do not pay for the services of others, then they will make sure to return the favour soon.

Sick people can take care themselves of their material needs by paying doctors, nurses, and homemakers, or having them paid by sickness funds or health insurance. However, a good part of such care is provided by close relatives who receive no pay for it and who can expect no immediate favours in return; sick persons become very much indebted to those around them. As the disease progresses, the expectation that such services can ever be compensated disappears.[17]

Increasing dependency goes with status anxiety and loss of

status: sick people become the lesser, the asking party, who need more from others while having less to offer them. And although usually people strenuously deny the asymmetry of their relations, their denials do not refute the fact.

But sick people can use their annoyance value, their capacity to invoke pity, shame, and a sense of obligation in others, feelings that are inspired by the idea that their condition is no fault of their own and that others may fall ill as well – feelings, therefore, that are instilled by excusation and identification. However, these remarks concern the strategies and counter-strategies that the sick may apply in order to compensate to some degree for their loss of bodily and social functions.

What occurs in the relation with the doctor reverberates in the other relations in which the patient is embedded. Every precept that the doctor gives implies a loss of social functions for the patients and limits their interaction with others. This appears most clearly and rigorously when patients are told to stay in bed, but it also applies when they are told not to smoke or drink, to keep a diet, to go to sleep early, to refrain from sport or travel, or to take it easy while at work. When the disease is chronic, and that means that it takes a long time before the process shows decisive improvement or deterioration, the course of the disease begins to determine the patient's temporal perspective. Plans for the near future are abandoned and all designs come to depend on the doctor's prognosis. The near future is charted according to the phases of the treatment and marked by the test results: until the next operation, the forthcoming hospital admission, the next laboratory analysis.

This perspective also permits a description of the relations of power and the forms of control that develop between the sick and their caretakers: how, for example, the sick are incorporated in the medical regime which for the duration of their illness governs their modes of interaction and forms of experience. Sick persons must compel themselves to comply with the doctor's precepts and to behave as the shifting relations of dependency demand. They are pressured into such self-limitations by the doctor and admonished by their closest relatives. Even as the temporal perspective of sick persons shrinks, much more than others they must think in everything they do of their near future: they should not tire themselves, neither eat nor drink too much, not get excited, take their medicine punctually, and so forth. Especially in the early phases of the disease process, when patients can still do much which they should no longer do, they are confronted with an acute problem of control in which the doctors occupy the role of the admonishing party, the agent of external compulsion: their precepts are emphasized once more by the patients' close relatives, and the sick comply because they care about their health. Compliance in the medical sense is a form of docility imposed and reinforced within a relational network. By subverting the doctor's precepts many patients force the people around them to intensify supervision and pressure, but these again are strategies and counter-strategies within given relations of dependency. (Such disobedience may carry the tacit meaning that someone who does not heed the doctor's orders does not really need them and is not really so ill. The rebellion against the doctor and against one's relatives who exert medical pressure by proxy is also the resistance of someone who has been forced to surrender positions of relative power in a shrinking network of increasing dependency.)

As the network of dependencies contracts, the temporal perspective shortens, and this again causes a loss of connections: vacation companions turn to others, colleagues seek others with whom to collaborate once they can no longer count on the sick person for the near future.

These phenomena are all too familiar, they need no confirmation from the professional literature, they are known from the everyday experience of sick people and those who are involved with them. Such observations are scarce in medical-sociological literature anyway, being too commonplace and considered as side effects, at best. But to a sociologist this social loss of function ought to represent the core of the disease process. Just as disease and ageing are catch-all labels for specific bodily processes which nevertheless may be described and understood in general biological terms, likewise increasing dependency is a catch-all label for specific social processes which are to be described and understood in general sociological terms of the balance of dependency and power within networks.

This view entails a programme for a radical sociological approach of the problems of disease and health care, and no more than that. What happens in actual fact must each time be investigated more closely. In the following essays this is done twice, once in depth and once in breadth.

The medical regime is exercised in the most incisive and encompassing manner in the hospital for chronic disease, where patients are immersed in a total order, an order which controls their complete functioning: their bodily functions, but also their affect management and their interaction with others.

But the medical regime not only controls the seriously ill, it also affects people who are not yet sick – all others – but who in their everyday lives and in their critical decisions follow medical guidelines. The expansion of this light medical regime is the unintended effect of countless incidental solutions to personal and social conflicts in which medical people have become involved. Both in the total form in which it is exercised in the hospital and in the light version in which it has expanded over society in its entirety, the medical regime serves not only recovery, but also the control of conflicts within and between people. At the same time, however, this management function of the medical establishment threatens to undermine its position of authority.

Chapter Two

AFFECT MANAGEMENT IN A CANCER WARD

In clinics or special wards for the treatment of diseases with a protracted course and a real risk of death, the people who together make up the hospital community face specific emotional and relational difficulties. In the collective effort of coping with these difficulties, certain ways of maintaining order emerge and certain forms of affect control are transmitted, constituting together the affect management of the hospital.

For anyone who has been part of this community for some time these shared modes of interaction and the corresponding forms of experience have come to be taken for granted, as part of oneself, and every encroachment is felt to be an assault upon the togetherness of the hospital community. Even the description of this order may be considered an attempt to tarnish it.

In the context of this form of affect management, continually recreated and re-confirmed by the others in the hospital, individual patients and staff may adopt various defence strategies to cope with the difficulties that may face them at any moment. A preference for one or another strategy corresponds to a particular personality structure: in any given episode, some will tend to withdraw or repress, and others may try to find a way out by manipulating or acting out, while still others succeed in creating an exceptional status for themselves. In this chapter, the shared affect management and some individually adopted defence strategies will be discussed in succeeding sections.[1]

In chronic disease the first danger signs are often trifles: congestion, continuing fatigue, blood in the stools, discharge, persistent bruises, or small lumps. This is not a characteristic of chronic disease, but a consequence of medical vigilance: doctors

31

and proto-professional patients tend to be on the alert for small signals pointing to dangerous diseases. That is why they will investigate these general and vague indications even before more specific symptoms appear, with an eye to the possibility of heart defects, multiple sclerosis, or cancer.

Interpretation of these general danger signs of course begins with the sufferers: they may or may not notice them, may be more or less worried, may talk about them with someone close to them who may then supply a different interpretation of the complaint. What meaning will be attributed to such minor ailments is unpredictable; it changes with the degree of proto-professionalization in the clients' circle of intimates, with their overall tendency to worry and complain, with the accessibility of a doctor and the expectations the sufferers hold of the diagnosis and treatment. The family physician may listen to the complaints, examine the patient and then either declare that there is nothing to worry about, or refer the sufferer to a specialist, 'just to make sure'. In increasing numbers people come to see specialists even without having noticed anything themselves, but because such danger signals were found during routine testing, mass check-ups, or periodic physicals. In such cases the initiative is entirely with the doctors.

The specialist, on his part, may decide that the complaint is innocuous or have the patient investigated further. If laboratory tests or clinical diagnostics do not reveal anything alarming, the patient is back at the family physician to have his minor ills cured. Even then the patient is not through with it, receiving extensive reassurance and some precepts for decreasing common health risks. But with a positive test result, the patient is drafted into the medical regime.

THE ORDER OF THE HOSPITAL AS A FORM OF AFFECT MANAGEMENT

The first notification is a double message: something serious is the matter and it may be helped. Patients who are referred to a special clinic may draw their conclusion as to the nature of their disease. Practically every adult in the area knows such a clinic by name and understands what it stands for. Yet, many patients succeed in not letting the indication sink in or give it an entirely different twist. In the case of cancer, for example, doctors will usually avoid this or related terms, such as 'malign tumour'; they prefer to talk about 'tumours' or 'growths' that might get worse. If the patients choose to call it a 'polyp' or a 'myoma', the doctors will not contradict them. But the ominous referral comes with the message that everything humanly possible will be done about the ailment. Frequently, cancer clinics are connected to a research institute and have some repute as institutions for technically advanced treatment. If there is a chance of a cure anywhere, then it must be there.

As threatening for the patient as is the message that something must be done, so reassuring is the message that something can be done. With this double hold of fear and expectation the patient is inducted in the medical regime.

The patient has been told that he or she is seriously ill: that the disease may get worse; that it is a chronic illness; that recovery and deterioration may occur over a period of many months and even years. But from the start the physician places this gloomy view in the perspective of treatment: a further prognosis can be had after the results of the first tests are known. Next, expectations are coupled to the outcome of succeeding trials, and then to the effects of subsequent interventions, and so forth.[2] The patient does not get to prepare for permanent loss of functions, let alone for approaching death, since new data are always on their way and must be awaited in the weeks to come. And, who knows, a new remedy will yet be found. Through the treatment process the course of the disease is fragmented into small episodes of hope, disappointment, and renewed expectations; the confrontation with fate is postponed time and again. In this manner, the medical treatment itself acquires a sedative function and serves to help the patients to push aside their anxieties and worries for the time being.[3]

In the case of serious, chronic disease, hospitalization may occur at any time, and patients must put aside all other activities for it. Admission often cannot be arranged ahead of time, nor can the period of treatment and recovery be planned in advance. All other projects in the patient's life thus become dependent on the disease agenda: study plans, vacations, career decisions, changes of address, or large purchases.

This in turn means that persons around the patient find it hard to make arrangements for the near future. Sports companions must find other company or accept the uncertainty, colleagues and superiors at work can no longer count on the patient's availability and must either risk that the work remains undone or find some replacement.

What matters in general is that in this phase patients cannot avoid making an appeal to the willingness of their colleagues, friends, and relatives to help them out and thus may find themselves increasingly indebted to them (or finally provide them with the occasion to make good on old debts of their own).

But as the patient is drafted into the medical regime, another, entirely new set of dependency relations becomes effective: the clientele relations with the arrangements of care – the health insurance in the first place, whether a public plan or some commercial scheme. In most European countries specialist care and hospital treatment are covered so completely that re-imbursement is well-nigh automatic, often without the patient having to do or know anything about it. For employed persons the same applies to income loss due to illness: reimbursements depend on medical-administrative formalities carried out by the doctor and insurance officials; the patients have hardly any part in it. This automatism is a triumph of bureaucracy and a great blessing of the system.

Matters are more complicated when coverage is not so complete, or when the patient needs material provisions and services that are not regulated as exactly and exhaustively: special facilities at home, nursing care, housekeeping assistance, and so on. Such provisions are granted only after special permission which does not come without some enquiry into the patients' means and circumstances. Usually a medical social worker or a community nurse must intervene and at the least interview the patient who may not know precisely which answers will help the request and which will not.

At best, bureaucratically organized and professionally provided care constitute 'an example, in practice, of what a compassionate society can achieve when a philosophy of social justice and public accountability is translated into a hundred and one detailed acts of imagination and tolerance'.[4] But it may fall short, far short, of this ideal.

Patients obtain these services and provisions without an immediate compensation on their part. They have paid insurance premiums or payroll taxes for them, but the size of their contribution is related only indirectly, if at all, to the costs of the provisions they now receive. This is a matter of course since insurances are involved, the patients having entered a stake as in a betting game, and also when social insurances are involved, where this stake is adapted to the patients' financial resources. But in the patients' experience, things may look very different. They receive costly services and an entirely unaffordable treatment, without doing anything in return: they 'receive' something and 'are being treated and cared for'.

For every problem which occurs in the course of the disease, a specialized expert is assigned to the patient. If an ailment requires adaptations in the home or work environment, the rehabilitation expert appears. If the patient's condition threatens to disturb family life, the family social worker intervenes. If the disease attacks new regions of the body the appropriate specialist is called to the bedside. If the patient panics, begins to rage, or completely withdraws – at any rate, becomes unmanageable – the psychiatrist is called in for consultation. In other words, the disease is factored out in as many separate factors as there are helping professions; every expert treats his or her case, one as an insurance problem, another as a matter of disturbed family relations, a third as a problem of special provisions, a fourth as a metastasis, and a fifth as a psychiatric complication.

While the patient's worries are thus dispersed among a multiplicity of experts, in the hospital attention remains focused on the physical disease process. Only when the patient has become a case in some other respect also, specialist help is recruited for that one added aspect, effectively separating it from medical care. This may degenerate into complete fragmentation and helpless confusion on the patient's part.

Clearly, patients usually do not feel that they hired the services of a medical doctor, but that they enjoy the privilege of the physician spending costly time and much-demanded expertise on their case. Not only do the doctors have to compete for the patients' favours, but also the patients need the doctors' help; the doctors prescribe medicine and treatment to the patients, the patients follow these instructions and are more or less compliant or docile.

Where in the perception of the patients and those around them there is no reciprocity and no equal exchange, there looms a sense of humiliation and degradation, of stigmatization. These feelings may be warded off by a show of gratitude or awe in 'compensation' of the helpers,[5] or, on the other hand, patients may over-compensate their feelings of dependency by demanding, complaining, and accusing. But much of this can be avoided by a better understanding of the exchange relations embedded in the wider context of the system of insurance premiums, taxes, disbursements, and fees. Ignorance and uncertainty[6] on the patients' part increase the asymmetry in the dependence relations with the doctors who monopolize information:

> certain kinds of goods and services may be of such a nature that they create marked inequalities of status between providers and users in any kind of exchange situation. This is especially likely to occur when one party has a monopoly, or near monopoly, of expert knowledge.
> Medical care offers a relevant example of this unequal distribution of knowledge.[7]

Doctors and especially medical specialists belong to the highest income category in the national economy. They earn more than the bulk of their patients. Their prolonged training and their special skills convey to them a prestige far exceeding that of the great majority of their patients. This preponderance of social prestige is further reinforced by the bedside manner of most medical doctors, a true rendition of the grand bourgeois customs of half a century ago, probably passed on by their professors as 'general medical decency'.

The hospital is a strongly hierarchical community, the specialists are above the interns, the nurses have less prestige than the doctors. Because of their age and experience, the head nurses are not simply the inferiors of the young doctors, who can only rely on formal knowledge. This status-inconsistency between the two different prestige hierarchies gives rise to the classic conflicts in which novice doctors clash with 'know-better' nurses. Such differences may allow patients with a gift for manipulation an opportunity to conquer marginal privileges, obtain more pain relievers, 'because the doctor says it's all right', longer visiting hours, greater freedom to move around the ward, or early dismissal, 'since the nurse did not mind at all'.[8] But in principle, the patient must accept staff judgement, not because young nurses should have more say than patients, but because they derive their authority from the doctor and the head nurse. Only when patients succeed in playing off the nurse against a superior – for example, by obtaining permission for some small privilege from senior staff – can they afford to ignore her instructions.

The young women serving the meals are held in lower esteem than the nurses, but they at least have had some training. At the bottom of the status ladder are the cleaners, often unskilled immigrants, complete outsiders to medical care and devoid of special responsibilities. They may deal more freely and candidly with the patients; without fear of being manipulated for favours or telling the patients more about their condition than they should know. They have no privileges or information to give out at all. The cleaners being so insignificant, patients on their part make less of an effort to keep up appearances in their presence, and that too makes interaction less contrived.

In principle all patients are equal to the medical profession and therefore also to the hospital. The distinction between first-class and lower-class wards, which persists in the Netherlands and else-where, conflicts with this professional approach and with contemporary ideals of equality. Interns and nurses tend to be offended by the difference and try to undo it by joking. Patients in the 'class' ward, trying to obtain extra privileges; may quickly meet with silent resistance inspired by a professional and democratic egalitarian ethos. Patients do not get preferential treatment by demanding privileges; they must be prominent, rich, famous to deserve them. Still other preferences operate in the clinic: the fate of young people affects fellow patients and the staff much more strongly than that of the aged. The decay of the elderly is accepted with greater equanimity, 'since dying is really something for old people'. The mostly young staff tends to identify more with young patients. Mothers and small children also evoke strong sympathies in the hospital, as does everyone who still stands in the midst of life, has a job, a family: 'Their time has not yet come.' The patients' 'social value' in the outside world also plays a role in the hospital.[9]

The hospital is a community in which the staff spends a good part of its days for many years and the patients all of their time for a brief period. The patients are expected to adapt to the customs of the hospital, and these rules are justified down to the smallest and sometimes most implausible detail with the requirements of medical treatment, hygiene, and the tranquillity indispensable for recovery: the new patient who unceremoniously throws his jacket on a chair is reminded that this is an 'unhygienic' thing to do.

That patients should stay in bed, even when they are still mobile and active, is for their own good. That they can have only few belongings with them is for the sake of order, not just domestic neatness, but medical order: to avoid contagion or to reserve space for their medicine. That everybody should have a fixed place at the table is not a matter of courteous arrangement, but permits everyone to be served without mistakes with the proper medication.

Hygiene as a rationalization of medical discipline is not a recent phenomenon. Norbert Elias has suggested and Johan Goudsblom documented that hygienic avoidance rules have served to rationalize an increasing sense of social embarrassment.[10]

Whereas in the hospices of old, codes of behaviour were based on religious considerations, and whereas at the beginning of this century common decency still served as the foundation for rules of conduct, modern hospitals invoke almost exclusively medical and organizational considerations for justifying their rules of behaviour, even if the connection may appear tenuous to the outsider. If nowadays people transgress against the hospital regime, indeed they do not violate God's commandments nor sin against propriety, but they risk being blamed with obstructing their treatment and thus harming their own chances of recovery and those of others.

In this manner the medical regime may maintain its house rules without having to invoke penalty clauses, or religious or moral norms, which after all might turn out to be controversial.

In human communities, such as hospitals for example, an order emerges which for everyone at any moment is a given. This insight reveals more understanding than the tendency to reduce all difficulties of interaction to unpleasant character traits or to the evil intent of the people with whom one must deal or, conversely, the belief that whatever goes well is the result of the commitment and qualities of those concerned.

In a schematic view, the hospital community might be rendered as a complicated network of dependency relations in which people must rely on one another for obtaining a scarce commodity: in contrast to the outside world, this scarce commodity cannot be had for money. Within the hospital walls, the money economy has been suspended and only the economic manager and the bookkeeper mind the finances. The main concern in the hospital, the medical treatment, is not the scarce commodity *par excellence*: patients usually get more or less what they need without too much delay, and the fight for adequate treatment facilities goes on elsewhere. But people in the hospital nevertheless unmistakably operate under pressure, and it is clear that patients, and staff also, one way or another try to obtain something that is hard to get, which all the time appears to be in short supply: that scarce commodity in the hospital is best designated as *attention*. Almost always a patient demands more attention from the nurses and doctors than they are ready to give. They experience this constant appeal being made on them as a claim on their time while they have other things to do: there are always other patients also requiring attention.

The nurses, in their turn, demand the attention of the head nurse and the doctors, who again are busy with other matters. The interns and head nurses, finally, must make an effort to get the attention of the specialists who must divide their scarce time over all sorts of concerns. At first sight it may appear that time is the scarce commodity in the hospital, but the patients who are left with least time to live, have more time than they like in the hospital, often having nothing to do but wait around to see the doctor.

The specialist's time is the most precious, measured in money, the standard that applies in the outside world, but also in terms of the demands made within the hospital. But again, once in the hospital, the specialist's time is gratis and as a rule nobody is lacking in medical intervention. What is lacking is something else, *attention*.

The attention which people seek in the hospital may be distinguished as of four kinds. The patients first of all require medical intervention in the strict sense, *treatment*; the nurses and junior doctors do not themselves need medical care but they demand proper guidance in fulfilling their tasks; that is, *task instruction*. Task instruction and treatment are closely related; both are manifest functions of the medical staff, and unambiguous rules exist for allocating responsibility for the various elements of the treatment and assigning competence to instruct different staff categories as to their tasks. In principle, the staff may not refuse an appeal for its attention when treatment is involved and – also in principle – senior personnel may not reject demands for their attention when it comes to task instruction: these claims have priority status. This will turn out to be important when it comes to choosing strategies for obtaining the desired attention.

The third kind of attention concerns *information*. Patients demand all kinds of facts and explanations about their condition, and that is why nurses and interns are constantly seeking additional data about the patients entrusted to their care. But the only authoritative information comes from the medical specialists; the assistant doctors and nurses may only speak on authority of the specialist and must be silent whenever the latter wants information to be withheld. That is why the junior staff continually tries to find out what the patient has been told and what has been withheld, what they may confirm, and what they too must keep back.

The fourth category is the hardest to define; it is of a kind that is always in short supply, and which gives attention in general its character of a scarce commodity: attention as *support*; no curative or informative intervention, but affective attention, emotional assistance through comfort, admonition, encouragement, sympathy, and understanding. In fact, patients may be very reluctant to accept such overtures and even reject them, but the hospital staff assumes that their need for support is in fact boundless and that anyone who gives in to it will have to provide that support for a long time. It is this idea of an essentially boundless need for support which turns attention in the hospital into a scarce commodity, constantly in short supply. This is much reinforced by the need among doctors and nurses, on their part, to seek support from colleagues and superiors, a need which is not always gratified and for which no regulations or facilities exist, which can only be met between the rules.[11]

This is why the hospital staff is always so busy; the more senior, the busier. A permanent appeal is made for the attention of superiors by inferiors and of staff by patients. As long as the appeal concerns task instruction or treatment it is regulated and limited; when it is about information, problems arise with secrecy and ambiguity; but once it comes to affective support, no division of tasks has been defined and the needs appear accordingly limitless.

It may appear that, high up in the hierarchy, the specialists only have to distribute their scarce attention over those who depend on them, without themselves being dependent on others. But, of course, the specialists on their part must rely on the other staff for the adequate treatment of patients, just as they are dependent on a continuous influx of patients to keep their practice, their research, and the clinic going. But the specialists are much less dependent on any individual nurse or patient than a patient or nurse is on them.

If what matters within this network of dependency relations is the allocation of scarce attention, the next question is what strategies people may adopt to acquire some of this attention or to lend or withhold their attention as they see fit. In the hospital the appeal for someone's attention very often takes the form of a complaint.

DEFENCE STRATEGIES IN THE CANCER WARD

The medical regime is justified in terms of the treatment. The problems which manifest themselves in the hospital are solvable only in so far as they can be defined in medical terms.

The first strategy for dealing with the difficulties that do not fit the medical context is to translate them into medical terms – displacement – in this case somatization or medicalization. Similar displacement on the part of the staff might imply translating emotional or relational difficulties into organizational terms, presenting them as difficulties with task allocation and instruction.

. At the beginning of their hospital career, the confrontation with the seriously ill and dying may still be terrifying to the interns. Newcomers suffering from the 'candidate's disease', the first year medical students' hypochondria, tend to imagine that every new disease they learn about afflicts them personally. But the new doctors hide such anxieties or reveal them to a chosen confidant. The intern who, after the staff briefing, believes there is a lump in his neck goes to see an experienced head nurse to reassure him; she tells him to 'go and have it looked at right away'. But the head nurse, in turn, confesses during an interview that when things get too much for her she goes to cry on a friendly surgeon's shoulder. The young nurse who gags while changing the tube in a patient's throat is sternly reprimanded by the head nurse and withdrawn from the ward. Intense emotions must be kept away from patients and colleagues: 'When the story of his death had been told, I could no longer control myself. I ran to the toilet and howled. One can't do that in the presence of other nurses. That is the unwritten law.' And in general: 'One doesn't talk about such things with others, we talk about work; other experiences one keeps to oneself.'

The conflicts that are fought out openly, albeit hidden from the patients, rarely refer to the need for support and comfort, but are couched in organizational terms and concern the division of tasks. An intern objects to his working schedule precisely at the time that he is confronted for the first time with the death of a patient; the lab assistants stage a protest campaign because of an increase in workload, but in group interviews they appear to be troubled by the fate of patients they are especially concerned about.

In such group conversations, specialists, interns, nurses, and assistants reveal some of the emotional pressures caused by the contact with gravely ill and doomed patients, but they do not want their patients and colleagues to notice. The support they do give one another and which does comfort them concerns mutual help at work: 'standing in for one another' or 'mutual consultation'. This collegial solidarity consists not so much of support by mutual solace and reassurance, but consists in re-distributing tasks and exchanging information, displacing emotional to organizational and medical aspects. Even more than the others, the specialists as the paramount bearers of the regime find themselves compelled to adhere to these defence strategies, for if they cannot overcome their fears and worries, who will?

If the junior staff tends to translate their uneasiness into organizational objections, the patients show a similar mechanism of displacement to an even stronger degree: they 'somatize' their discontent, translate it into physical complaints and demand action in terms of treatment. This tendency to somatization is usually understood as an individual characteristic of the patient concerned, a personality trait which is connected with social background and education. But the hospital patient is also embedded in dependency relations which provoke such displacement. The hospital staff has a professional obligation to react to the patient's physical complaints, even more so with chronic patients whose seemingly insignificant pains and discomforts may indicate deterioration of the disease – a metastasis, for example. With a somatic complaint the patient is certain to get the staff's attention. The staff, on their part, are well aware of this, and among colleagues they brush aside such complaints about a sleepless night, a pressing bandage, a lame sensation, or a painful spot as so many attempts to 'attract attention', to be comforted, reassured, or encouraged – and therefore, 'Nothing is the matter'. A physical complaint is always taken seriously, but when the suspicion of displacement arises, the complaint is ignored or rewarded with minor, friendly service that leaves the somatic translation intact: 'People sometimes suffer so much from trifles. One should give the patient what he needs, a beer, a sleeping pill, a prescription, shake his pillow once again.' The nurses are well aware that this is not what the complaining is about, that it springs from the patient's fear and solitude, but they also believe that a sick person is not helped by the expression of affection or by confidential conversation.

Patients may raise anxiety in those who care for them and this may again be translated into factual insecurity: the patients ask for information about the disease and its treatment and the interns, nurses, and assistants pass on the queries. They too would like to know more about the patient's chances of survival and cure. But at the same time the nurses and analysts admit that they could hardly cope with such knowledge and would not know how to remain silent to the patients about their prospects. This ambiguity again has to do with displacement: the patient's anxious insecurity worries the caretakers and they pass on their concern as a request for factual information which at the same time they do not want to know, because, just like the patients, what they want is reassurance.

Dependency on the medical regime operates partly by translating complaints of a different origin into medical and organizational terms. Other complaints are ignored and rejected. Patients may keep their complaints to themselves, if only because – just like healthy persons – they are reluctant to make an appeal to others. But the seriously ill have an added reason to remain silent about their troubles: articulating their anxieties may make them real, said, heard, remembered. And, worst of all, such forebodings once articulated may not be contradicted, or the answer may be so ambiguous that anxieties surge even higher: 'Nurse, what did the doctor tell you in the corridor? Will I die? – No, you have a one-way ticket.'

If patients remain silent in order to protect themselves, they also do not wish to burden fellow patients or staff; they are having such a hard time anyway: 'It is a problem of one's own and one must solve it by oneself.' And if a patient dares to bring up the subject, the dismay of the audience may frighten even more: 'Is it that bad?' More often than not the people around the patient are themselves at a loss to deal with the matter, are startled, embarrassed, making a frenetic attempt to control themselves, and change the subject with a cliché or a forced joke. When the patient does not broach the subject, others will not do it on their own account. What is thus being concealed jointly the patient may try to forget.

Patients among themselves may exert subtle pressures to silence one another. One patient told a newcomer how in another hospital the nurses would pick on a patient who kept on complaining: 'Pull yourself together, missis', the nurses had said, 'take an example from the lady over there' – none other than the patient telling the story. Patients are often afraid that their lamentations and grief will alienate them from others. In fact, not much is known about the support that the closest relatives – the last remaining network connections – give to a patient. But in many conversations among chronic patients one may detect a warning: 'There are people who talk about nothing else but their illness, and they will be shunned for it by the others.' In this way the sick teach one another to control their emotions.

In this reciprocal control of affect, the key notion is 'to be strong': 'I thought, now I must be strong and show what I am worth.' To be strong implies control, the concealment of anxiety and worry, a display of good humour, patience, confidence in the treatment, and ready compliance with doctors' and nurses' orders. To be strong is not only the duty of the sick and proof of moral force and character, in the hospital folklore yet another connotation is concealed behind the term; patients may influence the course of their illness by being strong: 'The doctor does one half of the job, the other half you do yourself.' Doctors would rarely say that with so many words, but neither will they deny that the patient through mental attitude alone may affect the disease process. And yet, the dominant medical doctrine holds that malign neoplasms are a strictly somatic phenomenon, independent of the patient's mood and mentality. Of course, patients may 'feel better' or even 'bear it longer' if they can find the mental attitude that fits their condition. Most likely, this is what nurses and doctors would say they mean when cheering up patients and telling them not to despair and take courage. But such encouragement acquires a life of its own, and for many patients 'being strong' comes to mean that they can affect the actual cell proliferation, that they can 'fight back'.

> And yet, I know for sure that I owe all this also to my own commitment. I worked at healing myself with an intransigence bordering on the impossible. I was amazed at all the things I could achieve at the time. It delighted me and it did not cost me any effort to be cheerful and happy.

Being strong also means living as if the life-threatening disease does not exist: 'For, if you give in, it will cost you years of your life.'

But against the background of these interwoven, concealed, connotations, the rule to be strong first of all also becomes somewhat menacing: control yourself, don't let go, for if you allow self-discipline to slacken and freely show your fears, you yourself may make your illness worse and, moreover, undermine the equanimity of your fellow patients and panic will spread through the ward. Few doctors would ever say it in these words, but nevertheless the encouragement and urging from the staff and among the patients themselves acquire this meaning, and the final effect is a reinforcement of order and decorum in the hospital.

The bodily cure is best served by patients controlling their emotions: this is not official and public medical opinion, but as an unrefuted, half-concealed, and pseudo-medical idea it does its work. To be strong means first of all not to complain. The staff's business-like and rather cool approach to the patients also serves to keep them from complaining. A researcher in the out-patient clinic of the cancer hospital reports: 'Observations indicate that in more than half the cases of a patient voicing a personal question or remark, the doctor does not respond to it.'

The patient's anxious complaints may not only be avoided by appearing vaguely absent-minded and preoccupied with medical and administrative concerns, but also by a more active demeanour, such as 'imperative cheerfulness', 'compelling jest', and 'overt censure'.

The first behaviour fits the classical repertoire of the stereotyped nurse. She enters with an emphatic salute, praises the day, applauds the appearance of the ward, acknowledges progress everywhere, and allows no one to be exempted from her cheerfulness: 'We already feel much better today, don't we!' No answer fits these exclamations, a denial least of all. In using 'we', the nurse conveys that she also speaks on behalf of the patients and expects no retort. The unspoken assumption in this compelling encouragement is that the patient will pick up just by taking it lying down. An equally unspoken consequence of such a demeanour is that it saves the nurse much whining and that the patient who might still dare to respond with a grumble is disqualified as an incorrigible moper: 'You are never happy.'

The second mode of conduct that should prevent complaining is jest: the nurse saying goodbye to a colleague in the ward before she goes off on vacation carries on a dialogue implying that everyone in turn leaves the hospital to travel to more pleasant places. A patient who is being asked by an assistant to come and get his radiation treatment threatens her with mock punches. The meal that is not tasty is qualified as high energy food that will hasten recovery. Small comedy that suggests that it is great fun to be here, but everyone knows better than that.

A third kind of behaviour occurs more rarely in the modern hospital: admonition. A minister tells a patient: 'You should be strong, imagine what your complaining must mean to your wife and children.' And the patients among themselves also remind one another at times of the codes of modesty and control, which ought to be observed in the hospital, often suggesting that it is the staff who insist on it. Young nurses and analysts who can no longer manage get the book thrown at them by a senior nurse: 'If you can't stand it, think how bad it must be for the patients. For their sake you ought to control yourself.'

During their training the nurses are constantly reminded to 'pull themselves together',[12] and medical students are taught this self-control from early on in the dissecting room where training also serves as an initiation ritual. Wouters and ten Kroode maintain 'that students learn "being strong" and practise it mostly by denial and repression of feelings characterized as "weak"'.[13] They add that it is precisely the medical doctors' dominant position in a hierarchical work setting which compels them to control their emotions so tightly towards patients and personnel of lower rank. The display of imperturbability is also a part of the medical professional ideal, a badge of occupational competence. The 'strong patient' is the complement of the 'imperturbable doctor'. The affect management of one party supports the other in controlling emotions.

The emotional distance between people in the cancer ward is further increased because so many people die there, often unexpectedly. That is why patients sometimes avoid friendship ties with their fellow patients, for fear of being confronted suddenly with their death. Some relatives and friends, too, stay away from a terminal patient: 'Thus dying friends are avoided by those who cannot face the physically altered person or even simply the torture of visiting.'[14] Doctors and nurses learn not to get attached to seriously ill or dying patients: 'The next morning I entered the ward and looked in Mr O.'s room to say hello. The room was empty. He was dead, of course! I was mad. Damn it. For weeks I spent all my energy on him and there he just croaked!' Such appalling experiences are a lesson to young nurses and serve to make them more detached.

The possibility that someone may soon die makes relatives and friends afraid of losing that person, frightened of the confrontation with suffering and death, and of being reminded of their own mortality. They are also bothered by

a peculiar embarrassment felt by the living in the presence of dying people. They often do not know what to say. The range of words available for use in this situation is relatively narrow. Feelings of embarrassment hold words back. For the dying this can be a bitter experience. While still alive, they are already deserted.[15]

For doctors and nurses this threatening presence of death is an added reason to guard their occupational detachment. In the last analysis, medical imperturbability is inspired by an identification with the patients: it is for their sake. The restraint is reassuring and it also conveys a cue to the patients to keep themselves in check. The forceful control of emotions has its parallel in the strong limitation of affect between higher and lower staff ranks. The relations of authority in the hospital also imply that the doctors and head nurses hide their vexation and fatigue in front of nurses, and that the nurses, in turn, rein in their indignation and anxiety towards their superiors.

Many doctors do possess the gift of establishing a contact that comforts and reassures without many words, with a single gesture, a skilful move, or a friendly touch. To patients it means much when doctors and nurses know how to handle their wounds competently and without fear and that is what medical people have been trained to do and demand from themselves. A general practitioner relates, still ashamed many years later, how on a visit to an aged cancer patient who wanted to show him her operation wounds, he had declined, and yet, that was what the patient needed at the time.

The normal course of affairs in the hospital is business-like, efficient, formal, and detached. The beds are made, food distributed, the radiation machines adjusted, conversation limited to what is strictly necessary. But not all support needs to be bestowed explicitly as emotional assistance. Basic nursing care as such may at times comfort and reassure. The nurse patiently washing a dilapidated patient, changing his clothes, is also the only one who dares face and touch him without disgust or fear, who quietly and competently handles the body which so torments and frightens the patient. Sick people see the healthy ones pass at a distance and hardly dare think of what their own bodies look like. The nurse can stand the sight of them and knows how to deal skilfully with the wounds and lumps, in doing so liberating the patients for the moment from their isolation.

Modern nurses advocate not only greater flexibility in dealing with patients, but also more democratic relations between higher and lower staff in the hospital. More flexible relations of authority assume that subordinate staff members will carry out their heavy and unpleasant tasks on their own account; more supple relations with the patients demand that nurses can endure more emotional claims from the patients: the emancipation of the nursing staff imposes heavier demands on the nurses' self-control and affect management. Apparently, contemporary nurses find it self-evident that they are equal to such tasks, and more so because they do not recognize these new requirements as demanding burdens at all, but rather as gifts which they possess 'of their own', and even 'by birth'. Protesting against a medical model experienced as rigid and hierarchical, neither they nor their superiors may be aware to what degree they already have become its bearers and disseminators, so much so that they believe they can now do without further direction.

Time is not the scarce commodity in the hospital, but attention. The patients have all the time, the staff is always short of it. The patients wait for the nurse to clean them, for the doctor to examine them. The nurses, in turn, must wait until the doctor gives them instructions or must go and find the specialist to tell them what to do. The inferiors wait for their superiors and the superiors are being sought by their inferiors.[16]

The staff's lack of time is not always a result of an overburdened work schedule. They are also busy because they are under pressure: the pressure to provide patients and subordinates with the affective attention they need. So as to protect themselves against a particular claim for support, doctors and nurses use the claims of others in general as an excuse: 'So much is still to be done, so many others need care, I cannot fulfil your demands.' Precisely because patients have all the time, doctors and nurses assume that they will make an unlimited claim upon their time if given half a chance: anyone who even begins to give in to a patient's demands cannot get rid of them any more.

This unlimited time claim is a metaphor for the boundless emotional appeal that patients are thought to make upon their caretakers, if ever they began to express their worries and anxieties. And precisely because so many emotions remain unspoken, the idea has taken hold that this wordless emotion is indeed boundless.

EXCEPTIONAL STATES

Sometimes events occur in the hospital that are felt not to belong there, that should be overlooked, and many researchers have let themselves be led along without registering them. This concerns exceptional cases such as laughing fits, anxiety attacks, and loss of decorum.

The casual manner in which jokers, panic-mongers, or the demented are assigned to an exceptional position within their environment and allow it to happen, confirms and conceals their functions in the maintenance of the order of the hospital regime.

Whenever eccentric behaviour occurs in the hospital, immediately social screens are drawn up around it and in extreme cases actual isolation in a separate room results.

The eccentrics in the clinic will be identified as such only cursorily; whatever the eccentric does or says no longer counts, he or she is the 'house comedian', or suffers from 'anxiety hysteria', is 'senile', 'demented', or suffers from 'loss of decorum'. And, it will immediately be added, it is of no importance, the eccentric is neither offensive nor dangerous. The outsider will be reassured nonchalantly and told not to pay any attention, to ignore the eccentric and not to mind. 'He is always joking, but he doesn't mean any harm, he isn't serious.' Or: 'She does not know what she says, she has an anxiety psychosis.' Or: 'He is getting demented, always been a decent person, knows no longer what he is doing.'

The eccentric comportment is put between brackets and divested of any significance. A person in this exceptional position is not taken seriously, and loses all prestige being neither 'strong' nor 'correct'. But the same position also affords one a greater freedom of expression, allows one to say and to do exactly what everyone else in the hospital tries not to express or to act out.

The role of the house comedian illustrates this best, precisely because it remains beyond any medical terminology and needs not to be winkled out of medical definitions. (After all, one does not suffer from humour, but makes others laugh.) The buffoon manoeuvres himself into his position with the aid of his audience: set formulas serve to begin the session and close it again. A comical welcome, 'Well, see who's here', invites a witty retort. There follows a reference to an earlier act: 'Let's have a good laugh again', or 'We are not going to be funny again, are we?' Every once in a while the comical definition of the situation is confirmed again: 'Just having fun, only fooling around', 'Better to laugh it off, what else can you do?' Such side remarks can also serve to close the act: 'Well, at least we had a good laugh.'

Among themselves doctors and nurses may also shift in and out of the comedian's role with ease, behind the wings and out of the patients' hearing. Very often their humour functions to convey what normally cannot be said, but between quotation marks, so that it will not count and may not be held against the speaker. This defensive function is unmistakable among students who are for the first time confronted with corpses in the dissecting room. Wouters and ten Kroode note: 'Coarse jokes abound, although we had been expecting worse.' They add: 'Nothing reminds them of any compassion with "the victim" or of an awareness of their own mortality.' And a little later: 'And yet, the dissecting room affects their emotional make-up, as appeared from the dreams they related.'[17] Apparently, medical imperturbability forbids the expression of disgust or fear, but allows daring pranks among peers so as to maintain defences through exaggeration of the opposite.

In the cancer ward also, exaggeration of the opposite turns out to be an accepted way in which to maintain one's impassivity: when during the nurses' coffee-break a junior enters to announce that a patient is suddenly complaining about pains in the arm, which might indicate a metastasis, the head nurse between sips of coffee retorts: 'Well, come and tell me when her arm turns black.' The nurses shriek with laughter.[18]

There is nothing clever in this remark; it is an exaggeration of the opposite. Because the student-nurse is a little upset, the head nurse displays complete impassivity, which also serves to initiate her junior colleagues into the occupational stance of imperturbability. But the exaggeration is also aggressive towards the patients who, with their eternal complaints and requests, pursue the nurses even during their coffee break. This vexation is harder to air, certainly for a head nurse. The sudden coarseness of her remark expresses the annoyance which all who are present try to control; the burst of laughter relieves their mood.

A new intern who has been confronted with his first dying patient, upon hearing that the relatives have just arrived, exclaims in mock despair: 'What do you want me to do for them? Give them a shovel!' Freely translated: 'Get them out of here, I can't deal with them.' But this comical elaboration of his own trials proves that the young doctor is already quite prepared.

In the wards and conversation rooms the patients complain to one another in a droll manner, often with a note of despondency, only by their exaggeration conveying that their remarks are not to be taken seriously, that they expect no solace for their grumbling, no annoyance from their teasing. The 'funny complainer' expresses what the others also think but do not say: 'Today's rolls are so stale, they bounce.'[19] This puts in words the disgust with the hospital fare, but need have no consequences. The patients' stories also serve to prepare newcomers for what is in store for them, but with such obvious exaggeration that at the same time it should reassure them: it won't be as bad as that.

These joking games conceal rage and envy against the healthy, most of all against the staff, and also anxiety about the future. Only when packaged as jokes can these emotions be expressed without anyone taking offence, or feeling the need to soothe and placate. One patient calls another an insect that should be sprayed away, a dog whose place is under the table; two men in the conversation room lose themselves in a surrealistic exchange in which the first qualifies the other as an after-birth and the other retorts, 'They must have forgotten to flush you.' Healthy visitors must be thrown in the canal, floored with a boxing punch, their necks twisted, put on the table and made to sing; it is all recited in a tired, resigned tone. These diatribes are closed with a sigh: ' . . . dare to laugh, a joke every once in a while . . .' This puts what has been said between quotation marks, it isn't serious, it should be of no consequence.

Once in a while, the entire company bursts into a song, is carried away by a TV comedy, loses itself in a card game. But as soon as it is over, the patients fall back on their own worries.

In more or less regular groups, one patient may develop into the comedian, another routinely feeds lines to the first, and a third allows himself to be the butt. Afterwards patients often say that they did not find it funny, but joined for the sake of the others, and anyway, it distracts, relieves. It creates exceptional positions that allow to be said, gratuitously, what otherwise must remain unsaid. That is the meaning of the role of the comical exception.

The comedian's role requires some talent: wit, nerve, vocabulary, and, most of all, tact (a sense of how far one can go). The comedian may switch into the role or step out of it again with no more than a few ritual phrases. The audience may easily tempt the comic into a performance and – with a bit more of an effort – goad her out of it. The comedian compels the listeners to retort with a joke or a sigh and sometimes to conceal their grievances.

An anxiety psychosis demands fewer skills but ties the sufferers more firmly to their position as it is defined in medical-psychiatric terms. (One might imagine a similar role, but outside the medical context, called 'chicken', for example, or 'cry-baby', which could be introduced and terminated, just like the comedian's part, with a few pat sentences, and would equally permit the expression of emotions that the audience wants to conceal.)

It is unknown how anxiety attacks are provoked and launched. But once such frightened patients have been qualified as a medical case, also in an emotional sense, their affect management becomes an object of treatment too, and their affects are henceforth regulated by medication.

What goes unnoticed is how the anxious patient initiates the performance, how others are drawn into it and may disentangle themselves again, and how it is terminated. Calling it a 'performance' already suggests that it might not be a 'disease' and that therefore it must be a pose: but it is anxiety.

For the duration of the anxiety attack, patients can afford to say whatever occurs to them: the ward is a hell hole, a snake pit, a slaughterhouse, a concentration camp; fellow patients are living corpses, yellow wrecks, the doctor is a hangman, a camp guard, a mechanic dentist. These are striking characterizations which may not openly be made in a hospital setting. For cancer patients especially, the doctors are not only the carriers of bad news, but also the perpetrators of a treatment which causes more pain and discomfort than does the incipient disease itself. It takes much rational reflection to accept that this is for one's own good. And that is why in jokes and anxiety fantasies a much more direct emotional connection is made: the doctor overwhelms the patient and the treatment is a punishment.

At the same time, these utterances are stripped of all significance, since the patient suffers from an anxiety attack and cannot mean anything by them. When patients in a panic report alarming bodily complaints they are immediately examined, but if no new physical symptoms can be found, their case is qualified as an 'anxiety psychosis' and medication, isolation, and possibly psychiatric consultation may follow. In this manner they are screened off socially and no one needs to be disturbed by what they say, no matter how striking it may be.

Patients suffering from loss of decorum or an initial dementia may take even greater liberties: they may not only openly express their anxieties, but also rage, scorn, and lust. The accepted wisdom is that physical decay somehow has caused a loss of mental control, that the physiological basis of social modesty has fallen away. The patients' conduct is considered a direct consequence of this damage and any meaning is therefore denied to it. But even if this lack of inhibition did result from physical deterioration, it is most unlikely that the uninhibited behaviour itself is entirely induced by the impairment. On the contrary, it may be that only now intentions and emotions are expressed that before with much effort remained concealed.

Weinstein and Kahn have investigated similar phenomena in brain patients, whose cerebral damage was a matter of record rather than conjecture, and concluded that even among them conduct was not solely determined by their physiological anomaly.[20] Time and again, they point to preceding social and psychological factors and find that the patients' conduct changes with the environment – for example, when they return home. The authors find similarities in the symbolic use of language by brain patients and language forms such as poetry, prayer, drama, myth, humour, and slang, and with the content of dreams: 'All these forms of language, whether occurring in people with brain disease or in the normal, provide important forms of adaptation to the stresses of human existence.'[21]

Concepts such as 'dementia' or 'loss of decorum' help to create a screened-off social space around patients within which they may say whatever they want, while all they say is immediately divested of its meaning by the audience.

Patients suffering from a loss of decorum often allow themselves erotic liberties with the nurses, talk freely about their sometimes rather peculiar sexual desires, and permit themselves infantile pleasures and pastimes. A demented patient can't find his bed and wanders into the women's ward. Another patient behaving so helplessly that the nurses have to treat him as a child, obviously enjoys it (and causes the nurses silent rage). Even incontinence has its social functions: 'If they treat me mean, I say nothing, but I pee in bed.' A man described by the staff as suffering from progressive loss of decorum had made it a habit to scribble words in the margin of newspapers. He wrote: 'One millimeter sometimes may hurt for a meter.' And another time he jotted down a children's joke: 'A man comes to the drugstore for a bag of Reckitt's blue balls. The druggist kicks him in the groin: "that will give you blue balls".' The first line, from a man who had suffered a succession of jaw operations, needs no comment. The second may well be read as: 'That's what you get, when you ask a healer for help.'

The medical regime strongly dampens the affects of patients and staff in the hospital. Patients regulate their affect by being strong, the staff by maintaining its imperturbability. But whoever cannot or will not conform to this demand may let himself be manoeuvred in an exceptional position gaining in freedom of expression and losing in meaning and prestige. The joker's role is the paramount exceptional position. The sufferer from an anxiety attack has got himself in a similar position, be it one that is mostly defined in medical terms. Even demented patients appear to gain opportunities of expression and comportment.

The people who make up the hospital community together maintain a social order which not only serves to further the due course of treatment and efficient management, but which should also help to allay the fear of death and disease. This order is kept by all involved, under the leadership of medical personnel and with medical arguments, even when the latter are irrelevant or not founded on medical expertise. The people in the hospital keep one another to an encompassing medical regime, that determines and limits their modes of interaction and forms of expression to the smallest detail and at the same time supplies them with a vocabulary and an etiquette for shaping their affect management and mutual interaction. This serves to reassure and even to soothe, it is also a form of repression, both collectively and individually, of different, possible modes of experience and interaction.

This total medical regime[22] was never designed by anyone, nor imposed unilaterally by doctors. It developed mostly unnoticed from incidental remedies for personal and group antagonisms in the hospital. Whenever conflicts occurred between or within people, these could be resolved by medical reasoning or intervention: problems of meaning could be temporarily solved by interposing considerations of medical treatment: problems of self-control could be solved with a pseudo-medical ethos of 'being strong'; problems of behaviour regulation and discipline became manageable with the arguments of hygiene, time, and information management, and with medico-psychiatric labels. The general helplessness of the seriously ill was thus transformed into a specific dependency upon the medical staff.

This medical regime has been attacked under the label 'medical model' as a conspiracy of medical people against the defenceless sick.[23] But patients, nurses, and doctors maintain this regime through a common, often concealed, effort and no one who is involved in it can withdraw unilaterally without becoming an exception.

The total medical regime operates within a wider society that has been increasingly medicalized and in which a medical regime in a lighter form has expanded further and further. In this society matters of disease and death have been entrusted to doctors, to professional helpers, also because other forms of support or comfort have been lost and others who might have cared for the ill are no longer willing, capable, or allowed to do so. Disease is dependency, and it did suit people well that medical and para-medical professionals adopted the dependent. In the confident awareness that the medical nexus ties every sick person to an extensive apparatus of care and treatment, the critics began to idealize the informal, spontaneous, and intimate support net-works. But what so many people really blame the doctors for is that they need them.

Now that the medical regime has been so firmly established, while moral and religious meanings have gradually been lost, the regime might be exercised with a little more flexibility and common sense; the massive repression is no longer required. The hospital no longer needs to be so strictly screened off from the outside world; there is more room for negotiation about modes of conduct between visitors, patients, nurses, and doctors; the control of affect might be a bit less rigid; and emotions may be expressed somewhat more freely. But such developments do not occur in the seclusion of the hospital: transitions in society at large determine the change in modes of interaction and experience, as well as inside the hospital.

Chapter Three

EXPANSION AND LIMITATION
OF THE MEDICAL REGIME

Everyone lives under medical supervision, at least in today's advanced and affluent societies. Some people – heart patients in intensive care or psychotics in crisis – are observed and cared for from one minute to the next in everything they do: for as long as it takes, they remain under a total medical regime. Others are admitted for years or the rest of their life into institutions under doctors' control and equally lead their existence under an all-encompassing medical regime. This regime also extends to out-patients who walk around freely but who, on account of a handicap or a chronic illness, live according to the doctor's precepts and regulate their existence and their expectations of the future accordingly. Still others spend their days in a state of heightened medical awareness; a danger signal is picked up during a routine check-up or a community examination, and henceforth they are aware of the small chance of a great misfortune and thus try to avoid risky habits. Sometimes there may not even be a danger signal, but their condition, or their youth or advanced age, is in itself a reason for increased watchfulness in medical matters.

The rest of the population is not so much healthy as not-yet-sick and live under a light medical regime: in more and more aspects of their daily life they mind their health, with regard to food and cleanliness, physical exercise, and their environment. Sometimes they do so at the urging of doctors, but frequently they talk one another into it in the name of (often imaginary) medical opinions.

'Everyone is always sick,' A. de Froe once remarked, 'but a serious sickness is one that gets worse.'[1] Sociologically speaking, everyone lives under the medical regime, a light regime for those who are not yet patients, stricter according to how dependent on doctors one becomes.

This medical intervention has expanded greatly over the last half century, including areas where medical expertise can offer no conclusive answers and where other approaches are conceivable. The expansion and establishment of the medical regime is not just a response to social and individual needs, nor the result of the drive for expansion of individual or organized doctors. The expansion of this regime is to a large extent the unintended effect of social contradictions which time and again appeared to be solvable by allowing medical people to decide. Doctors often benefited from it, but the final result of all these incidental interventions created legitimation problems for the medical profession as a whole, both internally and in relation to the outside world.

For a proper understanding of the nature, operation, and scope of this medical regime, it is useful to explore how in the last half century a multiplicity of new intersections has emerged between doctors and other members of society. It is striking that people encounter doctors at a greater number of critical moments in their lives and follow medical directions for a greater number of facets of their lives, that more people come under medical supervision for lengthier periods, and that ever new categories of people are placed under permanent medical tutelage.

THE MEDICALIZATION OF DAILY LIFE

Even when there is no question of an illness, in ordinary daily life people now orient themselves more than ever before to general behavioural precepts proclaimed or at least supported by doctors.[2] Hygienic habits are observed quite widely and taken for granted by all even when their medical justification is in fact inadequate (as it is for washing hands, for example); people want to be 'clean' and not 'dirty', and simply assume that the demarcation corresponds to that between 'healthy' and 'unhealthy', as it was previously regarded as a magical or religious distinction between 'pure' and 'impure'.

Eating habits, too, are largely dictated by health considerations, although here 'tasty' is often experienced precisely as 'unhealthy'. People impose all sorts of limitations upon themselves, desire or shun a variety of additives for the sake of health, while seeking support from medical advice or, in any case, medical rationalization. While doctors nowadays tend to be fairly restrained in giving dietary recommendations to healthy people, an abundant fantasy world has emerged, supported by a lively literature and commerce that caters to 'pure', 'natural', or 'healthy' eating habits, according to the medical model but in the absence of medical support. The preoccupation with body weight, also, is hardly sustained by doctors and yet is experienced largely in terms of 'healthy' and 'unhealthy'.[3] Dieting is probably the strictest form of self-coercion, day by day, hour by hour, in which people in modern society engage. Only stopping smoking, and the agonizing determination to do so, presents a comparable problem of control, in which medical considerations again predominate, but this time with much more urging on the part of doctors.

This 'medicalization' of daily life can also be found in the recent preoccupation with physical condition, with 'fitness', and this concern, too, is reinforced by medical advice: for the sake of their heart and lungs people must walk and jog, jump and tumble. Old-fashioned notions like 'character formation' or 'experiencing nature' have receded into the background, and even *Funktionslust*, the pleasure of functioning, one good reason for movement, hardly plays a role any more.

The concern with the immediate environment, which may be viewed either as threatening or, rather, as conducive to health, is a fourth example of the medicalization of daily life. In this respect, too, people seek medical arguments, and argue less in terms of aesthetics, morality, or social distinction when shaping their immediate surroundings. The initiative in this case is not so much with the doctors, but when asked they provide the arguments to denounce air pollution, noise, lack of light or air, lack of living and playing space. Cleanliness, good diet, physical exercise, and concern for the environment all are aspects of a civilized life in accordance with the demands of the present day, and these demands are often, increasingly often, posed in medical terms, even when doctors remain non-committal, even when the connection with sickness and health is tenuous or ambiguous.

EARLY WARNINGS OF HEALTH RISKS

A second development confronts people with medical precepts long before they are aware of any discomfort: the premonitions of potential illness are detected at a much earlier stage in many more people. This is a consequence of technological and organizational innovations in medicine: the technical progress concerns the improvement and refinement of diagnostic machinery: with electronic measurements and laboratory trials, small aberrations are discovered long before symptoms appear which the patient themselves might notice and which might prompt them to visit a doctor on their own initiative. The organizational innovations concern the mass examinations of complete populations in preventive campaigns, or of doctors' clienteles in their entirety in 'anticipatory health care'.[4] The mass studies presuppose the existence of a census bureaucracy, the availability of simple, quick, and reliable test techniques, of large computers to process the results, and also of easy access to all those people who are to report for examination and to return when the results are positive. The studies also presume the extensive support of doctors and nursing staff, and the willingness of many tens of thousands to turn up on call. With all their awe for technical invention, people marvel too little at the resourcefulness and determination underlying these organizational improvements, and at the ready compliance found among the citizenry.

As a result, every year many thousands of people are confronted with a peculiar finding: the 'distant early warning system' has done its work and tiny, early danger signs have been detected: signals of a small risk of a great misfortune. It is up to the doctor to interpret these portents. The people concerned may not be patients yet, they are already 'proto-patients'. The doctors now have to get these proto-patients to follow their directions without upsetting them too much: after some time they should report back for examination, they should change their habits, give up salt or tobacco, work less hard or diet harder, and so on. In short, they are now in a state of heightened watchfulness. From now on they will be living under a light medical regime.

In order to get some insight into the degree of dependency brought about by this early warning, it is necessary to examine the paradoxical nature of the message more closely. All these cases concern the small chance of a great misfortune. Although the odds will be known to some extent, but rarely with great accuracy, this does not establish the meaning of the early danger signals for the proto-patient and the doctor. 'The limited predictive value of a test result or of some irregular finding puts the doctor in a predicament. For the patient, the examination result must always be translated into an all or nothing: someone is either sick or healthy.'[5] A small chance of a great misfortune has no emotional significance as such in psychodynamic terms: people either let themselves be overwhelmed with anxiety about the great misfortune, or they repress all thoughts of the threat. But these emotional tendencies on the part of the patients (and their doctors) raise an interactional dilemma, because 'people without complaints are more difficult to mobilize towards the "medical model" than people who are clearly sick'.[6] The doctor will first reassure the patient, but also attempt to promote docility, 'compliance'. This leads to a 'double-bind' interaction in which the doctor's spoken message is contradicted by the style of presentation (the meta-communication).[7] The doctor will play down the likelihood of misfortune, but at the same time will give precepts in a manner which should guarantee compliance so as to prevent the possible misfortune. Blood pressure is a bit high, but not dangerous, the patient should not be upset at all and might from now on avoid salt and excitement and report back in three months. These guidelines and follow-up appointments are perceived by the patient as implicitly giving the lie to the reassurances.

This analysis may explain why the increasingly frequent 'early-warning' consultations run aground so often and result either in apparently unjustified anxiety or in 'non-compliance' (and repression). If doctors want to bring their proto-patients under a medical regime they must leave them with some anxiety which, on the other hand, as the patients' protectors they want to talk away. With all these early signals what matters is not so much the statistical odds of the misfortune, or its objective seriousness, but the balance between manifest anxiety and repression, between reassurance and the doctor's gaining compliance.

LENGTHIER LIVES, LENGTHIER ILLNESSES

With the extension of the average life-span a category of people has been brought under a light medical regime and a state of increased watchfulness solely because of their age: these are the elderly. Medical supervision of the aged has recently developed into a separate specialism, geriatrics. The chance of various afflictions increases with age, but even when none has manifested itself, the everyday existence of the elderly is more medicalized than the daily life of the young, and periodic medical check-ups alert old people to the early signs of possible serious illness. The greying of the population itself causes further medicalization of ordinary life. If old people can no longer manage on their own, they are often admitted to a home, again on medical advice, and there they live under a regime which may not be directly controlled by doctors but is always supervised by them.

Another category of people is also on the increase: patients whose condition does not permanently improve or deteriorate, the chronically ill. Some very protracted diseases, such as tuberculosis, have disappeared, while others which might cause permanent dependence have likewise been eradicated, such as poliomyelitis. But precisely because people live longer and are not threatened by acute infections, they now run a greater risk of heart disease or cancer. The risks have also increased as a result of modern sedentary life-styles, eating and smoking habits, and the polluting side effects of industrial production.

As a result, a large category of people lives permanently in a state of medical exception. They are ill, unable to work full time, they may be bed-ridden or require all sorts of special adaptations at home, they must always consider the doctor's advice when making short-term plans, and cannot make long-term arrangements since they may not live to carry them out. They are admitted to the hospital for shorter or longer periods, must undergo tests and operations, swallow the medicine as prescribed by the doctor, and often ultimately end up in a nursing home. This process of deterioration may take years, alternating with and sometimes terminated by a period of improvement, or else by a final decline. But all this time the chronically ill, in and out of hospital, find themselves under a total or a light medical regime, and as their numbers increase the regime expands accordingly.

After a long period of growth, some forms of institutionalization seem to have reached saturation point. Hospital admissions are now shorter on the average than some years ago; psychiatric institutions contain fewer long-term inmates; admission to old people's homes is delayed longer than before; here and there juvenile cases and the mentally disabled are entrusted to family custody rather than institutional care.

Undoubtedly, the mad, the retarded, the disabled, and the diseased are a burden on their environment and are themselves at risk from neglect and ill-treatment. However, this does not make the protection, supervision, and care of the needy a matter of medical expertise alone and need not come under the medical regime in its most incisive form of admission in a 'total institution'. It is a matter of controversy whether admission to one institution or another is desirable in each case. But apart from that, it is contested in how far medical expertise is of itself adequate to determine and justify the regime in such institutions. And yet, whenever a social conflict erupts with some vehemence, clamour arises to put another category of people under medical tutelage – and this has included at one time or another sex criminals, violent delinquents, narcotics addicts, venereal patients, and so on. The medical establishment, however, rarely made such proposals its own.

MEDICAL ADVICE

At critical moments in the life-cycle, with controversial measures about working conditions, with the allocation of scarce provisions, in the assessment of collective risks, medical doctors have found themselves in a position where their advice is sought and where often it turns out to be decisive. In nearly every case medical expertise may provide relevant information, but rarely may all relevant considerations be inferred from it alone, and almost never can a reasonable assessment of the interests involved be based solely on that expertise.

This may well be illustrated with the example of abortion, a measure best carried out under medical supervision. And yet, in the large majority of cases, the decision whether to act or not cannot be taken on the basis of medical expertise alone (and even in health-endangering situations the risks cannot be weighed purely on the basis of medical knowledge).The socially contested nature of the decision to abort prompts medical involvement in the decision and the delegation of competence to medical people serves the purpose of reconciling and concealing social contradictions. Similar developments occur in relation, for example, to euthanasia, suicide, and transsexuality. In other areas, such as contraception and sexual variations, medical involvement decreased with growing social acceptance; that is to say, to the degree that social contradictions on these issues eased.

The assessment of the inability to work equally involves an essentially contested appraisal of interests, which is turned into a matter of medical expertise: the question of how far people are indeed unable to carry out their present tasks predominates; the issue to what extent these tasks might be modified or which alternative tasks are available remains unasked. In so far as the disability cannot be determined exclusively on the basis of physical examination, independent of the foreknowledge and the intentions of the patient, it involves a residual category of 'vague complaints' and 'mental problems'.[8] In fact, there usually is a conflict between an employee who under the circumstances will not or cannot work and management which will not or cannot change the circumstances. Unwillingness and inability are inextricable, on both sides, and the doctor brings a potential conflict under a medical regime by determining disability. And all the time, broader developments on the labour market remain almost completely beyond consideration.

The system of medical allocations for scarce provisions, such as public housing, placement in nursing homes, material aid, and so forth, functions essentially in the same manner. In these cases, too, an essentially subjective need is apparently objectified by turning it into a necessity on the basis of a medical argument which is usually inadequate for the purpose and which in every case ignores the overall problem of distribution, again with a conflict dampening function. Analogous is the operation of medical advice in personnel selection, whether in military service or for private enterprise; the examining doctor receives a power of veto which may serve whenever necessary to protect the organization from a series of conflicts. Wherever the selection is less contested, has lesser consequences, as in sports physicals, medical advice tends to be more specific and concrete, since it does not have to serve the purpose of conflict management (and as soon as the conflict potential increases again – for example, in examining sports participants for drug use – medical expertise is once more stretched far beyond the limits of its validity).

The problem of evaluating small chances of a great misfortune has already been mentioned in the context of the doctor–patient encounter, but it appears also in medical advice about the risks of industrial waste, food toxicity, environmental pollution, and radiation dangers. The problems involved are two orders of magnitude larger than in the early diagnosis of individual patients at risk: the odds are smaller, the calamities larger – that is, they affect many more people. The same applies to estimating the side-effects of medication and other therapies. Time and again complex social problems of estimating and appraising risks and of attributing external effects are being dissembled through the construction of safety norms which are then presented as the result of medical expertise, where in fact they could not have been deduced from such expertise and in many cases turned out much later to imply a risk appraisal that deviated very far from what was socially acceptable.

To sum up, everyday life has become medicalized through a heightened concern with fitness and hygiene. Growing numbers of proto-patients are brought under medical watchfulness after early warning signs have been found on them in the mass or routine tests that have become ever more frequent. The aged, the chronically sick, the disabled survive longer with their ailments and throughout are the object of medical supervision. And, finally, scarce resources are increasingly distributed, social conflicts resolved, and societal risks appraised according to medical criteria.

THE EXPANSION OF THE MEDICAL REGIME

This increasing medical intervention, the growing sway of the professions, and the scientific outlook over social life has been well documented and discussed in the literature, increasingly with a critical slant. The ideological,[9] disciplining,[10] class-reproducing[11] character of expert dominance is a central theme in contemporary sociology. The process of professionalization has been described, especially since Freidson,[12] in terms of the monopolization of knowledge and service supply, in terms of the accumulation of power and profit.

This is a justified and necessary correction of a description of medical professionalization, solely as the growth and improvement of knowledge and practice. That a demystifying and critical tendency is now so predominant in the literature on professional occupations, especially in medical sociology, is also a consequence of the rise of the social sciences as a relatively autonomous discipline which initially put itself at the service of a mightier profession as a *sociology in medicine* and now more and more confronts it as a *sociology of medicine*.[13]

Yet, the earlier discussions of the professionalizing process in terms of the growth of knowledge and service as well as the modern analyses in terms of monopolization and control suffer from the same fault: they overestimate the conscious, active part of the individual practitioners and the professional corps as a whole in the course of the professionalizing process. Whether the tenor of the discourse is apologetic or accusatory, whether, for example, medical people are portrayed as saviours or exploiters, what is lacking is an understanding of the unintended, often unnoticed, compulsive aspects of the development.

One remarkable pattern in this development remains unmentioned in the literature: the hesitation and often the aversion of the managerial and academic elites within the medical corps to take upon themselves the power of decision in those fields where individual doctors were already active, where social groups insisted on such medical intervention, and where the government or the administrative apparatus thrust this competence upon doctors. This remarkable reluctance on the part of medical elites provides the key for an analysis of medical power formation for an understanding of its internal contradictions and external limitations.

A summary of the areas in which medical intervention has increased permits the conclusion that a medical regime is exercised over modern society, over some people totally and even permanently, over almost everyone for many aspects of daily life, and at decisive moments in the life-cycle. This medical regime can be conceived of as the totality of all precepts imposed by doctors on their patients and potential patients. The totality of precepts also involves an authority relation and a hierarchy, a professional ethos and a world-view.

The medical regime is not the only one that is exercised over the population; young people live under a strict pedagogical regime, those in military service under a military regime, those in the labour force under a work regime, and convicts under a penitentiary regime. With the expansion of social security and public assistance, beneficiaries increasingly must account for their doings and non-doings under a welfare regime administered by social workers and public assistance officials. And, finally, almost all adults find themselves under the scrutiny and compulsion of the fiscal regime.

The professional bodies which manage, control, and treat their clientele owe their monopoly and thus their power base in the last analysis to the state; they permeate the state apparatus through an osmosis of professional organizations and administrative apparatuses, but they do not rule. The ultimate title to their exercise of power rests upon their special expertise. In principle, the domain of their specific competence is circumscribed and their knowledge founded upon explicit theories and demonstrable results of research. In practice, not all precepts promulgated under a given regime are justified by its technical–scientific knowledge.[14] As a regime is established and expands, situations will occur more often in which measures are taken that cannot be adequately grounded on that expertise: this creates a problem in legitimizing the exercise of professional power and this legitimation problem causes internal contradictions and imposes external limitations. The legitimacy deficit compels the educational and administrative elites within the profession to restraint in the extension of the domain of professional competence.

The medical regime was established and extended in good part as the unintended result of the strivings of individual doctors on the one hand, and on the other as a consequence of social conflicts which appeared more manageable through medical intervention. Within the medical profession a constant pressure operates to extend the intervention by doctors, because new generations of medical people seek employment and because all individual doctors strive to increase their social chances for income, prestige, and the realization of occupational ideals. In this respect they are no different from others in the political arena and on the labour market, even though the realization of occupational ideals is an ambition which has a chance of success only in the highly skilled and somewhat autonomous occupations.

Doctors individually or in specific groups are continually busy trying new possibilities and opening up new work areas, formulating and realizing new ideals of medical care. And at the same time all sorts of conflicts occur in society where the parties involved look for support from the experts to settle their differences. Such a re-formulation of their dispute in technical–scientific terms already presupposes a certain degree of familiarity with the basic notions and fundamental stances of the profession which is to offer a solution: it presupposes a certain degree of 'proto-professionalization'.[15] The re-definition, for example, of a labour conflict as a medical problem strengthens the bargaining position of an employee because his or her personal demands may now be couched as medical requirements; thus they are object-ified, but at the same time individualized, reduced to the specific but now clearly defined problem of that employee. This restriction of the dispute may prompt the management to accept a medical approach to the conflict of interests. The best-known manner of the medicalization of discontent is, of course, absence from work in the form of sick leave.

This reduction of social conflicts to problems that may be managed by medical doctors occurs time and again, in all the fields mentioned in the preceding sections: in personnel selection and the distribution of services; in referring people to medical insti-tutions, whether it be the disabled, the chronically or the termi-nally ill, the feeble-minded, psychotics, addicts, or the dependent elderly. Such social conflict often appears to individuals as a personal conflict, in which conflicting desires must be weighed against one another by a single person. In these personal conflict situations, too, which once counsellors and pastoral workers had to solve, the doctor can provide a solution by re-defining the conflict as a manageable, because medical, problem.

Whenever social contradictions are involved, also in their individual form as personal conflicts, the reduction to a medical problem is a derivative application of medical knowledge; medical expertise is used as cover for conflict management.

This function of doctors has been described in the literature in countless situations, but it has often been mistaken for control pure and simple. This is wrong in two respects. First, what is involved is not just disciplining, but in the first place conflict management, the resolution of social controversies and personal conflicts in a particular manner, by re-defining them as medical problems. Second, this form of medical intervention is not solely initiated by doctors, has not been imposed by the ruling class or the state apparatus, but comes from a collusion, a hidden complicity between the parties to the conflict, with one another and with the doctor. The weakest party in the conflict gains from having its wants re-defined as medical necessities; the strongest party gains by the 'individualization'[16] thus realized, by the social isolation of the conflict. Medicalization automatically creates a state of exception, even if it applies to many millions as in the case of disability to work. The gain for the third in this alliance, the doctor, comes from the chances of prestige, income, and the realization of occupational ideals.

However, all these triangular collusions are incidental, occur in separate episodes, without the parties involved being aware of what the effect of their strategies of conflict control will be in the longer term and in a wider context. The elites among medical managers and educators are the ones who are confronted in due time with the accumulated effects of the incidental expansions of medical intervention. What gradually becomes the generally known and accepted practice of individual doctors and separate groupings of doctors in the end requires the articulation of a general policy. Once such policy becomes a topic for discussion within the medical profession and beyond, almost inevitably problems of legitimation occur. Whenever the practice cannot be adequately justified on the basis of consensual medical knowledge, as many differences of opinion will turn out to exist within the medical organizations as among the population at large: this was amply demonstrated by the abortion debate, or by the discussion on euthanasia, and becomes apparent each time new grounds for sick leave or for occupational disability have to be defined, or again, when doctors concern themselves with suicide, addiction, or the prevention of nuclear war and so forth.

When the medical regime expands into aspects of life or categories of people while medical expertise remains insufficient to justify the precepts, opposing world-views within the medical profession threaten to come into open conflict. Medical managers and educators see their power base in the membership being

69

eroded and fear divisiveness in the ranks, which could undermine their bargaining position towards the state and its advisory bodies.[17] But the same extension of the medical regime beyond the confines of its legitimacy also affects the authority of the medical corps towards outsiders, exposes the exercise of medical power to public discussion and political criticism, on an issue where the profession is vulnerable by definition because its policy turns out not to be justifiable on the grounds of medical expertise, the only base of legitimacy for its exercise of power.

These problems of legitimation explain the reluctance of the managerial and academic elites in the profession to extend the medical regime under their control. The fact that it expands nevertheless, is the unintended aggregated result of myriads of medical interventions in social controversies and personal conflicts in collusion with those concerned.

The complement of the expansion of the medical regime is the increasing dependence of patients and potential patients upon doctors; it also implies the contraction and even the disappearance of other networks for support, aid, and conflict management. This was not the outcome of machinations by a conspiracy of experts lusting for power and profit, much less the result of a scheme to mobilize these professionals in order to expand state power or discipline the working class; nor was it the triumph of the united efforts of life-savers and microbe hunters; it was for a good part the unintended and unnoticed result of countless incidental collusions among mutually opposing and internally divided people with doctors in search of social opportunity.

The pervasive nature of the medical regime and its mostly latent function in the regulation of social conflict convey a unique position to the medical profession. And ironically, even though this position surpasses the most grandiose schemes of the great medical reformers, it has not come about by their design, but mostly as the unintended aggregate consequence of the efforts of individuals and small groups, an outcome to which the profession has adapted itself only reluctantly. As modern medicine is coupled with the management of ever-expanding institutions, staff, and clientele, and with the control over vast and growing sums of money, state bureaucracies and large corporations become more and more intertwined with the administration of medical care: individual medical doctors may become powerful bureaucrats, but by the same token powerful bureaucrats increasingly control doctors and their patients.

The development of this medical regime may be checked and directed, first of all through public criticism of the legitimation of medical power. But even the critics may catch themselves at other moments advocating social reform with arguments of medical necessity. And, the acceptance of a 'social' instead of a 'medical' model may equally lead to an expansion of professional intervention in everyday life, legitimated this time by social science rather than medical expertise.[18]

The medical regime may also be reformed by increasing control by its clients. While doctors are expert in medical matters, the conditions under which they apply their expertise may be determined to a larger degree by the people concerned and they may also be the final arbiter in appraising the risks and interests with the aid of expertise contributed by doctors, among others. But such a renewed politicization of health care, in which social contradictions and personal conflicts are discussed as such and not as medical problems, cannot be effectively pursued at the level of the central state alone; it must be carried out at the level where the contradictions and conflicts arise, within the social context where people live and work and pursue their beliefs, leisure, and friendship.

Part Two

THE PSYCHOTHERAPY TRADE

Chapter Four

ON THE SOCIOGENESIS OF THE PSYCHOANALYTIC SITUATION

Freud's *Recommendations*[1] contain a clear and rather complete design for the practice of psychoanalysis. In these brief writings, the sociologist will find a blueprint for the then-novel profession of psychotherapy. Yet these four articles, so easily accessible to the uninitiated reader, are relatively unknown outside the circle of psychoanalytic practitioners and have never been the subject of sociological enquiry.

From the beginning of this century, sociologists in Europe and the United States have studied Freud's works, but they have mostly been interested in his general views on human psychology and, especially, in his own application of psychoanalytic theory to social problems.[2] Others have investigated the general application of psychoanalytic ideas to the design of sociological research and analysis.[3] Although the relation to Freud's thought remains mostly implicit, in Elias's *The Civilizing Process*[4] one can perceive an early and very thorough osmosis of psychoanalytic thinking into sociological analysis. Another area of confluence lies in the adoption of sociological and anthropological concerns by psychoanalysis, initiated by Freud himself in *Totem and Taboo* (1913b), *Group Psychology and the Analysis of the Ego* (1921), *Civilization and Its Discontents* (1930), and *Moses and Monotheism* (1939).

In the last 80 years the uses of psychoanalysis *in* sociology have been greatly extended, and so have, to a lesser degree, those of sociology *in* psychoanalysis (for example, community psychiatry, family therapy). Nevertheless, there remains a surprising scarcity of sociology *of* psychoanalysis, and a complete absence of psychoanalysis *of* sociology.[5]

Yet Freudian analysis has become one of the great intellectual currents of this century,[6] and the study of this development rightfully belongs in the sociological domain. One important course of research would follow the emergence, development, and distribution of psychoanalytic ideas – a sociology of psychoanalytic knowledge.[7] Another area of enquiry would focus on the ways in which people come to experience and express their troubles in psychoanalytic terms and may even come to consider themselves 'suitable cases for treatment'.[8] A third path of investigation would trace the development of the psychoanalytic movement and profession from the early days in Vienna to the present, with an eye to the change in its status and the related ramifications. The last approach deserves heuristic precedence: both the professional and intellectual body of psychoanalytic ideas and the layman's notions about symptoms and complexes are best understood in the context of the early circle and the later psychoanalytic community where they originated and evolved.[9] To this end, it is necessary to investigate and trace the origins of the concrete, day-to-day aspects of the psychoanalytic trade – the 'psychoanalytic situation' that Freud first described in his *Recommendations*. In line with this, the subject of my enquiry is Freud's gradual adoption between 1886 and 1912 of certain practices that, taken together, shaped the psychoanalytic craft, through which Freud made his great psychological discoveries. For a sociologist, the psycho-analytic situation itself – understood here as a particular, novel form of interaction, which constituted the social matrix for the body of psychoanalytic knowledge – represents as great an invention as any other Freud made.

My argument can be summarized in four basic propositions:

(1) The psychoanalytic situation was in many respects an extension of practices already emerging in the general medical profession.

(2) Psychoanalysis was, however, a 'pure' practice, in the sense that all forms of interaction (or other occurrences) that could serve as alternative explanations of the patient's reactions were, as far as possible, and in principle, eliminated – analogous to a natural science experiment in which all variables are controlled so that the resulting

process can be explained in terms of the *agens* and *reagens* alone.

(3) The new practice of office consultation appeared to Freud and his contemporaries to be a form of interaction devoid of all exchanges that did not immediately serve the business to be transacted – a 'social null-situation'.

(4) In the *Recommendations*, Freud proposed two complementary ground rules, one for the analysand and one for the analyst: the rule of free association and the rule of abstinence. These rules constituted the very essence of psychoanalytic practice, and they transformed office consultation into an entirely new interactional situation.

The remainder of this chapter is devoted to a justification of these propositions based on historical evidence and on material from Freud's writings, especially his early technical works, first among them the *Recommendations*.

THE ORIGINS OF OFFICE PRACTICE

In the 1880s, when Freud established his neurological practice, the medical profession was being transformed by a succession of scientific discoveries and therapeutic innovations. It was the heroic epoch of Koch and Pasteur; yet very few quick and sure-fire cures existed at the time. In neurology, Freud's speciality, a number of new treatments were introduced, practically all of them now abandoned as ineffective: Erb's electrotherapy, faradization, Weir Mitchell's rest cure, and so on.[10] The young Freud tried his hand at all of them, as well as older therapies such as massages, vapours, purges, baths, and also hypnosis, which, especially in France, was coming back into respectability.[11] One of the unintended consequences of the new therapies, with their necessary equipment, was that physicians found it harder to travel to see their patients, even though transportation had improved. The tools of their trade had become too heavy and too bulky to carry along in a carriage, let alone on horseback along country roads.[12]

Thus, many of the new treatments could be administered only in the doctor's surgery or in a clinic. It became more necessary for doctors to be available every day at a fixed place and at an appointed hour. Also, as physicians had more remedies at their disposal, their services came to be in greater and more urgent demand. Moreover, once doctors were widely known to achieve cures, their prestige grew.

Even so, in the early nineteenth century the doctor is still pictured as a man on the go, a man about town: 'The more the physician makes himself noticed around town, the larger will appear his clientele, the more competent and beloved will he be held to be.'[13] In the early days that was the way to win patients, or, according to a satirist of the times: 'Always drive about town, even if initially you lack patients, as if you were very busy.'[14] Initially, the physician received at home only during the *Audienzstunde* for the poor, who could not afford a doctor's visit. Sometimes the maids and valets of the rich came to describe their patrons' illnesses and to take back counsel and medicine, without the doctor ever having seen the patient. These arrangements changed in the course of the nineteenth century as a consequence of the new treatments and, from a broader perspective, with the rise of the professions, the improvement of university education, the imposition of standards of practice, and the relative ascent of bourgeois occupations in general.

As early as 1829, Samuel Hahnemann received his patients, regardless of their worldly status, in consultation for some five office hours a day.

> In order to save our noble time [*edle Zeit*] and so as to maintain our dignity, we must not visit chronically ill patients at their homes, not even princes, if they are able to come to our house. We must only visit acute, bed-ridden patients at their homes. Anyone who can move about and does not want to seek your advice at your home may stay away; otherwise it won't work.[15]

Clearly, it is a matter of both efficiency (noble time) and prestige (dignity). Interestingly enough, the difference between home and surgery consultation is no longer between the rich and the poor, but between medical categories, between chronic and acute, bed-ridden patients – even princes ('und wäre er ein Fürst'). The standards of professional practice should cut right across the boundaries of rank.

But Hahnemann, known for his arrogance (as a medical practitioner), was ahead of his colleagues; he had few followers in this practice for some time to come.[16] The 'luxury' of surgery hours was apparently reserved for those physicians who had achieved such a good reputation that patients came to them, rather than their having to visit their patients. It is a fair speculation that the developments in Austria, and especially in Vienna, were similar and roughly synchronous to those in German cities, documented here.

THE EARLY PSYCHOANALYTIC SETTING

Dr Sigmund Freud, Privatdozent Neuropathologie, opened his practice on Easter Sunday 1886, having recently returned from his studies with Charcot in Paris and from a brief visit to Berlin.[17] Freud's first years in practice form one of the least accessible periods in his life, since his rich correspondence with Martha Bernays ceased with their marriage in September 1886. Freud's equally informative correspondence with his friend Fliess, on the other hand, got off to a slow start, warming up only gradually.[18] No admirers or students came yet to visit Freud so that we find no published recollections to enlighten us. Freud's biographers have paid scant attention to his manner of practice during this period; they have been preoccupied with a different theme: the reception of Freud's ideas on hysteria by the Viennese Society of Physicians.[19]

After a few months at the Rathausstrasse Freud moved to an apartment in the Imperial Memorial House. About the arrangements there little is known, but by 1891 the family had settled at 19 Berggasse. There Freud would live and work until 1938, in 1907 moving his working quarters from the ground to the first floor, where the family dwelt at the other side of the landing.[20] Many of Freud's visitors have described him in his work surroundings, but these accounts prove to be disappointing to the sociologist. Each time one might wish such a witness to stoop, if only for a moment, to record more mundane observations on procedure or schedule, the witness has another flash of insight and moves on. In any case, the premises at Berggasse have been variously described as 'une maison de médiocre apparence dans un quartier perdu de Vienne'[21] and 'a large apartment in one of the best residential quarters in Vienna'.[22] But in the judgement of a fellow-Viennese contemporary, a 'pupil and friend', Hanns Sachs, the house was 'in a quiet and respectable, if not exactly distinguished neighborhood'.[23]

Freud's working quarters there consisted of three rooms and an anteroom: a waiting room; a consultation room, where Freud received his patients; and a study, which could be entered through his consultation room and which housed the famous antique collection.[24]

At first very few patients came to see Freud, paying patients even less. Freud's friend and mentor, Josef Breuer, had advised him at the start of his practice 'to take low fees, treat a good many people gratis, and count on earning only 5 gulden ($2) a day for the first two years'.[25] Three times a week Freud worked as director of the neurological department at the Institute of Children's Diseases of his acquaintance Kassowitz. He held an office hour (*Ordinationsstunde*) daily from 2 to 3 p.m., seeing patients who were often referred to him by friendly colleagues, such as Nothnagel, and foremost, Breuer.[26] Freud applied the stock-in-trade remedies of the neurological profession, but he gradually became known as a specialist in hypnosis with an interest in hysteria. He had, after all, studied with Charcot, lectured on the subject of hysteria, translated and edited works by Charcot (1886) and Bernheim (1888), and visited the clinic of Bernheim and Liébeault in Nancy in 1889.[27] Gradually, more and more patients with disorders that had resisted all attempts at organic treatment and were thought to be of psychic origin were referred to Freud.

In tracing the development of the physical psychoanalytic setting, it is significant that Freud received very few of these patients at his office; he usually went to see them. Apparently, he considered this a matter of no importance, if he considered it at all, since he rarely even mentions where the treatment of a patient took place. In the earliest case study (1892-3), the reader finds him visiting the home of his hysterical patient: 'Far from being welcomed as a saviour in the hour of need, I was obviously being received with a bad grace and I could not count on the patient's having much confidence in me'. In the *Studies on Hysteria*, we again find Freud treating most of his patients at their homes, in nursing homes, or in clinics, but two, at least, were received in his office: Lucy R. 'came to visit me from time to time in my consulting hours'[28] and so, apparently, did Rosalie H.: 'One day the patient came for her session'.[29] Thus, with some exceptions, daily visits to homes or clinics seem to have been the normal pattern in the early nineties. A turning point in the treatment of Elisabeth von R., for instance, occurred when, during the session, she overheard her brother-in-law in the adjoining room, with the implication that this disturbance took place in the patient's home.[30] In clinics and rest homes consultations sometimes took place at the bedside, but, especially in later years, they were also given in a special treatment room or office on the premises. In 1910, when the Wolf Man began his treatment, it was all apparently still a matter of convenience, albeit, at that time, Freud's convenience. At first Freud conducted the Wolf Man's treatment at the sanitorium, but a few weeks later he began to receive his patient at his Berggasse office.

One may speculate about the reasons that brought Freud and his patients together in his office, rather than at their homes or elsewhere. It certainly was not a matter of cumbersome equipment, as in other medical specialities. Freud gave up the use of one implement after another and finally abandoned all manipulations. But the savings in time and energy spent moving here and there must have been a great relief for a man with Freud's schedule, which covered a working day from 9 a.m. until after midnight.[31] As noted earlier, in the late nineteenth century, conducting one's medical practice at an office instead of making home visits was also connected to a gain in professional reputation, a 'luxury' one could afford once one had established a name, and an arrangement that, in turn, enhanced one's prestige. (This reputational aspect of the changes in Freud's practice will be discussed later.)

But foremost in this transition to office practice must have been the need for physical and social seclusion and for constant surroundings. An office setting greatly increased the possibility of controlling the scene of the treatment.

THE EVOLUTION OF THE PSYCHOANALYTIC SITUATION: TOWARDS A 'SOCIAL NULL-SITUATION'

The development of Freud's therapeutic procedure involved the gradual abandonment of almost everything reminiscent of medical technique, and finally, of all manipulation and every instruction, except one: the basic rule of free association. In the first five years or so Freud gave up the standard neurological therapies, maintaining only rest cures until about 1910 (Breuer and Freud 1893-5: 267). In December 1887, he turned to hypnotic suggestion (1887-1902: 53), but with this technique, too, he moved towards doing less and less, replacing suggestion with the simple instruction to the patient to concentrate and remember the circumstances under which the complaints first appeared (p. 105). In the following years Freud gradually abandoned even the attempt to induce hypnosis, partly because of the imperviousness of some patients to this treatment, partly because he found it tiresome, and also because he discovered he could do without it: 'When, therefore, my first attempt did not lead to somnambulism or to a degree of hypnosis involving marked physical changes, I ostensibly dropped hypnosis and only used concentration' (p. 109). Under this 'pressing technique', Freud would place his hand on the patient's forehead, inviting the patient to say whatever came to mind, with the assurance that this was what he had been looking for (pp. 110-11). But the 'pressing technique' was abandoned in its turn, probably some time before 1900. Patients were still invited to lie down and shut their eyes, although even the latter request was soon dropped (by 1900). In his next description (1904), only the supine position on the couch remained from the neurological and hypnotic origins of Freud's method.

The transition from hypnosis to the cathartic method and from there to psychoanalysis implies a gradual elimination of activity on Freud's part. Manipulations and instructions were abandoned as ineffective and superfluous. They also conflicted with the emerging paradigm of the psychoanalytic situation: whatever patients did or said during their sessions was to be understood from the perspective of their own psychical conflicts and thus should not be influenced in any way, or even appear to be influenced, by the therapist or the surroundings. As Freud instructs, the patient 'is spared every muscular exertion and every distracting sensory impression'.[32] Thus, the locus of the psychoanalytic encounter shifted to the constancy and seclusion of the office and its choreography was reduced to well-nigh zero.

Before however broaching the complementary ground rules of free association and abstinence, it may be useful to trace the evolution of several other elements of the psychoanalytic situation in relation to common medical practice in Freud's time: arrangements concerning money, time, discretion, and acquaintance. In each case, we find a general movement towards a social null-situation.

PAYMENT AND THE PROBLEM OF REPUTATION

In his *Recommendations,* Freud assumes an uncompromising stance on matters of money, which not only underlines the distinction of psychoanalytic practice from pastoral and charitable care, but also represents a break with the medical tradition of honorary fees from the rich and gratis treatment of the poor. Money matters were to be dealt with right at the start of treatment, and a fee set, to be paid regularly, with no exceptions allowed. According to Freud, this simple, strict arrangement stems not only from the obvious necessity to earn a living, but from the fact 'that money matters are treated by civilized people in the same way as sexual matters – with the same inconsistency, prudishness and hypocrisy'.[33] The psychoanalyst should counter this tendency: 'He shows them that he himself has cast off false shame on these topics, by voluntarily telling them the price at which he values his time'.[34]

This stance on matters of payment may not have been unique or even uncommon in Freud's time, but it appears to have been quite controversial: 'This is, of course, not the usual practice of nerve specialists or other physicians in our European cities. But the psycho-analyst may put himself in the position of a surgeon, who is frank and expensive because he has at his disposal methods of treatment which can be of use.'[35] As a matter of fact, Freud's attitude also constituted a departure from the practice of hypnotizers and magnetizers. Liébeault, for instance, treated his patients without remuneration, having already assembled a small fortune in earlier occupations.[36]

A vivid illustration of this 'inconsistency, prudishness and hypocrisy' on money matters among 'civilized people' (*Kulturmenschen*) can be found more than a century earlier in the remarks of a medical professor from Tübingen, D.W.G. Ploucquet (1797): 'It is somehow repugnant, somehow indelicate to receive a reward, a piece of money from someone's hand, even though it certainly is the payment of a debt and not a gift'.[37] It is not fitting to bring up the subject of payment; moreover, it is not very smart, as 'voluntary contributions often exceed the amount of the fee ... not only in money but also with precious things'.[12]

Almost half a century later the embarrassment over compensation had not diminished at all: 'One more topic remains for discussion, one which we would rather pass over silently ... the doctor's fee.' With this caution,[39] Dr B. Liehrsch (1842) offers his financial advice: 'In every instance of payment, the physician should maintain the decency [*Anstand*] that goes with his rank, which is not the craftsman's rank.'[40] These last words present a clue to the motives behind this embarrassment. To demand *quid pro quo* payment at set rates would make the doctor similar to a craftsman, and, although craftsmen held a lower status, apparently the distance was not great enough to prevent anxiety. As Liehrsch points out, 'By such actions one unintentionally brings one's art down to the level of the manual crafts.'[41]

Thus, a sociologist might explain the consistent and rather intense embarrassment about financial matters in the nineteenth-century medical profession in terms of status anxieties. In contrast, a psychoanalyst might emphasize the symbolic connotations of money, as did Freud in his *New Introductory Lectures*.[42] Of course, no psychoanalyst would offer an explanation *in abstracto*, but these connotations might be assumed as a 'search strategy' in the given context of a patient's productions or in an autobiographical fragment.[43]

The apparent gap between sociological and psychoanalytic explanations may, however, be bridged by looking somewhat more closely at these remarks. Liehrsch exclaims: 'How could a gift of money or precious things ever be an adequate compensation' compared with the life-saving efforts of the ever-ready physician.[44] But he does not rule out payment: 'The physician is *entitled* to demand a fee and that is why he should accept even the greatest gifts without embarrassed or submissive gratitude.'[45] In other words, even though asking for a fee or accepting a gift might appear to lower a doctor's status, at the same time none of this is true compensation for the gift of health that the doctor bestows on the patient.

Another physician, William Hooker, notes: 'The wealthy by no means discharge in full their obligations to the Physician, who attends upon them in all their sickness with unwearied fidelity, when they pay him for his attendance. They owe to him the affection of a true friendship and the gratitude due to something more than a professional performance of duty on their behalf.'[46] With these words, Hooker points to a moral hierarchy, in which the conscientious, self-sacrificing efforts of doctors make them the betters of their social superiors, who receive their care. Such a reversal of values, in which a tangible, immediate gain (money) is forsaken for a less apparent, often secret, or even unconscious reward (glory), might be called in psychoanalytic terms a moral masochistic manoeuvre.[47] By insisting on prompt and proper payment, doctors risked being ranked in status with lower occupations; in contrast, by waiving their claims, they not only avoided this loss of status, but attempted to place themselves outside the prevailing status hierarchy, in a different, moral hierarchy. This had to be done tacitly, as it is not fitting for benefactors to proclaim their position too loudly.

Evidence of this moral masochistic stance, with the corresponding fantasy of virtuous nobility, is found throughout the medical manuals of the time. And, in the long run, this self-abnegating stance both enhanced the reputation of doctors and earned them patients, with consequent material rewards. Indeed, from the viewpoint of gaining and maintaining a reputation, the seigneurial codes on financial matters appear quite entrepreneurial in themselves. The Ploucquet and Liehrsch manuals may be read in their entirety as guides to the conquest of a reputation (and thus a clientele) through the ostentatious display of moral character, kindness and empathy, reliability, discretion, knowledgeability, and so on. The 'other-directedness' of this advice is sometimes striking: the young doctor was instructed to display modesty towards more established or senior colleagues and arrogance towards the 'lower ranks' of the helping professions, surgeons, and midwives. In these manuals the early-nineteenth-century doctor emerges as an entrepreneur who invests in a reputation at the short-term cost of initially providing gratis or low-fee treatment.[48]

In his study of court society in France, Elias (1969) points out that from the courtier's perspective the acceptance of a loss in financial opportunities for the sake of a gain in opportunities for status and prestige might appear 'rational' or 'realistic'. In contrast, the same action might be termed 'irrational' or 'unrealistic' by the mercantile bourgeoisie. Both groups oriented their actions according to their particular perceptions of power opportunities, and these perceptions were shaped by the specific position of each group in the social configuration which they together constituted. It is not the kind of gain people seek that determines their rationality, Elias argues, but the way in which they seek it: rationality is characterized by the precedence of long-term considerations of 'observable realities' over immediate impulses. Forms of behaviour that are rational in this sense can only occur in those social configurations in which external compulsions (*Fremdzwänge*) are transformed into self-controls (*Selbstzwänge*) to a relatively high degree – in societies, that is, in which people are not forced by others to bridle their impulses, but in which the 'social compulsion to self-compulsion' has taught them to control these impulses with some autonomy and constancy, and according to long-term objectives.[49]

This view allows us to understand some of the contradictions in nineteenth-century medical practice. Throughout, a primary concern for the individual doctor was the establishment of a reputation. At first the emphasis was on moral excellence. Thus, each physician was forced to be as self-abnegating as the next in advancing both his own and the profession's reputation. During the course of the century, the prestige of the medical profession as a whole was enhanced, among other reasons, because of an increase in therapeutic possibilities. Yet the rise in status of the medical profession relative to other occupations did not solve the problem of achieving an individual reputation in competition with one's colleagues. As moral grandeur came to play a diminishing role, technical competence began to count for more and more in the establishment of a reputation. In either case, the gaining of a reputation can be seen as an end in itself, beyond the opportunities it afforded for financial reward and personal prestige. The social constellation in which medical professionals found themselves imposed on them what might be called a 'reputational' rationality. Only with the recent advent of large-scale public or semi-public medical insurance schemes, which assure doctors of a steady income and a fair share of patients, has this competition for reputation within the profession been mitigated to any appreciable degree.

Thus, Freud began his practice in a social figuration in which he had to make a name for himself if he wished to survive as a doctor, or even as a middle-class family man. It was in this context of establishing a reputation that Breuer advised Freud to start with low fees. Eventually Freud gained an almost uniquely wide margin of free movement within Viennese professional society, even turning some adverse conditions in his favour. Yet he could only achieve this within the constraints of the social figuration of his day. As a man without independent means, and perhaps because he was a Jew,[50] he had to build his reputation as quickly as possible. At first, the prospects of success appeared gloomy. Freud even considered emigrating after six months because he was earning so little, 'but Breuer thought there was no hope in that either unless he went as a waiter'.[51]

Since a university career did not pay enough to support a family, there were only two avenues open to Freud: accepting referrals and financial aid from a few friendly senior colleagues, or making a great discovery, a kind of short-cut to fame. Freud travelled both. As a keen observer, he had discerned some of the tactics of the reputation game, but he avoided the moral dilemma by creating his own version: 'Freud observed that all these men [Viennese colleagues] had a certain characteristic "manner", so that he had better decide to adopt one also. He chose to exploit his native tendency to uprightness and honesty: he would make a "mannerism" of that, and the various people would have to get used to it. If he didn't succeed, at least he would not have lowered himself.'[52] In later years Freud may have found that a controversial reputation was not necessarily harmful in a cosmopolitan centre such as Vienna around the turn of the century. In any case, by approaching Freud's early years from the perspective of the social figuration of which he was a part, we can see how this figuration compelled him to establish a reputation quickly. We may thus explain many of his actions without reference to his moral or personal characteristics, such as his ambition, his concern about priority, his interest in money, or any of those other traits that have been the subject of so many acrimonious, essentially moralistic, polemics. Given the existing social figuration, no one would have heard of Freud had he not pursued a reputation, and this he understood very clearly, as his letters to Martha Bernays and Fliess testify.[53]

The same struggle for a reputation may have impelled some of Freud's followers to present their ideas as *new forms* of treatment and thus acquire a name for themselves. This may also be true today, especially where governmental regulation of payment for psychotherapy is lacking and therapists depend on the free market to find a clientele. Careful investigation of the means of existence, the recruitment and distribution of patients, and the ways of disseminating new treatments is needed to determine the validity of this conjecture.

In addition to clarifying the social forces Freud had to cope with, this extensive discussion of financial mores may shed some light on payment. Freud clearly counters a posture of moral grandeur in stating:

> It seems to me more respectable and ethically less objection-able to acknowledge one's actual claims and needs rather than, as is still the practice among physicians, to act the part of the disinterested philanthropist – a position which one is not, in fact, able to fill, with the result that one is secretly aggrieved, or complains aloud, at the lack of consideration and the desire for exploitation evinced by one's patients.[54]

In his *Recommendations*, Freud also warns against taking gratis patients, even against the custom of treating colleagues or their relatives without recompense. First of all, analytic treatment involves 'the sacrifice of a considerable portion – an eighth or a seventh part, perhaps – of the time available to [the analyst] for earning his living, over a period of many months'.[55] (Note the brevity of the treatment.) There is, however, another reason: 'Free treatment enormously increases some of a neurotic's resistances.' And, third: 'the whole relationship is removed from the real world, and the patient is deprived of a strong motive for endeavouring to bring the treatment to an end.'[56] Freud admits that he himself did take gratis patients for ten years, 'one hour daily, and sometimes two', but this was only 'to study the neuroses' with the least possible hindrance. Nevertheless, in later years Freud at times exempted himself from his own recommendations and treated some patients gratis, among them the Wolf Man, whom he even assisted financially.[57]

With paying patients, too, Freud may have been less strict than his *Recommendations* suggest, at least in the early years. In 1898, in a letter to Breuer, he noted that for several years he had been earning more than he spent, but that he still lacked cash, since in his profession one had to accept long delays in payment. And he went on to explain an arrangement he had with one of his female patients, whom he was treating at a greatly reduced fee; full payment would be made only after this young woman inherited money on her mother's death. Freud justified the arrangement with therapeutic motives: 'I was interested in preventing any excessive gratitude from arising; on the other hand I had no intention of depriving the poor girl of her modest means.'[58]

Freud's attitude towards payment reveals his firm intention both to survive as a practitioner and family man and to sweep aside all those, mostly tacit, partly contradictory, moral and social obligations which might encumber the psychoanalytic relationship. Thus, the psychoanalytic situation was stripped of the trappings *Kulturmenschen* had previously adhered to. All financial complication was, in principle, reduced to a minimum in an agreement of maximum clarity: prompt monthly payment at a fixed rate – one further approximation of a social null-situation.[59]

Having detailed the evolution of the office consultation and the payment of a set fee, we can examine more briefly the temporal arrangements of psychoanalysis, as well as those arrangements that served to isolate the psychoanalytic dyad as much as possible from outside interference.

THE MANAGEMENT OF TIME

'In regard to time, I adhere strictly to the principle of leasing a definite hour.'[60] This flat declaration is immediately followed by a comparison to practitioners of somewhat lower status, 'teachers of music or languages in good society'. Freud notes that his rule may offend medical dignity; it 'may perhaps seem too rigorous in a doctor, or even unworthy of his profession'.[61] Yet, as he points out, a physician's very material existence may be threatened if patients are allowed to miss sessions with all sorts of excuses.

Again, with these firm rules, Freud slashes a knot that had tied many nineteenth-century doctors in a reputational predicament. Liehrsch, for instance, remarked: 'Young physicians and quacks make it a habit to keep their visits short so as to appear very busy. Those who are in fact very busy have to do so anyway; others try to ingratiate themselves by staying long.'[62]

Usually, Freud worked with a patient six days a week, one hour a day. On the length of treatment, however, Freud tended to be somewhat reticent, finding the question 'almost unanswerable'. This was one of the few unspecified clauses in the implicit treatment contract; it had to be fully explained to the patient that psychoanalysis always takes a long time: six months, a year, or more. On the other hand, with his usual consistency, Freud did not 'bind patients to continue the treatment for a certain length of time'. The analysis could be broken off whenever the patient wished, although Freud cautions that this might leave the patient in an 'unsatisfactory state'.[63]

Freud's recommendations on precise temporal arrangements appear to be more in line with his personal inclinations than the equally strict prescriptions for financial matters. One of Freud's servants indicates: 'The Herr Professor is always *sehr punktlich* – very punctual – in everything he does.'[64] This punctiliousness enabled him to manage an extraordinarily busy schedule, including 'eight or nine hours of therapeutical or training analysis'.[65] His evenings were devoted to the many chores of a researcher, writer, and teacher, as well as to his extensive correspondence. In addition, Freud was the leader of a gradually expanding movement, with its own journals and publishing houses, and a variety of managerial bodies.[66]

THE SOCIAL ISOLATION OF THE PSYCHOANALYTIC ENCOUNTER

The psychoanalytic situation gradually also became more sharply defined in its social setting. It was divested of anything that was superfluous, anything that might introduce ambiguity between the analyst and the analysand, anything that might contaminate the patient's contributions, so that nothing other than the patient's own psychic conflicts could be held accountable for his or her reactions. This isolated dyadic encounter has been called here a 'social null-situation', analogous to the expression 'null-hypothesis'. The conceptual structuring of this relationship is similar to a natural science experiment: all relevant variables, except the independent variable (the patient), are controlled, so that whatever occurs in the experiment (the analysis) can be explained on the basis of this remaining factor (the patient reproducing his or her own psychic conflicts).

Under this conceptual structure all direct and indirect relationships between the analyst and the analysand are to be eliminated, except for that of the analytic dyad. Of paramount importance is the integrity of the dyad and, in line with this, the analyst's discretion. Historically, doctors had practised a certain reservation in talking to patients' relatives and friends and had set themselves high standards of discretion, especially in matters pertaining to venereal diseases and gynaecological afflictions. 'The physician's silent breast is often like a grave in which one lets sink the matters of the past', writes Liehrsch,[67] therefore 'silence is among the doctor's first duties'. This oldest of medical obligations weighed heavily with Freud: 'With the neurotics, then, we make our pact: complete candour on one side and strict discretion on the other.'[68] For the medical audience addressed in the *Recommendations*, the matter went almost without saying. It was so much common knowledge that even the innkeeper's daughter in the Alp hotel, Katharina, trustfully began her confession on the mountain top with: 'You can say *anything* to a doctor, I suppose.'[69]

Freud, however, learned at an early point in his career that even the closest relatives must be excluded, no matter whether they might possibly clarify matters. He conscientiously reports an incident at the end of the treatment of Elisabeth von R., after he had discussed with the mother an infatuation on the part of his patient: 'She was indignant with me for having betrayed her secret. She was entirely inaccessible, and the treatment had been a complete failure.'[70]

Beyond the medical tradition of discretion, early-nineteenth-century handbooks warn physicians to be guarded in their relations with female patients.[71] And Liehrsch[72] warns physicians against 'ladies who often consider them as suitors, or at least that is what they would like'. Clearly, the phenomenon of transference love had been widely recognized for a long time, especially in the relations between hypnotizers and their clients, and even in the much less frequent and less intimate contacts between physicians and their patients.[73] But this situation, which had chased Breuer from Anna O.'s house, had not been understood. It was Freud's *coup de génie* to turn this familiar subject of embarrassment and jokes into the very vehicle of therapy. To do so, however, necessitated some strict rules of conduct, which Freud had to discover on his own, by trial and error. In the *Studies on Hysteria*,[74] for instance, the reader finds Freud engaging freely in social intercourse with his patients, staying at Frau Emmy von N.'s country house, or – be it stealthily – visiting a ball where Elisabeth von R. whirls past in a lively dance.

Of course, since for some time Freud was the only psychoanalyst, and for many years the analyst of all other analysts, he himself had to be exempt from the rule prohibiting friendship.[75] Be that as it may, as early as 1900, in the *Interpretation of Dreams*, Freud warns against the entanglements in treating patients from one's own circle of acquaintances, and he is adamant on the subject in the *Recommendations* :[76] 'Special difficulties arise when the analyst and his new patient or their families are on terms of friendship or have social ties with one another. The psychoanalyst who is asked to undertake the treatment of the wife or child of a friend must be prepared for it to cost him that friendship, no matter what the outcome of the treatment may be: nevertheless he must make the sacrifice if he cannot find a trustworthy substitute. [77] Not only 'previous acquaintance' but also 'lengthy preliminary discussions' may result in a disadvantageous, preestablished 'transference attitude', which must be uncovered before the actual work can begin. Freud also advised his patients to tell as few people as possible about the analysis: 'That in consequence the world hears nothing of some of the most successful cures is, of course, a consideration that cannot be taken into account.'[78]

Knowledge acquired about analysis outside the treatment proper is considered harmless but not helpful, and previous reading useless. By the time Freud wrote the *Recommendations*, he had come to abandon the habit of giving his patients lengthy expositions of psychoanalytic theory.[79] 'I require them to learn by personal experience' – within the psychoanalytic situation itself, that is.[80]

As we have seen, the adoption of office practice and a consultation hour in the nineteenth century was one aspect of a rationalization process that transformed the medical profession, a rationalization directly bearing on the nature of the relations between doctors and their patients. In many respects, Freud's design of the psychoanalytic situation was a continuation and a consistent elaboration of these rationalized patterns of exchange between an expert, the therapist, and the patient. The strict regulation of payment and timing, the isolation of the interaction from other contacts, and the analyst's discretion, all served further to purify a pattern of interaction that had evolved among *fin de siècle* physicians.

For Freud, however, the psychoanalytic situation was not simply his own version of contemporary professional trends; it was essential to both his working technique and this theorizing. It allowed him to confront both the patient and the scientific public – Freud's double audience – with the fact that the patient's productions could not be dismissed as artefacts of the particular situation, nor as having been induced by the therapist, but had, instead, to be explained on the basis of the patient's own psychic activities. The analysis took place in a social null-situation, which of itself would not lead anyone to expect the kind of behaviour on the part of his patients that Freud observed and reported. Therefore, according to the basic structure of Freud's argument, the behaviour had to be understood from the patient's earlier experiences.

THE TWO GROUND RULES: FREE ASSOCIATION AND ABSTINENCE

It is against this background of a social null-situation that Freud prescribes two rules to guide the behaviour of the actors, the analyst and the analysand. These two complementary rules – the rule of free association and the rule of abstinence – represent a true innovation; they appear almost entirely without precedent.

In describing what is known as the 'basic rule', Freud writes:

> My patients were pledged to communicate to me every idea or thought that occurred to them in connection with some particular subject . . . . [The] success of psycho-analysis depends on his noticing and reporting whatever comes into his head and not being misled, for instance, into suppressing an idea because it strikes him as unimportant or irrelevant or because it seems to him meaningless. He must adopt a completely impartial attitude to what occurs to him.[81]

To this day the requirement of free association stands as the *sine qua non* of psychoanalysis. 'Everyone really reacts to the statement of the ground rule as if he had already been familiar with it,' Fain remarks.[82] Somehow, somewhere there should be an opportunity to say whatever one pleases, and the basic rule embodies an invitation to do precisely that. Little has changed in the application of this fundamental rule, though some of Freud's phrasings might now be replaced by different words.

Freud's primary interest, at first, was in the repressed content, rather than in the defence mechanisms with which this repression was carried out and sustained. Thus, his instruction that 'whatever comes into one's head must be reported without criticizing it'[83] might be misconstrued as forbidding any hesitation, protestation, or apology – phenomena which later became themselves a focus of interest. Another misunderstanding might arise from Freud's use of terms such as 'pledge' (*verpflichtet, versprochen*), which suggest a moral obligation, whereas what is at stake is a '*technical* instrumentality'.[84] To repeat: 'the success of psycho-analysis depends on' the patient's adherence to the basic rule; this is quite aside from any ethical considerations. Finally, Freud's formula has been criticized for promoting a kind of dissociation between the speaker and what the speaker speaks about, between 'him' and 'what comes into his head'.[85] Whatever the astuteness of these criticisms of Freud's theoretical writing, they are outwitted by Freud's words in practice: 'And now', Freud began treatment with Wortis,[86] 'you can start and say what you like.'

The second prescription, the rule of abstinence, is more difficult to define and has provoked much controversy.

> The treatment must be carried out in abstinence . . . . I shall state it as a fundamental principle that the patient's need and longing should be allowed to persist in her, in order that they may serve as forces impelling her to do work and to make changes, and that we must beware of appeasing those forces by means of surrogates.[87]

At first sight, the rule seems to impose limitations on the patient. Freud (1919) makes it very clear that he does not expect the patient to forgo sexual satisfaction in daily life.[88] One of his concerns, however, is that cravings unsatisfied in the treatment may be acted on outside it with harmful consequences. In this regard, he advises: 'One best protects the patient from injuries brought about through carrying out one of his impulses by making him promise not to take any important decisions affecting his life during the time of his treatment – for instance, not choose any profession or definitive love-object – but to postpone all such plans until after his recovery.'[89]

Promises of this kind are nowadays less often demanded from patients, perhaps because life decisions, such as marriage and choice of occupation, no longer seem so definitive. Van der Sterren also suggests technical reasons for this: 'in fact it might well have quite harmful effects, because it means the introduction of a certain measure, a prohibition, which may provoke the patient to act out and which brings with it the danger of our missing a valuable interpretation.'[90] Van der Sterren's argument represents a further purification of the psychoanalytic situation through the elimination of 'a certain measure, a prohibition'.

It is also necessary for patients to verbalize their fears and longings, rather than act on them *within* the psychoanalytic situation. The analyst 'is prepared for a perpetual struggle with his patient to keep in the psychical sphere all the impulses which the patient would like to direct into the motor sphere'.[91] This limitation – that the patient, while intensely feeling and verbalizing longings and anxieties, should refrain from acting them out through bodily movements – is the abstinence required of the patient. And it may be that an analysand cannot even express these strivings until he or she has discovered that it is possible to express them without physically (or magically) realizing them, and without being punished for giving voice to them. This gradual discovery is part of the psychoanalytic process.

On further reflection, it is apparent that the rule of abstinence imposes restrictions, first of all, on the analyst. Freud's 'Observations on Transference-Love' contains a lengthy list of what analysts should refrain from doing.[92] They should not proceed to satisfy a longing through actual action, nor should they prohibit, condemn, or even justify their patients' desires with juridical or ethical arguments, as these are external to the psychoanalytic situation. Analysts should neither encourage nor discourage their patients by referring to what they themselves like or dislike. And, perhaps the most subtle point in Freud's discussion, analysts should not dismiss these longings by denying their authenticity. Analysts should limit themselves to one activity only – to interpreting the patient's verbalizations in the context of the autobiographical material already given by the patient. This interpretation is arrived at by using all those rules of transformation that together constitute the body of psychoanalytic technique. Again, these limitations are not imposed on the analyst for moral reasons, but because the technique of treatment requires them. As Freud explains, 'I am on this occasion in the happy position of being able to replace the moral embargo by considerations of analytic technique, without any alteration in the outcome.'[93]

In their entirety, Freud's recommendations certainly created a new kind of relationship between two people, and a new form of dealing with the strivings of one of them: 'it is one for which there is no model in real life.'[94] In theory, at least, a perfect social null-situation has been brought about, and one might expect that such a completely rationalized relationship would lead only to correspondingly business-like, perhaps polite and friendly, behaviour on the part of the patient. 'We believed, to be sure', writes Freud, 'that we had reckoned with all the motives concerned in the treatment, that we had completely rationalized the situation between us and the patients so that it could be looked over at a glance like a sum in arithmetic; yet, in spite of all this, something seems to creep in which has not been taken into account in our sum.'[95]

With this 'something', Freud alludes to the transference. These emotional attachments appear to be so strongly connected to the person of the analyst and to the specifics of the treatment situation that every effort is necessary to convince the patient (and the scientific audience) that they cannot have been induced by either and that, therefore, they must be a compulsive repetition of the patient's earlier, conflict-laden experiences. Of course, there remains an element of suggestion, in so far as the therapist makes him- or herself available as an object for the patient's fantasies, without immediately correcting or contradicting them as someone in the outside world might do. But no active intervention is required to achieve this: 'nothing need be done but to give [the patient] time.'[96] Thus, the psychoanalytic situation, fully rationalized, comparable to an arithmetic sum, or, in the terms of this chapter, to a social null-situation, nevertheless produces deviations from the calculated pattern. And it is precisely these deviations that are significant expressions of the patient's psychic conflicts. Habermas captures this idea very neatly: 'The – in a sense – experimental control of the "repetition" [*Wiederholung*] under the conditions of the analytic situation offers the physician an opportunity to both carry out treatment and gain knowledge'.[97]

CONCLUSION

The premeditated and manipulated nature of the psychoanalytic situation and of the therapist's behaviour within it represents an extension of rationalization – in the sociological sense – into new fields of human experience and activity. Its origins may be traced to developments within the medical profession, which itself was becoming more rationalized both in the invention and application of therapies and in the mode of communication with patients. But Freud's creation of the basic rule of free association, as well as the rule of abstinence, goes far beyond the developments in the sphere of medicine proper.

As to the sociogenesis of the psychoanalytic situation, part of its social origin may be explained by the particular figuration in which physicians found themselves at the end of the nineteenth century. They saw themselves compelled to build a reputation based increasingly on technical competence rather than on moral character – each of them in competition with others, but all of them helped by the increasing prestige of the profession as a whole. The growth in professional prestige owed much to scientific advances. Within this constellation, Freud achieved his reputation through original discoveries, which he had to present and defend according to the canons of science. He did so, on the one hand, by postulating a model of the mind that, at least in principle, would allow a reduction to neurological concepts. On the other hand, he arranged his treatment in such a manner that he could convince his patients and his scientific colleagues that neither the situation itself nor the therapist's demeanour had in any way induced his findings, and that instead they were the product of the patient's psychic conflicts. Herein lies the meaning of the recommendations that together constitute the social null-situation in psychoanalysis.

Chapter Five

FROM TROUBLES TO PROBLEMS

In the course of the structural transformations that have shaped contemporary society, new dependence relations between people and new forms of conflict between and within individuals have emerged. One of these encompassing transformations concerns the rise of the helping professions, in which people make it their trade to solve other people's troubles. As the helping professions evolved, these troubles were re-defined and re-classified, the relations with colleagues and clients were codified, and definite methods of treatment emerged, requiring special training and excluding the uninitiated as unqualified. This process is referred to in one of those professional jargons, the sociological vocabulary, as 'professionalization'. These professionalizing occupational circles come to be organized in associations and treatment institutions, arranging among themselves a division of tasks and of spheres of competence, and providing for a regulated system of supervision, of remuneration and subsidy. A process takes place which, in that same sociological vocabulary, is referred to as 'bureaucratization', without this necessarily implying that inflexibility or indifference set in.

These processes occur in close conjunction with the state apparatus which grants the occupational circle its legal recognition, provides for binding regulation of occupational training and practice, and subsidizes its services, a development which is part of a wider 'collectivization of care arrangements'.[1]

Similar events have occurred in medical care and in the fields of education and social work, of 'psychosocial care' and 'mental health'. In this manifold development of care arrangements, one occupational circle has gradually emerged which claims as its province the treatment of troubles that people experience with themselves and with others in their intimate circle of close acquaintances and relatives – that is, the occupational circle of psychotherapy – and these problems are referred to as 'psychic problems'.[2] People make trouble with themselves and with others in a family setting, in love relationships, and in their everyday work. In these troubles, psychotherapists recognize psychic problems, they have theories to describe and classify them, methods to treat them, training courses to teach about them, and organizations that regulate collegial co-operation and professional practice in dealing with these problems. And in these respects they are very much like other helping professions.

The professional classifications and conceptions of troubles as problems that may then be categorized and treated by members of a certain profession are next adopted by outsiders; first by people who are socially close to the profession – for example, because they work in adjacent professions, as colleagues, referring clients to members of this profession, as assistants to members of the profession, or next because they have made contact as a client. These insights spread in ever-widening circles of laymen by means of personal conversations, literature, and the media, and also because people pick up such notions in passing in the course of their formal education.

With respect to the various professions, this spreading process is referred to as 'medicalization',[3] 'legalization',[4] 'psychologization', and even as 'professionalization of the client'.[5] In general, these external effects of professionalization upon the conceptualization among laymen may be referred to as their *protoprofessionalization*: in the course of this development, laymen adopt the fundamental stances and basic concepts which are circulating within the profession and, in this way, become 'protoprofessionals' themselves. The process does not take place at the same pace or to an equal degree within all segments of society. On the contrary, it occurs sooner among people who are socially close to the profession or at an intellectual advantage because of their extensive education.

People make troubles with themselves and with one another, and psychotherapists regard these troubles as psychic problems; as this professional concept spreads, people redefine their troubles as psychic problems suitable for treatment by the psychotherapist. But the troubles were already there. The service supply creates the demand, but it doesn't create the misery.

In this way, the division of labour which has evolved among the helping professions also serves as a guideline in the everyday experience of laymen when putting their troubles into words and categorizing them; often there is hardly any other way to talk about these troubles than in the vocabulary that each profession has developed for its problem area and has conveyed to adjacent circles of laymen.

The way these troubles are articulated and the manner in which they are experienced are determined in part by the division of labour and by the treatment claims that have emerged between the various helping professions. In this sense, the very fact that people live in society as potential therapy clients, welfare clients, and patients of one profession or another shapes the troubles they experience.

The entire area of troubled modes of experience and inter-action has become the working terrain of the fairly new profession of psychotherapy, and in circles of people who are closely related to it, laymen have begun to recognize their troubles as psychic problems, whereas they were previously accustomed to speaking of bad behaviour and evil moods, of sin and of illness, of deliriums and rage, of bewitchment or destiny, of the usual imperfections of human existence – if they took any note of these troubles and considered them worth discussing at all. Psychotherapy did not exist yet, and psychic problems were not recognized or experienced as such, but in many different ways.

The profession exerts an educating and proselytizing impact on the outside world. The external effect of professionalization is the formation of a clientele: the professionalization process operates in the surrounding society as proto-professionalization. And as people spend a greater part of their lives in circles where it is common practice to label one's everyday experience in accordance with the categories of psychotherapy and to put the basic concepts of the profession of psychotherapy into practice in everyday life, they will be the more likely to seek psychotherapeutic treatment and to benefit from it.

Given this starting point, it follows that what is to be studied first is not the population at large and its suitability or needs, but the professional circles themselves and the way they categorize clients to be treated.

THE INCOMPLETE PROFESSIONALIZATION OF PSYCHOTHERAPY

Some occupations are characterized by the special knowledge they require: it is usually impossible for the clients to judge the quality of the services provided. In this way, they can become the innocent victims of quacks, who, moreover, also harm the competitive chances and the prestige of those who do possess and apply this special knowledge. The latter will want to protect themselves by making certain agreements with one another, by setting certain fees, by drawing up certain educational requirements, by mutual recognition and the exclusion of unqualified non-members, by deciding upon certain methods of treatment and ways of dealing with clients. Processes like these are referred to collectively as professionalization, disputed as the term may be.[6] Wilensky described the typical professionalization process as follows:[7] First, the new profession must turn into a full-time occupation, not a secondary task for people in some other profession; a training institute is founded, and later on teaching is taken over by the university; local, and subsequently national, professional organizations are established; the state begins to give credentials to qualified practitioners; the professional circle imposes a binding code of behavior upon its members. In this way, or more or less so, a number of occupations have turned into full-fledged professions.

Particularly in the American literature on the subject, there has been a somewhat moralizing emphasis on the professionals' commitment to serving their neighbours and the common good, but in fact the professionalizing process tended to be quite conflict-ridden.[8] Practitioners from different occupational backgrounds often clashed, and, moreover, there never was a ready blueprint for the emergent profession which evolved in 'a process of trial and error, in which people attempt to match occupational techniques or institutions and human needs'.[9]

It is not difficult to detect many of these features of the professionalization process in the field of mental health care. The controversies in the area are still too great even to find a generally accepted framework for discussion. On the one hand there is the family of concepts related to 'psychosocial assistance', which suggests a close connection with community action, social work, and even remedial teaching. On the other hand there is the cluster of 'ambulatory mental health care', conveying that what is involved here is a subdivision of mental health care and a sub-subdivision of health care; the subject then comes under the overall heading of medicine. If, finally, 'psychotherapy' is selected as 'the unit of place, time and action', then this already indicates that neither psychiatrists nor social workers as such are included in the development, and that what is involved here is a profession *sui generis.*

Some researchers indeed have come to the conclusion that a synthesis of psychology, social work, psychiatry, and psychoanalysis has led to 'the emergence of a fifth profession': psychotherapy.[10] Even though these 'helpers' have arrived at this fifth profession along very different educational routes, they often come from very comparable backgrounds and in the course of their similar professional practice, they acquire ways of thinking and working which have more in common than they might think.

'In this battle of convictions, the social scientist may also take sides and he frequently does. But he need not.' One possible approach lies in 'taking as his very subject matter this battle of positions'.[11] Instead of taking sides in the controversy or speculating about how it will turn out in the end, one might also draw up a diagram of all the (more or less professional) occupations which entail helping people with their troubles with themselves and with other people.

It holds true for all occupations which comprise a sector in the circle in Figure 1 that some of their members perform activities that in many respects strongly resemble psychotherapy in the strictest sense of the word, while others in the same sector have virtually nothing to do with it. Clinical psychologists, for example, or medical and psychiatric social workers are active within their occupational sectors in specialities more closely related to psychotherapy than other specialists in the same sector. It may even be the case that in one of these closely related specialities some practitioners come to use mainly psychotherapy techniques; their position then borders the inner circle of psychotherapy in the narrow sense of the word. Clearly, tensions will spring up

Figure 1: The circle of therapeutic occupations

around these intermediary specialists, who may claim adherence to the field of psychotherapy proper, or to their original occupational sector, and these claims may be rejected by either side, while one or the other side may contend that the practice of these specialists is irregular, that they should either seek admission to the appropriate occupational circle or abandon their practices, leaving them to others who are better qualified.

The question now arises as to what may be called psychotherapy in the narrow sense of the word, a question which also depends on the particular school of psychotherapy involved. In psychoanalysis and behaviour therapy, the entire body of theoretical knowledge is structured in such a way – and the practice of the profession is regulated sufficiently – as to provide an indication of the degree to which an individual practises psychotherapy in the manner of that particular school. In other, less structured and regulated schools of psychotherapy, this may not be quite as clear.

The points which are now disputed by various groups of professionals are whether an inner circle of psychotherapy can and should exist, how admission is to be gained to this inner circle from the adjacent specialisms in every professional sector, and whether there should be a specialized training programme for psychotherapists, granting direct admission to the inner circle. Actually, there exists an occupational circle of practitioners from different schools who have combined in associations and institutes as psychotherapists in the strict sense, and psychotherapy training programmes have been established granting admission to them. The question remains how those specialists who were trained in other, adjacent occupations but now practise some kind of psychotherapy will be classified: whether and how they are to gain admission to the inner circle of psychotherapy. In other words, there is an occupational circle of psychotherapy, divided into various schools, which is professional in many respects but has not yet succeeded in closing itself off to the adjacent professions and struggles to guard its borders. The umpires in this conflict are the state's subsidizing agencies. That does not make the final outcome of the development any more predictable.

THE PARTIAL PROTO-PROFESSIONALIZATION OF LAY CIRCLES

The claim of every profession – not of every occupation – is that its services are better than the work of a layman. With the rise of the professions, all sorts of mutual support among relatives, neighbours, or colleagues have become less common, since they are now viewed as the professionals' task. Thus the professionalizing process has also altered the customs and categories of everyday experience. With the professionalization of the medical vocation, certain symptoms became 'medical' problems, a new category among all the many discomforts of daily life: something for the doctor. Among the numerous disputes or conflicts between people some came to be classified as 'a case for a lawyer'. The everyday orientation of laymen follows the classification of professional areas (just as the classification of consumer goods corresponds with the stores where they can be bought). What is involved here is not only cognitive orientation, but also the acquisition of habits, of stances that correspond to the basic attitude of the profession.

The adherence to the avoidance rules of hygiene is the most striking example of the medicalization of daily life, with each individual practising his or her own disease prevention. In a quite similar way, people have become more cautious in handling conflicts, referring to general rules (rather than directly to their own interests or feelings), and managing the dispute as if they were a lawyer in their own case.

Proto-medical hygienic avoidance behaviour and proto-legal self-control go much deeper than just a cognitive orientation; they affect the very emotions, feelings of repugnance and embarrassment, the control of rage and violence.

Thus, this process of proto-professionalization involves alterations in the everyday orientation patterns and daily habits of laymen as an external effect of a professionalization process, an effect which may well take place more rapidly and profoundly in circles which are closer to the professional circles – clients and ex-clients are the most important transmitters of the knowledge and the customs of the profession – and among people who have received a more extended and a more closely related education. The media also contribute to the process of dissemination; whenever television programmes deal with a subject that can be considered part of some professional area, a recognized authority in the field is allowed to have the last word.

But for the greater part, the actual process of proto-professionalization occurs in an informal, spontaneous, and diffuse way: in the course of conversations and gossip, people tell one another about their own and other people's troubles, what can be done about them and whether it helps: a trade directory for everyday troubles. In a society where so many and such serious troubles are entrusted to professionals, people must learn to select the right helpers for their troubles: this turns laymen into experts on the division of expertise.

With the development of the medical profession, the medicalization of everyday life has also advanced greatly; the legalization of daily life has taken place in a similar manner, though less drastically and less uniformly.[12] The 'Circle of Friends and Supporters of Psychotherapy'[13] was an early setting for proto-professionalization with respect to psychotherapy.

Since one's chances of proto-professionalization are greater the closer one is to a circle of professionals or the higher one's level of educational training is, the process does not take place at the same rate in all circles and with respect to all individuals. But the differences do not coincide with differences in income or property, religion, age, sex, or other characteristics that are easy to measure statistically, nor do these differences coincide with categories which are familiar from sociological theories, such as social class or personal prestige. The individual characteristic which coincides most strongly is the level of education. It will be clear now that especially people who are capable of categorizing their own life experiences in such a way that they correspond to some degree with the division of labour among the various helping professions, and who have made the basic stances of these professions their own, will seek help in these professions.

So there is no point in speaking of a 'need' for any given type of professional help, unrelated to the way in which this help is organized, and unrelated to what people in general know about it and how they view it. An individual has already had to view his or her own life as one in which events may call for lawyers or doctors or psychotherapists, as she or he conceives of these professional people and as they operate in the society in which that person lives. There is no natural 'need for legal advice' unrelated to the actual existence of the legal profession, nor do physical ailments in themselves inspire a 'need for medical treatment' unrelated to the actual conditions of the medical profession, how patients view their doctors, and how they approach them.

Since the medical and legal professions seem to be indisputably established, whatever is 'medical' or 'legal' also seems to be indisputable. In these long-established professions, the division into fields of work and, consequently, into problem areas, seems so self-evident that the existing apportionment appears to be vested in the nature of things, and it is quite difficult to view it instead as the result of relations which have gradually come into being among people seeking to cope with all sorts of difficulties. However, in a profession which is still in an earlier stage of development, the borderlines are still flexible and disputed, and lay persons do not automatically categorize their everyday experiences according to the classifications which have been drawn up by the new profession.

This is the stage at which psychotherapy finds itself, as do mental health care and psychosocial work also. These professional circles are under constant pressure to justify themselves to their own ranks as well as to the outside world by stressing the needs

107

which they fulfil, as if these were measurable entities, independent of their own impact on them. Their opponents can then raise the objection that when this kind of help does not exist, no one seems to miss it, but wherever it appears the demand soon increases, and therefore, it is understood, the need cannot be real. Both sides hold to the idea that human needs can be described without any reference to the social context within which they arise and are to be satisfied. It is partly an external effect of the development of the psychotherapy profession that people have come to view and to express their troubles and psychic problems. This psychotherapy proto-professionalization involves a certain amount of knowledge of which troubles are treated by psychotherapists and members of related helping professions, as well as a tendency to adopt certain attitudes and basic concepts of the field of psychotherapy. But in order to be able to recognize everyday troubles as problems for a therapist, it is necessary to see a certain pattern and a repetition in a whole range of actions and events. It is also necessary to recognize, in oneself or in someone else, intentions and feelings which might not be explicitly expressed, or even consciously perceived at all, and to be able to identify these emotions and intentions with some degree of accuracy. All this presupposes that such feelings and intentions are considered important in themselves, that they matter, that they may be expressed even if they cannot be gratified, that it is possible to achieve some understanding of people and that they are capable of explaining themselves to someone else and that this is worth trying for.

This attitude to proto-professional psychotherapy also pre-supposes that individuals are capable of suspending their reactions to their own or to someone else's behaviour, or can at least reflect upon their reactions afterwards and try to understand what occurred, regardless of what they would or would not like to be the case on the grounds of their opinions, religious beliefs, convictions, artistic, political, or erotic preferences, or because of their own fear, shame, and irritation.

Chapter Six

THE INITIAL INTERVIEW AS A TASK

'What is the question?
That is the question!'

The initial interviews at a psychotherapy institute are a critical episode on the potential client's path to treatment, serving as they do as the last (or penultimate) phase in the selection procedure.[1] Moreover, this phase is set up and controlled by psychotherapists themselves, whereas the client's earlier steps were mostly outside of their sphere of influence.

These initial interviews may be viewed as a conversational genre, comparable to other genres of dialogues, such as a police interrogation, a chat between friends, a dialogue between a personnel manager and a job applicant, a medical consultation, an oral exam at school. Each of these conversational genres has its own rules, as does every literary genre. The initial interview in psychotherapy is a form of the genre of conversations between a client and an expert, characterized by the discrepancy in the expertise of the two partners. Moreover, a selection is taking place: a decision whether to accept the client for psychotherapeutic treatment, based on the experts' opinion of their clients' suitability according to the selection criteria valid in the professional circle.

In the following sections the main characteristics of these interviews will be discussed.

THE INSCRUTABILITY OF THE TASK

A typical feature of initial interviews in psychotherapy is the particular inscrutability, to lay persons, of the task they are faced with. To the majority of clients, it is unclear what the interview will be about, what course it will take, and what their role in it is to be, what the standards are for treatment or for referral elsewhere. If clients telephone an institute to make an appointment, they rarely receive information on those aspects, and the brochure which is then sent to them does not much clarify matters. Nor does the doctor conducting the initial interview give an explanation at the start of the interview itself, at least not in the cases studied here. Of course, there are proto-professional clients who already have some idea of what to expect, and most other clients base their expectations on experiences with their family doctor. To most clients, the task of the initial interview becomes clear only in the course of the conversation, from the very deliberate vagueness of the doctors, from their reluctance to contribute to the conversation. This inscrutability of the task of the initial interview is partially intentional and deliberate, a technique which allows the therapist to determine what the clients themselves consider important enough to tell and how they structure their account. But there are other reasons for making the initial interview episode so very inscrutable.

In the first place, there is the difference in knowledge evident in all confrontations between clients and professionals of any kind. In the second place, in the case of psychotherapy, the selection criteria have taken shape in the course of a precarious and complicated process of demarcating the spheres of competence of a series of professional circles; it is to this origin that the criteria owe their complex and diffuse nature. In the third place, the professional circle protects itself from deceit or conflicts, and its clients from being offended by keeping the grounds for their acceptance or rejection as vague as they are.

These three reasons for the inscrutability of the initial interview are dealt with in this section. This and the next section – about the structure of the initial interview – are intended to link a historical-sociological analysis of the profession and the analysis of interaction in the initial interview to which the rest of this chapter is devoted.

To return to the first reason for inscrutability; the inaccessibility of professional knowledge is a general and defining characteristic of the professions: lay persons are not considered capable of performing professional operations themselves, nor are they considered qualified to arrive at a competent opinion on the quality of the professional care. Within the framework of these relations of inequality, the clients are protected through the recognition of bona fide members of the profession by a professional organization or by state authorities, closing the profession and excluding quacks, by formalizing professional training, by regulating professional practice, and by subsidizing these recognized services with public or other collective funds. Such developments have also taken place in the psychotherapy trade and related branches of social care.

The second reason for the inscrutability of the criteria in the selection procedure for psychotherapy is related to the development of psychosocial care, including psychotherapy services. In the United States in the thirties and somewhat later in other countries, such as the United Kingdom and the Netherlands, professionals from different academic backgrounds and from various schools of therapy attempted, within a variety of institutions and associations, to demarcate their spheres of competence with respect to one another and to other helpers. In the course of the years, a division of tasks and claims emerged, and rules were adopted for allocating categories of clients to certain kinds of therapists and institutes. Even though these borders do keep changing, and sometimes quite rapidly, for each separate initial interview they hold true as a given fact at that moment. In the initial interview episode, the aim is therefore to determine whether a specific client belongs to those specific client categories that the institute considers as within its area of treatment and sphere of competence.

Viewed in a sociological perspective, and independently of their merits as selective criteria for psychotherapy, these norms emerged from the competitive relations between helpers from the sphere of psychiatry and those from the ranks of the church; between helpers trained as psychiatrists, psychologists, social or pastoral workers; and between helpers with a theoretical orientation in psychoanalysis, learning theory, medical psychiatry, religious ethics, or some other field. Once again, regardless of the intrinsic merits of the discussion, what was at stake too was the prestige of one's own circle, one's own educational background and theoretical specialization, and equally, the access to a clientele, the attainment of recognition and subsidies from local and national authorities.

In this conflict-ridden process, a provisional demarcation of treatment areas gradually developed: problematical and contested in the interplay with claims made by others – each set of claims complex in itself, and always diffuse and abstract in nature. These very institutional claims, each staking out an area of treatment, operate in every initial interview as given facts, as compelling criteria of selection. Without insight into the development and the present state of the division of labour within psychosocial care, these criteria cannot be understood.

For example, there are the contra-indications (negative selection criteria) of 'psychosis' and 'addiction'. Regardless of their complex, abstract, and diffuse substantive meaning, they also came to apply to specific categories of clients as they were defined by certain institutes: psychiatric clinics, or consultation centres for alcohol and drugs. Of course, intrinsic considerations of treatment also played a role in the development of the division of labour among these institutions, but once this division of labour has come about, the criteria in turn come to refer to the field of operation of some established institute and acquire a different meaning. In other words, initially 'addicts' were supposed to suffer from a compulsion to ingest drugs or spirits, and in order to treat them institutions were established. But once these agencies existed 'addicts' were re-defined as those persons who were especially suited for treatment at those institutions.

In view of the problematical and contested nature of the division of labour within the facilities for psychosocial care, and in view of the complex, abstract, and diffuse nature of each set of selection criteria, proto-professionalization outside of the immediate environment of the professional circle must be quite rare and limited.

In those cases where proto-professionalization did grow to maturity, it includes knowledge of the division of labour among the facilities for psychosocial care and – in addition to this cognitive aspect – the habit of introspection and the suspension of one's judgements and impulses, the proto-professional counter-parts of the professional stance in psychotherapy: one's own experiences and those of others are classified according to categories such as 'inner conflicts' and 'defence mechanisms', as the proto-professional counterpart of how psychotherapists classify these experiences. But even though this became a generally accepted stance, it still is much rarer than legal and medical proto-professionalization, although by now it has far transcended the original, sophisticated 'Circle of Friends and Supporters of Psychotherapy'.[2]

Thus, social proximity to the professional circle of psychotherapy promotes a familiarity with its treatment criteria, an introspective attitude, and a habit of describing oneself in psychologizing terms. A system of diagnosis which takes such categories as introspection, insight, vitality, and motivation into consideration implicitly also measures the social proximity to the psychotherapy profession and the degree of protoprofessionalization of a client. At the same time, in this system of diagnosis, the lack of familiarity with the profession almost inevitably contributes to unsuitability for treatment.

There is also a third set of reasons for the inscrutability of the selection criteria; reasons not unique, but very typical of psychotherapy services. The diagnosis, no matter how devoid of any value judgement in the eyes of the professional, often contains, in the eyes of the clients, a statement about their worth, their social status – in other words, their value relative to and in the eyes of others imagined or real. 'Unsuitable for treatment' also means 'incorrigible', bordering on 'irremediable' or 'incurable'. Even though the diagnosis is made in co-operation with the clients, it is essentially a statement about them, not intended for them. Perhaps the type of misunderstanding described here cannot be cleared up with clients; it may not even be a misunderstanding, but at any rate it saves the clients heartache, and the therapist a headache, if they do not know why they have been rejected or even that they have not been accepted. As long as the criteria for acceptance remain inscrutable, clients who have been rejected cannot object to the decision, nor will they feel very bad about it. Here the protection of clients definitely coincides with the self-protection of therapists.

Since all information is provided by the clients themselves, if clients were able to handle the criteria skilfully and to adjust their presentation accordingly, they would win every discussion with the therapist about the diagnosis. As matters stand now, in the initial interview the decision-making therapist is familiar with the criteria

113

and their application, but the clients are not; the clients, in turn, know the facts about their own life which the interviewer wants to find out.

Thus, when highly proto-professionalized clients come for diagnosis – for instance, workers in other helping professions – a contest ensues of presentation with foreknowledge against diagnosis with surplus knowledge, and at stake are the ratings of 'good patient' and 'authenticity'.

Students applying for admission into training therapy are known to have rehearsed their self-presentation for the selection interview. In this sense, for once, proto-professionalization can also make the diagnosis more difficult; the social proximity can be 'too close for comfort'. A certain degree of unfamiliarity with the selection criteria, on the other hand, promotes a naïve presentation – in a psychotherapeutic sense – and facilitates diagnosis.

This third group of reasons for the inscrutability of treatment criteria is partially prompted by interests within the psychotherapy services themselves (and by interests of the clients, too). They can also serve as a possible explanation of the scarceness and ineffectiveness of information campaigns about psychotherapy.

THE STRUCTURE OF THE INITIAL INTERVIEW AND THAT OF THE PROFESSIONAL HIERARCHY

Within the hierarchy of psychotherapy professions, psychiatrists reserve the right to draw the borders of their own competence, and consequently of the other professions as well, and they are also the ones who determine which psychiatric or psychotherapeutic specialism is to treat any given client. The professed reason for this is the legal regulation of recognition and subsidy, which often requires a medical specialist – that is, a psychiatrist – to supervise treatment.

But there is another major reason why psychiatrists are appointed to conduct the initial interviews: it is 'the principle of medical self-elimination'. First, the psychiatrist eliminates him- or herself as a doctor by ascertaining that no somatic factors play a role in the complaints, or that these physical complaints are already being treated elsewhere. Usually this medical screening has already taken place prior to the initial interview:[3]

C: So that was the final breakdown, when I couldn't
   breathe any more.
T: You couldn't breathe any more . . .
C: . . . Through my family doctor, I had my blood tested –
   so they looked and I also looked for what it might
   be . . .
T: May I ask, these symptoms that you mention, these
   physical symptoms, are they also accompanied by fear,
   fear that something is wrong with you, that you are
   seriously ill, that you might faint, lose consciousness?

From a series of conversations between a family doctor and a
patient who imagines he has a cardiac disorder:

D: You are still wondering if there isn't something wrong
   with you . . . ?
P: (*laughs*) I don't know, doctor, there might be . . . I
   can't look inside my own body, can I?
D: But what we have been doing these past three weeks is
   really assuming that the pain doesn't have to do with
   illness, but that it's a signal from your body that
   something is the matter.

If predominantly somatic symptoms or untreated physical disorders are presented, then the client will be referred back to a
medical doctor. In the material studied there was not a single
example of a patient being sent back to a physician. Referrals by
medical doctors to the initial psychotherapy interview are usually
accompanied by a letter describing the somatic symptoms and
their treatment, so that this information is rarely a subject of
discussion at the interview itself. Obviously, in the chronological
sequence of the patient's life and in the logical structure of the
initial interview, somatic symptoms precede psychic difficulties.

Once psychiatrists who are conducting the initial interview have
ascertained, on appropriate medical grounds, that a patient is not
a case for a medical doctor, they then switch themselves off in their
medical capacity.

The second self-elimination has to do with psychiatric expertise.
Psychiatrists are considered more capable than anyone else of
recognizing psychotic or psychopathic patients in the initial interview. And thus they apply a criterion which has been maintained

throughout the history of ambulatory psychotherapy: admit no psychotics, no severe cases requiring lengthy treatment.

C: Well, a couple of months back I spent some time in [a mental institution], I have epilepsy and I have the idea that those attacks that I have, when I lose consciousness, that they are somehow provoked when I get excited, when I get nervous –

D: May I interrupt you, I'll keep in mind what you just told me. I see there is a letter here from [a mental institution]. I haven't seen it yet – shall I read it first? – May I ask, do you take any medicine?

The course of the initial interview is interrupted, and priority is given to written psychiatric information. Only if the client is not then eliminated as a psychiatric case, the initial interviewer next professionally eliminates herself as a psychiatrist and becomes a psychotherapist performing the selection.

The initial interview has an implicit lexicographic structure, it contains an orderly succession of decision-making rules: the initial interviewers, in their capacity as medical doctors, decide whether the client is mainly a medical case; if not, then the initial interviewers, in their capacity as psychiatrists, decide whether the client is a psychiatric case; if not, the initial interviewers, in their capacity as a psychotherapist, decide whether the client is suitable for psychotherapy treatment, and what type of treatment. This implicit lexicographic structure of the initial interview is a reflection of the hierarchic structure within the helping professions. In a society where community workers dominated the helping services, community workers specializing in psychotherapy would conduct the interview and first ascertain whether the client's problems in the work environment or the neighbourhood community required referral of the client system to a union or neighbourhood organizer; if not, then they would eliminate themselves in their capacity as a community worker and continue the interview as a psychotherapist. And equally, in an arrangement of helping services dominated by priests, an analogous pastoral self-elimination would have priority. There seems to be a very compelling reason behind the set of priorities maintained by the psychotherapy institutes: people may die of physical diseases, which is why this risk should be eliminated first; psychiatric disorders can lead to violence, nervous breakdowns, and suicide, and these dangers must be averted immediately after. Problems of coping with others' and one's own feelings take a less drastic and usually less tragic course, and are therefore dealt with after the rest.

The fact that this line of reasoning sounds so convincing reveals something about the degree to which the reading public has been secularized and medicalized: a religious crisis or a loss of faith can lead to hell and damnation, and in a theocratic society these would have to be averted before any other dangers. Just as there are societies where a lack of political conviction or fervour is taken more seriously than contagious or even fatal disease.

Interviewers are hardly influenced by information obtained outside the context of the initial interview itself. Referral letters apparently play a preliminary role in the medical and psychiatric self-elimination. During the initial interview for psychotherapy they are very rarely mentioned, and are either read silently or have been read beforehand:

T: And I also see you are married . . . and that you have
    two children and there is also something about fear of
    someday being all alone and then there are a few other
    points ...
C: So what the whole problem is really all about is ...
T: Just tell me in your own words, that's better.

This disregard of documentary information is in accordance with a fundamental feature of the psychoanalytic tradition:

The psychoanalyst is, for good or for evil, at the mercy of the patient's statements. He does not even seek objective data. Documents, interviews from present or past witnesses are not just ignored, they are forbidden.[4]

Records and reports from other institutes are usually not taken into consideration during the initial interview; this type of information is sometimes requested afterwards, once the client's permission has been obtained. Nor do psychological tests play a role of any significance in the selection procedures studied here. Other documentary material, such as letters, diaries, references, and autobiographical notes written especially for the occasion, also fail to influence the decision-making process.[5]

THE INITIAL INTERVIEW AS A CONVERSATIONAL GENRE

The patients' inability to give an ordered history of their lives in so far as it coincides with the history of their illness is not merely characteristic of the neurosis. It also possesses great theoretical significance.[6]

The manner in which clients present themselves is in part based on their familiarity with the concepts and stances of psychotherapy – their individual proto-professionalization in psychotherapy – and in part on their experience with professional conversation situations in general, situations that could serve to prepare them for the psychotherapy initial interview. Both of these types of 'foreknowledge' are not so much personal characteristics of individual clients as properties of the social networks within which these clients have moved in the course of their life, networks in which they have been and still are a node, and where they had the opportunity to develop social skills such as conversing with professional helpers, or become proto-professionals, conversant with the categories and interactions of psychotherapy.

In the following section, the aim is to ascertain what the joint task of the client and the decision-making therapist consists of in the initial interview, viewed as a certain conversational genre.[7] The achievements and failures of a given client in fulfilling this task might also provide the initial interviewer with cues upon which to base the final decision, without doing so explicitly or even realizing that it is being done at all. The material does not allow firm conclusions in this respect, since it does not contain the considerations that led the interviewing therapist to a decision. But the analysis may show that the failure of a client to deal with the various problems posed by the conversation in the initial interview also conveys to the reader an impression that there is something 'wrong' that might make the client unsuitable for psychotherapy, and this on the basis of sociological, or at any rate, interactional factors. It still remains an open question whether this unsuitability is due to a lack of opportunities for learning experiences within the networks in which the client moves, or to the fact that the client did not make effective use of the opportunities available, perhaps again because of past experiences, or lack of them, in earlier networks all the way back to the earliest family matrix. This issue may be settled within the initial interview of a given client, and the more effectively the more the course of the actual conversation is directed towards such earlier experiences. But the question is crucial since it can also serve as the basis for a prognosis of the client's ability to learn and to change in the psycho-therapeutic treatment to come.

The task that an initial interviewer and a client are faced with in the initial interview is to construct together a fragmentary version of the life story of the client, a presentation in which the client emerges as the 'teller' and the 'told', as the person accountable for whatever went wrong in the past. It is a task, moreover, which the client must manage to define, without the initial interviewer explicitly pointing it out. This fragmentary negative autobiography has to be presented within a very limited time span; it must be comprehensible to someone who, though an expert, is a complete stranger, it must be accomplished with all the concomitant emotions, but with enough self-control to maintain the proper decorum and go home unassisted after the ceremonial conclusion of the interview. It is the task of the initial interviewer to provide the client with the few implicit cues that enable him or her to present this fragmentary negative autobiography within the res-trictive framework of a short initial interview. To the client, this is a critical episode in his or her life, and on the road to the helping services; though to the initial interviewer, this is routine work, repeated many times each day.

For reasons which have been gone into above, the selection criteria are not made clear to the client in so many words. Nor can the client be told what the interview is supposed to be about: 'the hidden agenda is never revealed'.[8] So it is also the client's task to find out what that task is, and the therapist's task is not to tell, but to provide the client with just as many or as few cues as needed to find a form for the story and to establish the relevance of the topics within it. Here proto-professional psychotherapy clients have the advantage of already being familiar with the genre; other clients will usually have to base their behaviour on the most closely related conversational genre that they are familiar with, usually a consultation with the family doctor.

The initial psychotherapy interview is divided into two parts, a rather formal period of factual questions and answers, and an open conversation, during which the actual task of the joint auto-biographical reconstruction is performed. Some therapists start the interview with the question and answer period, others prefer to do it at the end; some therapists want very detailed and exact answers, others are very casual and nonchalant about these set questions.

The question and answer period covers the referral, previous psychiatric and psychotherapy experience, medical-somatic symptoms and treatment, addiction, the use of drugs and medicine, sometimes also housing conditions and smoking habits. What occurs here is mainly selection by elimination. A number of questions have to do with name, place of birth, age, other members of the household, domicile, income, and religion. Facts which are also registered elsewhere (by the receptionist or the financial administration) often seem to have as their main function, be it a latent one, the construction of a general professional setting in a more or less familiar, almost ceremonial manner, facilitating the beginning of the meeting and reducing anxiety for both parties. Van Schaik mentions the 'diligent recording of the anamnesis' as the first of 'several widely used defence techniques' by therapists, and also emphasizes the importance of the professional ceremony in the reduction of anxiety: 'It seems quite clear that in the initial interview, there are two people with problems, the doctor and the patient.'[9]

Negative elements in the autobiography may emerge in this period of routine official questions and answers. These elements are not tactfully ignored, as they would be in a general professional setting; they are clearly stressed.

T: So you were married for four years ?
C: Yes.
T: Do you have any children ?
C: Yes, a girl.
T: How old is she ?
C: She is six.
T: She was born in 1973 ?
C: No, a girl, six years old, 1969.
T: Were you pregnant before you got married ?
C: Yes.

The client is not very helpful in ascertaining this pre-marital pregnancy, but might have thought that she was co-operating in tactfully ignoring the fact. This dialogue contains an implicit cue on the nature of the interview: that one does not beat around the bush, but that facts are brought into the open without the therapist expressing any opinion or emotion. The opening move of the decision-making therapist is often a reference to the 'red booklet' that is sent to the clients after their first call.

T: You got the red leaflet ...
C: Yes.
T: You read it ?
C: Yes.
T: You have an idea what the purpose of this talk is ?
C: Yes.

Three times the client cannot be made to start talking. Now the therapist gives a cue:

T: And that it's different for you than for me. I want to get an idea and see if the problems are within the framework of this institute . . . and whether I think what you want is to find as much understanding as possible. Then you have come to the right place and you'll have a chance to go into it in greater detail later.
C: Yes.
T: Yes . . . Maybe you can tell me in a few words what the reason is for your coming here.
C: The reason?
T: Or what are the problems?

The client is a very antagonistic actor. Every 'Yes' can also be taken to mean 'No, unless you tell me first what you want from me'. There seems to be a thinly concealed counter-questioning going on on the part of the client – just as at the beginning of a bicycle sprinting contest, when the cyclists remain motionless 'sur place' and wait to see who will start first and give away his riding plan.

FRAGMENTARY PRESENTATION OF A NEGATIVE AUTOBIOGRAPHY

In the introduction to the initial interview, there is usually a reference to 'problems', but in the next coaxing sentence the initial interviewer keeps the invitation as vague as possible:

T: All right, then you can say it now.
T: Perhaps you can tell me about it now.

Some cues may be added:

> T: Perhaps you can tell me in your own words why you
> have come here.
> T: What made you come?
> C: Uh, what made me come? Well, it is horrible . . . .
> Actually it is a long story and I don't know whether
> you have that much time – well, let me try to say it as
> concisely as possible.

The therapist may give a clear cue to present a negative autobiography:

> T: And then the most important point is . . . what are the
> things that you want to have changed, or that you have
> the most difficulty with?

That even the most neutral opening sentence can provoke a
presentation of the problems is clear from the consultations with
family doctors:

> D: Come in . . . . Sit down . . . . Now then.
> P: Well, I came about my eye.

Similarly, in the psychotherapy initial interview, even the slightest
hint of an invitation is usually sufficient to start the presentation of
the problems, and if it fails to do so, then what is needed is perhaps
not so much further cues as reassurance.

With very few exceptions, the things that a client enjoys or does
well and easily are not mentioned in the material studied. A
passing reference might be made to a world of capabilities, a
college education completed, a job held successfully, children
raised. It goes without saying. The fact alone that someone appears
at the initial interview on time, shod, dressed, and groomed, sits it
out, and manages to carry it to a conclusion, proves that more goes
well than could be described in hefty volumes. It also indicates how
well adjusted the interviewee is to society in comparison with all
kinds of other categories such as imbeciles, psychopaths, addicts,
and patients with brain damage.

Another example is as follows:

> T: You are still going to night school, I see. (*Apparently
> mentioned in the report*)

C: Yes.
T: What are your plans?
C: It's an academic high school and I'm in the senior class now, sometimes I do all right and sometimes I don't and, uh, next year I want to go to college.
T: All right. I'd like to leave it at that.

In this passage, a conversational theme is put to an abrupt end, typical of the fragmentation technique used by initial interviewers, which makes stringent demands on the narrative talents of their clients. The selecting psychotherapists deal with the story of a client in much the same way as experienced readers with a book in a store, browsing through it, glancing at the foreword and the table of contents, leafing through it and reading an incidental paragraph to get an idea of the story and the style.

ACCOUNTABILITY

Under the influence of psychoanalysis, current views on accountability have obviously changed:

> It is strange that the strongest hostile response Freud evoked was, at least to begin with, moral indignation .... A profounder criticism would have been to show that, on the contrary, he extended a person's responsibility so immeasurably that it became in practice all but unworkable.[10]

Particularly in more recent psychoanalytic writings, with the introduction of the concepts of 'action' and 'disclaimed action' as fundamental notions, the accountability of clients for their behaviour, and the manner in which they experience things, have become a core issue:[11]

> that feature of psychoanalytic interpretation from which its transformative significance stems, namely, its bringing home to the analysand the extent to which, and the terms in which, he has been the author of his own life, unconsciously and preconsciously, and the extent to which, and the terms in which, he has been disclaiming this activity.

The very existence of some therapy for sick people or for neurotics serves to extend the range of human accountability, simply because someone can either seek or not seek such therapy, live on with a front tooth lacking or have a bridge made, continue to live with an agoraphobia, or seek help. The statements of a client must be seen against the background of generally accepted views on the range of an individual's accountability, views which are held by the client as well, and against the background of psychotherapy views on the matter which a client may hold, depending on his degree of proto-professionalism. What is not taken into consideration are the fantasies which clients do not talk about, or which they are not conscious of in so many words and in which they may attribute completely different limitations to accountability. In so far as these ideas do come up in the initial interview, it is important to note the phrases with which they are, or are not, introduced as 'fantasies'.

The paradox here is that in order for clients to be deemed suitable for psychotherapy, they must accept accountability for feelings and behaviour patterns which they will only learn to recognize in themselves during the course of the treatment. This paradox also holds true for other aspects of the selection procedure: in order to fulfil the task of the initial interview, clients must be able to do the things they should learn to do in the course of the psychotherapy. This paradox can be solved only by focusing the selection on an estimation of the clients' learning potential as it appears during the interview episode, and seen in the context of the relational network in which they led their lives.

Within the framework of the views held in the circles in which a client moves, he or she can accept a margin of accountability which can serve as a starting point for further development in the course of the psychotherapy treatment. In order to be able to assess the usability of this margin in the treatment, it is important to compare a client with her or his peers. After all, it is essential to see what use a client has made of the current interpretations, given the opportunities available in the environment, or how she or he has utilized the available leeway of the figuration in which the client lives. In this connection, it is important to know whether clients have chosen these specific conceptions of life from a variety of conceptions in circulation, and internalized them, or whether what is involved is a conception almost inescapably forced upon them in the course of his life. Someone who is born into a family of Jehovah's Witnesses has handled these convictions differently from someone who joined the Jehovah's Witnesses when she moved to a big city and entered college. Whether clients have sought out a set of convictions or have had it more or less forced upon them, and whether they deal with it rigidly or flexibly in comparison with their peers, may all reveal something about the uses they will make of the opportunities in psychotherapy to learn to recognize and use their own strivings.

In the following quotation, the client expresses her ideas about people in general, and the therapist tries to get her to make some comment about her own share in her life's vicissitudes:

C: Well, and I also always have a very hard time with men, because I really do think that we are living in a time when we don't understand anything any more. What it really amounts to is that I think people are terribly cold, they don't have any warmth at all, uh, they don't give anything either. But, but uh, and everything is just dismissed so easily, sex and things like that. And I just couldn't care less. I really don't feel any liking for people any more. So as a matter of fact I don't go to anybody any more – the only place I go is a bar maybe once a week. But that always turns out wrong, because then I drink such an awful lot and I end up in an argument.

T: Are you trying to say that somehow it must be your own fault, that you end up in an argument wherever you go?

A preliminary broaching of the theme of accountability has to do with the presentation of the reasons why the client is there, whether he or she has 'been sent' or just 'came'. In conversations with helping professionals, it is not uncommon for clients to state that they have been 'referred' or 'sent', without themselves playing any role in this process, but this type of reaction was not recorded in the material studied. A detailed description of the client's own role in his decision to come to the initial interview can be found in this quotation:

C: Yes, God, I've already gone over it, again and again, by myself, what could be wrong. Because I'm not the type to just rush into therapy like that. Because it really is the last resort. That's what we said to each other.

> Because I once said to her [his wife], I'm not doing
> this any more. Then she says she's ready to quit too. It
> was really her that got me to come here. Because I
> don't like to talk about these things. But it's our last
> chance and . . . then we did everything we could.

To summarize, the task is to present a negative autobiography in which the client emerges as accountable for the things that 'didn't work out'. The presentations of a majority of the clients do meet with the requirements, sometimes after an implicit cue by the decision-making psychotherapist.

THE TELLER AND THE TOLD

'La narration double en effet
le drame d'un commentaire' (J. Lacan).[12]

The client, who draws up the initial interview story (together with the therapist), is the teller and the told at the same time:[13] the person who is telling the story and the person whom it is told about. If the client were only the person whom the story is told about, then during the initial interview he or she would be doing what now is being told; if the client were only the person who is telling the story, then the story told during the initial interview would be about someone else who existed outside the initial interview episode, perhaps before it or after, or at the same time somewhere else, but not as the client in the initial interview.

Sometimes clients actually do come to the initial interview to talk about somebody else. The therapist promptly responds by giving these clients an instruction to talk about their own feelings and behaviour towards the person who is not present.

C: She pretty much feels that I made her the way she is . . .
T: But that is her feeling?
C: That is her feeling – and I think she's right.

Only the problems of the client himself can be treated, and they are what is to be discussed.

The double presence of the client in the initial interview episode is a preview of the 'therapeutic split', as it is referred to in psychoanalytic literature: 'the patient's reasonable ego, the observing, analyzing ego is separated from his experiencing ego'.[14]

This double presence is a prerequisite for the 'therapeutic alliance', without which no treatment can succeed. What matters here is which modes are used in daily life and in the initial interview to create the double presence of the teller and the told, and to maintain it in the presentation of an autobiographical fragment. In everyday conversations an objectifying or alienating self-referral is often used for comical effect: 'that became too much for this here youth'. And similarly, distancing terms are used in the context of journalism ('your reporter'), the law ('defendant'), or academic research (where the author never speaks in the first person but always in the third, as 'the author', just as here). Such distancing forms of speech do not occur in the research material, clients are not in function, they speak for themselves, and yet they try to maintain a certain distance from themselves as the subject of their story. One mode they may use is a generalizing mode whereby the client's own experiences and observations are attributed to someone or everyone else: instead of referring to themselves or speaking in the first person, they use 'one' or 'you', as is very common in colloquial speech, in the sense of 'people like you and me':

C: You really want to put an end to it but – this is the
     point – you are powerless to stop it.

Or:

C: Yes, and then you have those periods, of course it's not
     always as bad, periods when you just can't deal with it.

The client's own experience is first attributed to other people:

C: I think my brother's death meant a great deal to an
     awful lot of people, then a lot of different things
     happened, that's when the relationship with my
     fiancée went wrong, then the family just fell apart.

A bit later:

C: My fiancée at the time once said to me, 'I wish I could
     mean to you what [your brother] meant to you'.

The therapist responds to this new effort at detachment, this time by means of the fiancée's comment – by referring to the feelings of the client himself.

T: Were you able to cry about it?

Another method used to achieve this detachment is to describe oneself as seen through the eyes of others:

C: Well, not that I'm the kind of man who visits people.

Which, in direct speech, means: 'I don't often visit people'.

A 'he-perspective' like this – seen by others – can sometimes be easily interchanged with an internal view, an 'I-perspective'.[15] In the following passage, a client tells about how other people see him, how he sees himself, and then how he feels in the process:

C: . . . that they talk about me behind my back, that they
      say [name of client] is homosexual, that makes it very
      clear that I didn't fit into that group. God, of course
      I'm very well aware that I make a gay impression. I
      think, I mean, that I act that way when I don't feel
      comfortable.

In contrast to the clients who talk about themselves as if they were talking about someone else, there are the clients who don't talk about themselves at all in the initial interview, but instead do, or do not do, precisely that which is the problem to be told: nag, sulk, protest, pick fights, or they do not appear at all (instead of coming and explaining how afraid they are of the interview – but, of course, such clients are not represented in the material). Sometimes clients do notice such traits in themselves and then talk about it; sometimes they can acknowledge it when the initial interviewer brings it up; and sometimes it remains without comment, as evidence of exhibited but unmentioned behaviour.

It is difficult to extract the silences, repetitions, or incoherent passages from the transcripts of the initial interviews as evidence of this kind of behaviour, displayed but not put into words: that would require a greater amount of interpretation of the available material than a sociological analysis allows for. The therapists themselves make very few comments about the portions of their clients' presentations that are not actually verbalized, perhaps so as to avoid making their clients feel even more ill at ease. But an intervention like this might provide a great deal of insight into a client's abilities to perceive himself and talk about himself. For example, a client who says very little about himself could be confronted with the fact of his own silence and prompted to give the reasons for it.[16] In this way, the initial interview would move a step in the direction of a trial therapy.

COMPREHENSIBILITY

The client and the decision-making therapist have to be able to make themselves comprehensible to each other. Consequently, they each have to have a vague notion of what the other will be able to understand, and they have to be able to alter this notion at the first sign of misunderstanding.

> Some things can be supposed as well known and self-explanatory and others as needing explanation, depending upon whether I talk to a person of my sex, age, and occupation, or to somebody not sharing with me this common situation with society, or whether I talk to a member of my family, a neighbour, or to a stranger, to a partner or a nonparticipant in a particular venture, etc.[17]

The experience clients have had with professional consultations and with formal meetings with strangers in general also help them in the initial interview to make an accurate estimation of the general knowledge which other people – in this case, the initial interviewer – already have at their disposal: 'In each of the above general conversational settings, members must assume the existence of an oral dictionary of "what everyone knows".'[18]

For the sake of comprehensibility, the story has to be told in the most specific terms in general usage, terms that 'everyone knows'. Characters who are mentioned must be promptly described in generally comprehensible terms in their relation to the teller:

T: Your husband had a girlfriend at that time?
C: Yes, he has had various women on and off, but at that time – it was a relative –
T: What do you mean by a relative?
C: It was my sister.
T: Why do you say everything so cautiously?
C: Cautiously . . . I don't know. Maybe because it makes me feel so tense now, a kind of tension I would rather not feel.

Here the client used a generally comprehensible term, but not the

most specific term, and that provided the therapist with a clue.
A bit later the therapist comments upon a similar vagueness:

T: When you say 'physical', then you mean 'sexual'?
C: Mmmmm.
T: And 'mental': that you don't talk to him any more?
C: We do talk, yes, just small talk . . . With the things that
   really bother us, we just keep going around in the same
   circle, we don't solve anything at least I don't, because
   I'm so discontented, and I'm so powerless, I just don't
   know what to do about it . . .
T: But you said: we are at a deadlock . . .
C: Yes, that's what I think, and we are trying to separate –

After a rather confused passage, which the therapist sums up, the
crux of the matter is revealed.

Jargon in psychotherapy produces specific problems of understanding; therapists generally avoid it during the interview; clients
do use it now and then, 'albeit in a respectfully lay version', says
Goffman:[19]

C: . . . he was a neurotic person; he had a stroke.
T: What is a neurotic person?
C: Well, that's what everybody called him, he suffered
   from a nervous disorder. I don't know what kind of
   old-fashioned term that is, but . . . he had been seeing
   psychiatrists all his life.

The therapist asks for a further explanation, he does not simply
assume that he and the client mean the same thing by the term.
Many terms are prevalent both in the professional jargon and in
ordinary usage, and the therapist also often asks just exactly what
the client means by these terms:

T: Could you try to tell me what's the matter?
C: Well, it's hard . . . I'm under an enormous stress.
T: What is that, stress? What kind of things do you feel?
C: Uh . . . pain . . . that my head is pressed flat –
T: And you've had that for a year and a half? And you say
   'I'm under an enormous stress'. Is that a sign of this
   stress?

A client seeks approval of her lay terminology:

C: But the bad case of nerves that I have . . . . Is it all right
     to call it that?
T: Yes.
C: It doesn't go away –

In certain cases, the therapist and the client make themselves
comprehensible to each other in professional terminology: there
is the start of a proto-professional understanding between them:

T: . . . you are a social worker yourself . . .
C: I'm divorced now . . . and things have gone very badly
     for me . . . just very depressed all the time . . .
T: Mmm . . . well, was she psychotic, confused or
     something like that?
C: No, not psychotic.

In this way, professional terms can function as badges of proto-
professionalization, but the therapist does test them out first.

ACCEPTABILITY

Clients come to the initial psychotherapy interview with difficulties
which they have a hard time accepting themselves, or which they
are afraid other people will not accept. They come to talk about
these difficulties, not to act them out, though their behaviour in
the initial interview will reveal certain aspects of their particular
problems, unintentionally and unknowingly.

The question which the clients now feel faced with is whether
they can actually talk about these difficulties without the therapist
disapproving of them or rejecting them for it (and some clients
may even wish for just that). The task of the therapist is, in the first
place, to avoid showing any sign of disapproval or rejection,
without giving too many assurances of his neutrality, since this
would only serve to imply that what was about to be brought up was
something requiring a special abstinence and thus something
considered objectionable by others, elsewhere.

The initial interview subjects the therapist and the client to the
numerous restrictions inherent in a conversation between urban
strangers, but it also exempts the client from a number of rules of
etiquette: the client does not have to avoid painful and embarrassing subjects, and can centre the whole conversation on his or

her own problems. The initial interviewers, on the other hand, are subject to very special restrictions: they have to avoid showing any sign of disapproval, and have to exhibit a constant display of attention. Moreover, they must refrain from repeating anything that they have heard to anyone outside the small circle of the institute staff.

The initial interview is arranged as a complete protective social shield that keeps social disapproval out and private information within. Its setting, private, secluded, safeguarded from interruptions by others, is already suggestive of the privacy that will be accorded to everything that is to be said.

Without exception, the clients were aware of the confidentiality of this setting from previous experience with family doctors and knew that they themselves would be expected to be frank:

> C: ... I am here now, I have to be completely candid and frank, otherwise there is no point to it –

Most clients will not expect any disapproval or reprimand from the psychotherapist, but whether they believe that the therapist does not sit in judgement on them or whether they think that he or she will judge them without showing it, is harder to decide; many people consider the diagnosis itself as testimony of their failure or as a moral judgement.

In order that they may nevertheless talk about subjects they fear will meet with aversion or disapproval from the therapist, clients may present their difficulties with an emphatic expression of their own reluctance and shame. This creates a distance between the teller and the told. A function of manifest shame is also to maintain a common judgement with the person in whose presence one is exposed: 'After all, I do feel very ashamed of this!' This is why, in a given episode, one individual cannot rid another of shame: the opinion of this one individual is not what matters; what is at stake is what the other individual assumes that everybody else thinks, on the grounds of implicit knowledge of general social norms. Therapists may deny this or simply ignore it, but they cannot suspend the general validity of these norms, nor are they in any way competent to grant a special pardon; they would be presuming an extraordinary authority if they were to exempt their client from shame. This is why selecting psychotherapists refrain from giving

far-reaching assurances of equanimity and explicit instructions for
frankness; they cannot give these instructions without constructing
a task in which they would presume for themselves an authority,
too extraordinary to be credible. The fact that they do not feel
disapproval or contempt for a client is not something that they can
state without thereby creating paradoxical consequences, it can
only become clear in the course of the initial interview episode and
in the course of treatment.

In this way, the feeling of shame functions as a divining rod for
social norms which remain implicit in the context of the initial
interview, but which are in danger of being violated. The clients
anticipate the judgement of the therapist with shame, and show, by
their shame, that they are aware of the norms and that they share
the judgement.

Many painful and shame-producing experiences are probably
not brought up at all in the initial interview. The task is to tell
enough to justify treatment, with sufficient frankness to give the
impression that the rest will follow in the course of the therapy,
and with sufficient reticence to make it clear that general social
norms also make themselves felt to this client. Thus the clients
probe the boundaries of what is still acceptable in the initial
interview, making it clear that they do not take it completely for
granted that the things they want to say are indeed acceptable to
the therapist.

The first reconnaissance of the possible limitations to do with
the boundaries of acceptable behaviour occurs in the initial interview itself. In principle, it is subject to all the rules of behaviour
that are valid for other formal conversations: the ceremonies of
greeting and parting, inhibited movement (both parties remain
seated during the entire conversation), restricted gesticulation,
subdued articulation (no screaming, peals of laughter, or weeping
and wailing), effective control of bodily functions (no coughing up
phlegm, no spitting, no farting), no immoderate use of blas-
phemous or obscene words. Except for a few unobtrusive manipulations of a handkerchief, a notebook, a pen, cigarettes, or a pipe,
the partners in the initial interview episode do not handle any
objects, and their acts involving their own bodies (scratching,
picking, stamping, rubbing, poking) also remain restricted to
gestures befitting urban strangers meeting for the first time.
Apparently all this is already clear to the clients prior to the initial

interview, it is not a subject of discussion, there are no records in the material of any violations of this type of rule.

Sometimes a client violates the rules of etiquette governing contact between strangers, though it does remain within the borders of acceptability in a medical or helping context:

C: He is so very understanding and that just makes it all much worse for me. I can cry here, can't I?

T: Do you really mean it, that question, I can cry here?

C: Yes, my tears come so easily, that's one thing I'm really good at, crying –

With a minimal amount of proto-professional prior knowledge, the client must have been aware that crying (as long as it was not too loud) is acceptable in a helping situation. The therapist does look slightly askance at the question, but 'understanding just makes it all much worse'.

There is another strict requirement to which decision-making psychotherapists apparently adhere in the initial interview: their undivided and willing attention for the entire duration of the conversation. This is also an implicit rule for ordinary conversations, but it is all the more strictly adhered to by the therapist during the initial interview:[20] 'Due to the ceremonial order in which his actions are embedded, he may find that any alternate allocation of involvement on his part will be taken as a discourtesy and cast an uncalled-for reflection upon the others, the setting, or himself.' It is clear that this undivided attention is generally expected by potential clients from a 'potentially helpful person',[21] whereas all kinds of other expectations on the part of these potential clients appear to coincide much less with the professional approach to the initial interview task (expectations such as the giving of useful information, frankness about the therapist's own family life, reassuring behaviour). Therapists can go to the most bizarre extremes, at least in experiments, before a client will put his foot down, as was illustrated in an experiment conducted by McHugh,[22] in which ten questions by the client were answered by a previously determined random selection of 'yeses' and 'nos', answers which most of the clients still managed to interpret as a directed helping intervention. One factor that makes it difficult to describe the behavioural norms in the initial interview, and in all kinds of social situations, is that many rules are taken so completely for granted that no one realizes their validity until they are violated – for example, by social scientists doing experiments. But even a minor infringement of implicit social norms, such as maintaining an appropriate physical distance, or a fitting volume of speech, creates immediate and strong responses. It is precisely such a type of deviance that creates the impression that something is wrong with the client that cannot be discussed and is hard to put in words at all.[23]

The task of the initial interview subjects the two participants to a number of strict rules, many of which also hold true for ordinary conversations and remain completely implicit, sometimes only coming out into the open in experimental research. Other requirements, such as the prohibition of any show of disapproval, and the necessity of a constant show of undivided attention, are mainly valid, and very strictly so, for the therapist; clients cannot take many more liberties than are customary in conversations between urban strangers, but they may exhibit their emotions more freely and are even prompted to be more frank, though not without some signs of diffidence. In general, clients may say practically anything, as long as they clearly indicate that they know how strange it may sound to others, including the initial interviewer. Clients with editorial skills may still manage to present an embarrassing or implausible story in an acceptable manner.

CONCLUSIONS

What counts most in this perspective is what takes place during the initial interview itself. Clients enter into this conversation with differing degrees of proto-professional equipment. They are faced with a problematic task; they may have had the opportunities for acquiring the skills needed to deal with this task in the course of their lifetime within networks of relations with others, in which learning opportunities were present in various degrees. In order to be able to estimate the treatment possibilities on the grounds of clients' presentations in the initial interview episode, it is necessary to gain some insight into the learning opportunities they had in the course of their life and the use that they made of them. For this purpose, a general understanding of society and of human character will serve a psychotherapist better than training in theoretical sociology (or psychology, for that matter). It is necessary to ask clients whether they have been able to discuss the difficulties that they are broaching in the initial interview with other people at any time in the past or present, whether the people in their circle are just as rigid, or as flexible, in their views, and whether it was possible for them to make these other people understand and accept their difficulties. Consequently, in order to gain insight into the opportunities which clients have had in their lifetime, and the use that they have made of these opportunities, a certain amount of social-anamnestic information about their life prior to and outside of the initial interview is indispensable.

It is generally assumed, and it is quite plausible, that these opportunities are available in very widely varying degrees to people from different social categories: to people from large cities, small provincial towns, or rural areas; to people who are orthodox in their religious beliefs, or people who are atheists; to men and women, and particularly to those from the lower middle or upper classes. In any case, there will be a close connection between the degree of proto-professionalization and the educational level. It is always tempting to make generalizations on the grounds of these general social categories and to assume that there is a direct correlation between the social category to which people belong and their tendency towards introspection, their aptness to describe their own and other people's behaviour in terms of feelings instead of in terms of commandments and taboos, their willingness to assume accountability for the events in their life, their ability to see their life as a continuous and coherent story, or their capacity to confront their impulses without acting upon them. However, generalizations like these are premature and result from an underestimation of the wide variety of forms of self-control, of experience, expression, and interaction which can exist in each network within such a vast social category. As generalizations, these assumptions are unfounded and are often more a reflection of the ideas held by professional academic sociologists and social psychologists about other groups, than conclusions validated by actual research. This is why it is advisable to ignore the clients' social category and see how they actually deal with the task of the initial interview, while asking them about the learning opportunities they have had, the use they have made of them, and the ways in which they experienced life in the networks of which they were part.

Part Three

EMOTIONS IN THEIR SOCIAL MATRIX

Chapter Seven

THE POLITICS OF AGORAPHOBIA: ON CHANGES IN EMOTIONAL AND RELATIONAL MANAGEMENT

The difficulties which people encounter with others and with themselves change as their relations with one another change. Within these relationships they develop a vocabulary and a conceptual system which allow them to verbalize their difficulties and thus to experience them in a specific manner. This also allows them to decide which difficulties are grave, and which are intolerable, which ones must be lived with, and which ones can be remedied and how. Some suffering may be conceived of as a punishment, some as an ordeal, a catharsis, a disgrace, a token of election, some as a consequence of fate, or of stupidity, some as merely sham. It was not until the past century that people came to describe some of the difficulties they encounter in living with themselves and with others as psychic problems.

The emergence of psychic problems in their present form is in part a consequence of the rise of the profession of psychotherapy and the spread of the corresponding stances and concepts among lay circles; in short, the psychotherapy proto-professionalization. This line of argument, stressing the part played by professionals and bureaucratic institutions in providing a vocabulary of troubles, in shaping lay definitions of everyday difficulties, in forming people's experiences of such vicissitudes, and in moulding the presentation of complaints as problems suitable for professional treatment, has been strongly advanced in the past thirty years by sociologists such as Becker, Goffman, Scheff, Cicourel, and Kadushin. But in another, more intrinsic aspect also, psychic problems are one kind of social problem: they are by their very nature problems in living with others, with intimate others, often with 'virtual' others; with those who are not actually present, but

139

who are remembered or repressed, feared, desired or fantasized, be it in a repressed or in a conscious manner. Thus, the 'virtual' relations of a person must be grasped together with the actual relations to understand his or her psychic existence completely as a social existence. This allows the treatment of the world of fantasies, including unconscious fantasies, as a 'virtual' part of social reality and the approach to it in terms both sociological and psychological.

The emergence of a profession of psychotherapy and the attendant external effects of proto-professionalization only explain part of the changes in the difficulties people experience. This emergence of a profession is itself part of a much wider social transformation in which the ways people care for one another have been profoundly altered, and in which the relations that bind and separate human beings have shifted, and with them, the difficulties between people. Hence, it is necessary to reconstruct the pattern of societal change that may correspond to the shifting difficulties people experience in intimate circles and, again, to the changing ways they verbalize and experience these difficulties.

The problem of the correspondence between societal change and the changing experiences of the people who make up a society is a classic theme of sociology. Sociologists have embarked upon their search by taking as a point of departure the encompassing institutions people constitute with and against one another in a society and by investigating how the compulsions and opportunities within these arrangements shape their intimate relations, emotions, and expressions. Sometimes they have stressed (as has Durkheim, for example), the facilitating and protective function of social institutions and of the rules that prevail there, rules which enable people to find a sense of direction and of confidence in others. Others have accentuated the limiting and repressive character of societal institutions (both Marx and Weber, for example). Nineteenth-century conservative observers bemoaned the disappearance of such structuring and moderating rules, the destruction of community and the expansion of anomie through 'commerce et industrie'[1] into all spheres of life. The modern mode of suffering was due to lack of direction. Radical and romantic authors, on the contrary, have interpreted societal development as an increase in regimentation and oppression; to socialists an ever-growing proletariat was *soldatisch organisiert*[2] in a military discipline of production, whereas outside the factory capitalist chaos reigned unfettered. Accordingly, the causes of human misery must be sought in the alienating effect of increasing capitalist oppression and exploitation. In a third interpretation, modern discontent is the result of a twofold institutional liberation, from oppression by the rule of law, and from want by industrial production: freed of fear and poverty, people can at last confront the remaining dissatisfaction with their intimate relations. Though this may be by far the most popular view, it has not met with systematic sociological treatment (though it is of course implicit in the writings of A. Maslow, and in the many liberal and social-democratic programmes calling for 'well-being' and stressing the 'quality' of life, now that a modicum of 'wealth' is thought to have been achieved for all, and the 'quantity' of production and consumption appears sufficient).[3]

Thus, modern discontent is understood by some as a consequence of licence, by others as an outcome of oppression, and by many as a token of progress beyond poverty and tyranny. But all three views share an immediate, all too immediate coupling of judgement and description of social developments. History is more complicated than that, and its outcome for each of us more ambiguous. A historical example of one small aspect of life may suggest some of the intricacy of the developmental lines, each one of which might be spun into a separate argument. The following study should illustrate some of the connections between large-scale societal transformations and shifts in emotional and relational management within intimate circles. In this manner the social pathogenesis of some highly idiosyncratic complaints can be demonstrated: the sociogenesis of agoraphobia. In a subsequent section the contemporary apparent relaxation of mores is interpreted in the context of a shift in the predominant modes of relational and emotional management within a bureaucratizing society. A concluding section confronts the argument with recent developments in the theory of the civilizing process and with Frankfurt and contemporary American social criticism.

NINETEENTH-CENTURY LIMITATIONS ON THE
MOVEMENT OF WOMEN IN PUBLIC

In the course of the nineteenth century, in the initial phase of
industrialization, many European cities went through a period of
accelerated growth: unemployed field-hands driven from their
villages by hunger and force flocked to the towns just as they still
do today in parts of Asia, Latin America, and Africa. This development also created new opportunities and new difficulties for the
petty bourgeoisie, still small in number in those days: new sales
outlets and forms of employment appeared for artisans and shopkeepers, clerks and functionaries.[4] But they found it increasingly
difficult to maintain a social and physical distance between
themselves and the invading masses of uncouth landfolk, an
appropriate distance between a middle class and a lumpen-
proletariat. Aristocrats and patricians could afford to surround
themselves with guards and to send their valets on errands; they
were in a position to avoid the rough and tumble of markets and
streets, but the small tradesmen found themselves in the midst of
it if they wished to carry on their daily business. Lyn Lofland vividly
describes the troubles the petty bourgeoisie encountered in trying
to keep beggars and job-hunters, ruffians and pickpockets at bay.[5]
Women were especially hard pressed by these new desperate and
insolent have-nots. The Dutch historians Jan and Annie Romein
mention the gradual disappearance of women from the streets
during the first half of the nineteenth century: 'never before had
women been more domestic and never more venerated'.[6] All kinds
of limitations on their appearance in public came to be imposed
upon bourgeois women so that they might avoid dangerous or
degrading contact with the lower classes. Little is known about
these restraints on the movement of women, which restricted their
lives so radically. Increasing restrictions on the movement of
women do not necessarily correlate with urban immigration
statistics, as they need not correlate narrowly with an increase in
street violence, much less with anxiety and concern over status
among the bourgeoisie. Finally, restrictions were adopted in
smaller cities, also because they were considered metropolitan:
'*das hab' ich in Paris gelernt*', as the song goes. And, these
limitations may have been considered too self-evident or not
important enough to merit much discussion or even description.

Knowledge of these rules has come to posterity mostly through novels, or the memoirs and biographies of the women who rebelled against them.[7] But little can be traced about their strictness or distribution according to age, class, married status, or domicile. Manuals on etiquette are the richest source: 'Another delicate matter pertains to the question whether your daughters may go out on the streets alone. There are cities, Brussels for example, where severity in this respect is so strict, that an unaccompanied woman under thirty may not visit further away than twelve houses from her home.'[8] Or: 'Even in the countryside I would not allow my daughter to go for walks alone, unless it be in the immediate vicinity of the home and even then only in a closed garden.'[9] And, 'A young girl may appear everywhere on her father's arm, but not alone.'[10] In diaries and letters of nineteenth-century women such restrictions are generally mentioned in passing, often with some amusement about a stealthy or ostentatious infraction and its consequences.[11]

This is not the place to trace the development and spread of these limitations throughout Europe and America, nor their gradual relaxation and final disappearance in most cities. What matters is that in the bourgeois mind the urban street, the urban market-place had become a threatened space, the scene of roughness, violent menace, and erotic seduction. A decent woman had no business there. In the recently emerging capitalist relationships, trade and craft were becoming men's jobs and a woman had her work within the domestic sphere.[12] Women appearing in the streets alone 'had to be' women who went to work of necessity, women whose husbands could not provide for their families single-handedly; such women could not possibly be decent. Once this line of demarcation had become established, it also came to imply a licence for men to allow themselves impertinences towards women who appeared in public unaccompanied. Thus, a woman could not afford to go out on those streets: a self-fulfilling prophecy if ever there was one.[13] A man's presence in the streets, on the other hand, was perfectly legitimate, and so was his accosting a woman in the street, as her presence there was unwarranted in the first place.[14] The limitations on movement in public for bourgeois daughters and wives thus accentuated differences in social standing and underlined the respectability of these ladies; this respectability was not so much a mark of the individual woman as it was a characteristic of her family, and of her husband in particular. Her domesticity demonstrated her economic and erotic dependence on her husband, and this in turn proved that he could provide for her material and erotic needs.

The economic considerations were expressed quite frankly – for example, by Stratenus,[15] warning the young woman against appearing in public, where she might be fatally infatuated with someone without sufficient means even for a humble existence: after one year of domestic chores and nursery care misery will have crept into the home, and poverty will have killed love. A woman who ignored these conventions risked exposing her husband to the twofold degradation of a suspicion of impotence and of insolvency. Such demeanour would undermine their common matrimonial prestige: husband and wife were tied together in their struggle to keep up the appearance of decency and respectability in the eyes of the outside world; at the same time they were involved in a struggle between themselves about her freedom or restriction of movement in public. Not much is known about how men and women coped with the difficulties that arose from this arrangement. Ego documents could provide some insight and so could the family novels and family dramas, genres that emerged during the same period.

In the end, this bourgeois concern with public order and security not only inspired the restrictions on women but also activated the nineteenth-century reform movements for the improvement of the working classes, against prostitution, begging, alcoholism, unmarried motherhood, disorderly conduct, and all those other vices which cause trouble for the bourgeoisie, and which continue to provoke urban bourgeois anguish and reformist zeal to this very day.

In this context, the resurgence in medical and psychiatric literature of hysteria as the woman's disease *par excellence* is most relevant. It provides the classic example of a terminology that allows people to express and experience difficulties of intimate living with themselves and with others in terms of psychic problems that could then be presented to professional practitioners as a case suitable for standardized forms of expert treatment. Hysteria may have been a way of coping with restrictions that were becoming unbearable; it may be understood as a revolt against the commands both from without and from within, but a revolt enacted as a mental disease.[16] Certain encompassing social developments, then, such as the advent of early capitalism, with the attendant processes of industrialization and urbanization, were accompanied by a political struggle concerned with public order in the cities and a social effort on the part of established petty bourgeois families to keep the surging ranks of outsiders at bay.[17] This effort to accentuate class differences involved struggles within the family *and* all kinds of fantasies about the street as a scene of potential violence and possible erotic encounters: both threatening and secretly seductive. (A double theme that was to return continually in regional, ethnic, and racial stereotypes about people considered alien or inferior.) Roughly in the last quarter of the nineteenth century, the tide began to turn. Increased employment and improved living conditions, street lighting, and better policing made for safer streets (as etiquette manuals began to point out).[18] Educated young women found employment in health care and social work, which, in turn, could only develop the way they did, because of the availability of these well-disciplined and well-trained daughters from bourgeois families.[19] Wouters has argued that actual street violence and its decrease were not even necessary conditions for these restrictions to appear and subside, the fear of violence and seduction being rationalizations of a 'fear of contagion', expressing the effort of the established class to close its ranks against the proletarian outsiders until class relations had become more secure.[20]

In any case, earnings of their own and a new occupational prestige, acquired independently of husbands and fathers, made working women less dependent upon their husbands and thus the balance of dependencies between spouses began to shift somewhat in favour of women. Around 1890, the limitations on public appearance by women were quickly disappearing (for example, in the Netherlands). During a transitional phase women acquired greater freedom of movement, but still remained partly segregated by sex: ladies' compartments in trains, separate coffee houses for women. Gradually these separations were abandoned and women began to appear freely in more and more places.[21] Even today women are warned to stay away from certain streets, but the emphasis is more on safety than on decency. And yet, at a time when restrictions on the movement of women in west European cities were decreasing, psychiatric publications began to include case descriptions of *Platzschwindel*: agoraphobia. Actions that had been socially prohibited before, remained unfeasible to some even after they had become permissible, out of an unreasoned anxiety – a vague fear that had lost its support in contemporary public discussion and could now only be expressed in psychiatric terms as a problem to be managed and treated by psychiatrists.

TWENTIETH-CENTURY AGORAPHOBIA

Westphal coined the term 'agoraphobia' and presented the first coherent case studies in 1872 (although similar symptoms had already been reported by Leuret in 1834).[22] The cases described by Westphal in his report – alas for the argument – all concerned men. The patients carefully reproduced with inexplicable personal anxieties the social taboos imposed upon bourgeois women.[23] And women patients soon followed, constituting a large majority of agoraphobic patients at that time. The patients complained of an inability to leave their home, cross a deserted street or square at night, or to enter a crowded concert hall, because of an intense but completely undefined anxiety (*Angst vor der Angst*),[24] an anxiety that would overwhelm them even as they continued to consider it unfounded: it was therefore not a delusion. In familiar company no such symptoms would appear. What had been not long before and what remained elsewhere a token of laudable modesty now gradually was losing encouragement and confirmation from others and began to appear as an inexplicable anxiety, an idiosyncratic inability to move around as everyone else did. The reporting psychiatrists describe their search for sensory, nervous, or cerebral ('epileptoid') defects, but Westphal[25] decides upon an 'isolated manifestation, under certain external circumstances, of a psychic symptom of a general neurosis of unknown character'.

Dr Barthélemy Brun mentions in his treatise on *L'agoraphobie, ses rapports avec les lésions auriculaires*[26] a Mademoiselle D., age 37, in Madrid: 'Following an unpleasant experience (*impression désagréable*) during a walk a sudden reappearance occurred of nervous and auricular symptoms.' He continues with fine psychiatric perception: 'A few days later, while leaving her home and before the memory of what had happened recurred to her, she began to experience a general discomfort (*malaise*) and since that day, each time she went out in Madrid she suffered the same symptoms –

This discomfort always occurred in the street, with anxiety, palpitations, and a fear of the movements of the crowd – The cause of these various manifestations resided in the ear.' Brun concludes his case description with: 'After six or eight sessions the patient, who at first demanded to be accompanied, came alone and soon enjoyed her steadiness of legs and head while in the street and never again experienced the slightest anxiety.' Apparently, the common state of affairs for unmarried ladies in Madrid was then to make such visits without a chaperon. What Dr Brun did during these sessions, except for applying '*lotions émollientes*', is lost to posterity, but the great otologist did leave one clue for psychiatric interpretation: the '*impression désagréable*' during the walk, quite unmentionable apparently, which had caused the sudden reappearance of the *malaise.*

Westphal's descriptions of the symptomatology in agoraphobia have remained largely unchanged for more than a century, and contemporary handbooks agree on the main symptoms: 'Several factor analyses confirmed the existence of an agoraphobic syndrome; according to Marks (1969) the clinical picture of 60 per cent of all phobics is dominated and controlled by: anxiety to leave the home, go in the streets, visit shops, crowded places, to travel or to be alone.'[27] The same *Handbuch* states, 'There is a high degree of unanimity in the literature that phobias (and agoraphobias even more so) occur significantly more frequently among women than among men',[28] and recent research reports mention percentages of 60 to 75 per cent of women among agoraphobics.[29] Professional opinion has it that the prevalence of agoraphobia is swiftly increasing, but this growth is difficult to document since statistics are influenced by the availability of psychiatric and psychotherapeutic aid and by the attendant process of proto-professionalization, discussed earlier, which prompts people to recognize and organize their anxieties according to professional categories and to present them as problems suitable for expert treatment.[30]

The developments in the understanding of agoraphobia are most germane to the central issues of this chapter. The psycho-analytic interpretation has been an elaboration of Freud's formula: 'Agoraphobia appears to be the fear of seduction', or, more precisely, the fear of punishment (castration) for giving in to repressed libidinous wishes with strangers.[31] This first theme in the etiology of agoraphobia repeats the collective preoccupation of nineteenth-century bourgeois families with the street as a place of threatening and seductive erotic encounters, a preoccupation gradually abandoned by most women, but maintained by some as a repressed and privatized fantasy. But, in Freud's account, the second theme of nineteenth-century concerns also re-emerges, the dependency of the woman on her husband as a fatherly protector: 'The agoraphobic can go out in the streets if accompanied as a little child by someone she trusts.'[32] The nineteenth-century child-woman disappeared, but the agoraphobic continues to compel others to protect her, as a child, and in so doing imposes her dependence upon others who find themselves forced to act in the family drama according to her directions. The chaperon may turn out to be the 'protected protector',[33] who is himself being supervised as he follows the agoraphobic on her ways, and who may himself need the reassurance of continually knowing her whereabouts. The psychoanalytic interpretation situated this struggle of dependencies mostly in the parental family: the agoraphobia repeated these earlier conflicts and represented difficulties with intimate 'virtual' relations, as they have been called before. Other contemporary authors stress the actual matrimonial relations and interpret agoraphobia as a collusion between spouses to prevent the marriage from coming apart by unbearable fears of infidelity and desertion: by appointing one of the couple as the phobic who dares not go out alone, the anxieties of the other party are allayed and may remain hidden. And thus the ideal nineteenth-century bourgeois family is compulsively reproduced by contemporary phobic couples.

Westphal mentions a man who would panic whenever his wife left the house and then developed an overwhelming fear of going in the street alone.[34] Barendregt and Bleeker vividly describe the matrimonial struggle going on underneath the agoraphobic relationship. Once the wife's fears have disappeared through treatment, the husband begins to object to her seeking employment and her complaints reappear. The husband 'had remained jealous. It had been and still was in his interest that A. remain home as much as possible, that A., like a Hindustani woman living in a purdah, would only go out into the lascivious world under guidance, preferably his own'.[35] Fry observes that the spouse, after encouraging the agoraphobic, often adds as an afterthought the warning that she should not venture too far alone. Or, he will follow his spouse wherever she goes, once she begins to move more freely: 'the symptoms serve to keep the couple united.'[36]

These observations do not imply that contemporary agoraphobics directly inherited these anxieties from their great-grandmothers who were prohibited from going where they now fear to tread. But they do convey that nineteenth-century society produced circumstances in which bourgeois families, out of concern for their safety and status, imposed restrictions on the movement of their womenfolk; these preoccupations soon acquired added meanings of respectability, chastity, and dependency, were transformed into collective fantasies about public order, sexuality, and violence in the street and about the family as the 'haven in a heartless world'. Such fantasies disappeared from public discourse but survived in the intimate family circle as available themes to be elaborated into a particular agoraphobic relationship. 'Thus the unconscious of modern women contains many remnants of the conscious misperceptions of her grandmother.'[37] Or, rather, all sorts of ideas that were taken very seriously in one generation are gradually abandoned as subjects of adult discussion in another, but these notions continue to be passed on as jokes, nursery tales, innuendoes, and threats and are added to the cultural heritage of later generations. Just as some poets use the themes of half-forgotten legends and folk tales to compose works of art, other people select themes from this shadowy childhood folklore to construct private fantasies that will guide them the more compulsively the more completely they have repressed them. In other words, there is no collective unconscious, there are the abandoned opinions and *idées reçues* of former generations surviving as inconsequential and unverifiable prattle, elaborated upon in infantile fantasy, repressed in a later stage. That may explain the striking similarity and constancy of so many very private fantasies. Although the nineteenth-century restrictions upon the movement of bourgeois women have relaxed, and her dependency on her husband has become less one-sided, the agoraphobic relationship reproduces such restrictions while denying any other motive except an inexplicable anxiety.

149

FROM MANAGEMENT BY COMMAND TO MANAGEMENT BY NEGOTIATION

It is now time to return to the general question in this chapter: how global developments of society may have altered the intimate relations between people, so that the difficulties they experience with themselves and one another may have become translatable into the vocabulary of psychotherapy and suitable for treatment as psychic problems. Rather than dealing with the problem directly in its full and formidable proportions, it was alluded to in an example: the restriction and relaxation of rules for the movement of women in public during the nineteenth century and the subsequent emergence of agoraphobia.

The early development of capitalism resulted in a strong limitation on the presence in public of urban bourgeois women, whereas bourgeois men could continue to move wherever they wished and, possibly, could allow themselves greater liberty than before towards women in public and with public women, since their own daughters and wives had disappeared from the streets. In the past hundred years, however, women have begun to move more freely in public and, possibly, bourgeois men have lost some of their privileges in approaching women in public. On balance, bourgeois urban men and women have become more equal, at least in this respect. This partial equalization of intimate relations in the course of the past hundred years, however, is not limited to this one aspect in the balance of dependencies between men and women, but covers almost all relations between the sexes. A degree of equalization has also occurred in the relations between parents and children, or between young and old in general. A similar decrease in social distance is developing between adjacent ranks in organizations, between those who used to be called 'superiors' and 'inferiors', and now often prefer to be viewed as members of a 'team'. But even as social distances between adjacent ranks within organizations decreased, with the growth of these organizations the number of such ranks increased, and with it the overall distance between the lowest echelons of production workers, consumers, clients, and the top echelon of company presidents, chairmen, and so on. This double movement may explain the conflicting reports on 'informalization'[38] and 'alienation', the former going on among adjacent ranks, the latter between the

150

lower and the uppermost strata. Finally, the distance between governments and their subjects has been decreasing, formerly in the long-term process of constitutional democratization and more recently in the dealings of participatory citizens' action groups with local and national authorities. A very gradual and slight equalization in the distribution of income and wealth in western countries provides a parallel undercurrent to these developments. In so far as these equalizing developments have occurred, they represent an aspect of the increasing mutual dependency of ever greater numbers of people upon one another, as more and more of their strivings are being taken care of within large organizations of production, reproduction, and government. By the same token, the multiple, intertwined ties that once united the members of relatively small communities have unfolded into the specific asymmetric relations with large organizations, the citizens being factored into different organizational memberships that each deal with separate aspects of individualized existences. And this again increases the asymmetric dependency of clients and claimants on these bureaucracies.

A second line of long-term development in European countries concerns the increasing control of infantile and bodily impulses. Marx and his followers have described extensively how a relatively independent agrarian population was regimented and disciplined into the strict rhythms and routines of the industrial workforce. Weber has demonstrated the intimate connection between a puritan abstinence and the entrepreneurial style of life in early capitalism. Freud has argued that the discontents of civilization constituted its very essence, because well-ordered society exacts the renunciation of drive satisfaction. The gradual process of state formation and the increasing control of domestic violence implied a more equable, more flexible and long-term management of emotions, as Norbert Elias has suggested in *The Civilizing Process*.[39]

Undoubtedly, the relations between people have become less volatile, impulsive, spontaneous, and violent since the Middle Ages, and people have found themselves compelled to steer their impulses more strictly, through external compulsion first, gradually through a social compulsion to self-compulsion,[40] and finally mainly through self-compulsion. By the end of the nineteenth century, this had resulted in rather strict and limiting patterns of intercourse among the bourgeoisie and in severe and restrictive superego formations in middle-class citizens – very much the type of families and the type of patients Freud was familiar with. Unmistakably, these patterns have changed in the course of the twentieth century. This presents a theoretical problem to historical sociologists concerned with problems of societal change, family life, and character formation: how is this recent shift in manners to be interpreted and how can it be explained in terms of societal transformations? Some authors have solved their dilemma simply by declaring that the changes were of no importance, or only apparent in nature, so that they might arrive at conclusions that fitted their view of societal development best. Their views will be discussed in the concluding section. But first, it is necessary to have a close look at these changes in the way people control themselves and others in expressing their impulses and emotions.

A first survey of contemporary mores suggests that the margins and the variety of acceptable behaviour have increased markedly since the First World War and even more quickly since the Second World War. Examples of the relaxation of restrictions on the movement of women in public are only one case in point. Many others may be added, especially in the realm of intimate relations: the practice of contraception, abortion, concubinage, promiscuity, divorce, homosexuality, pornography, masturbation . . . a wide gamut of sexual relations with oneself and with others has become mentionable, acceptable in many circles, thinkable for most people. But this observation often leads to the conclusion that the relaxation of restrictions also applies to other spheres of life. Although most people believe that violent behaviour is on the increase everywhere in the world, as a general statement this is unlikely to be true. Here, what is most relevant is not the violence between states, nor the violence of a state apparatus against its own or a foreign citizenry, nor even organized violent opposition to a state apparatus, but especially violent actions by individuals. Statistics over long periods of time, covering all crimes of violence and comparing several countries, are rare, the problems of interpretation well-nigh unsolvable. In France, for example, the homicide rate has varied with periods of social upheaval and tranquillity, until in the early 1970s it reached a level as low as the low point in the nineteenth century, around 1865.[41] In the Netherlands, rates for violent crimes declined steadily throughout this century until the sixties when the number of assaults continued to decline, but the incidence of manslaughter increased (probably a result of the spread of lethal arms).[42] Comparing recent statistics from five European countries, Selosse concludes that 'although violent crime shows a tendency to increase slightly in absolute terms, it is outstripped to a greater or lesser extent in certain countries by the increase in crime in general, and by the almost universal rise in crime committed for gain, in particular'.[43] Such criminal violence as occurs is overwhelmingly used as a means of intimidation to acquire material gain.

The social acceptability of violent behaviour has probably not increased. In most countries fraternity initiation rites and bar brawls are quickly disappearing as male rituals. On the other hand, gangs of soccer supporters have become almost as violent as they used to be before spectator sports became organized and broadcast. Paradoxically, an increased aversion among the public against violent behaviour may result in an increased visibility of such violence both in newspaper reporting of shocking incidents and in official statistics: indignant citizens are more prone to report, police to investigate, and courts to convict in cases that before went unremarked as routine roughness.[44] Increasing sexual tolerance does not extend at all to violent forms of sexual conduct such as rape or flagellation; rather, the contrary is true: mounting indignation should not be interpreted as increasing incidence. People, including young, strong, and volatile people, are still being pressured to surrender the advantages and pleasures of physical strength and not to lay hands on others. Even as violence and torture are continually depicted in novels and on the screen, these scenes are without exception accompanied by messages of disapproval and by the punishment of whoever has abandoned himself to such lustful violence. This simultaneous excitation and its denial, this hypocrisy, used to be a characteristic of sexual pornography until recently; it conveys the severity of the prohibition and at the same time the effort it takes for people to give up these pleasures under the moral condemnation by others and their own conscience. This intertwining of disgrace and lust finally comes to characterize the pleasure itself. Chertok and de Saussure point out how nineteenth-century scientific publications on sexual pathology served prurient ends, no matter how vehemently their authors and readers denied it.[45] In Michael

Herr's novel, *Dispatches*, on the Vietnam War, a character receives 'a letter from a British publisher asking him to do a book whose working title would be "Through with War" and whose purpose would be to once and for all "take the glamour out of war". Page couldn't get over it, "Take the glamour out of war! I mean, how the bloody hell can you do *that!*"'[46]

People, then, are not only supposed to contain their violent impulses, but there are other emotions they also must inhibit: all those manners of feeling and conduct with which one puts oneself above others are increasingly becoming unacceptable. Scorn for the defects of others, for their ugliness, disability, or indigence only serves to discredit the scoffer in the eyes of most contemporaries. The self-satisfied awareness and ostentatious display of one's superior social position, be it through wealth, descent, rank, or education, do not necessarily add to the deference one will receive, but may be held against one. Even the awareness that such rankings play a role at all in one's own and other people's thoughts is more and more denied. People pretend to be 'colour-blind', not to notice class differences in speech, dress, and demeanour, not to prescribe behaviour but to arrive at a definition of the problem together with the client, to discuss alternatives with co-workers rather than order their assistants around. Differences in social position are denied in every possible way, yet are betrayed in this very denial at the same time that the denial also contributes to diminishing the social distance. Equally, people are expected not to apply themselves in an effort to outdo others, through ambition and competition,[47] because of a desire for fame, glory, honour, power, or the domination over others. This is not to say that people in fact no longer attempt to rise above others, but that they try to control the expression of these strivings in themselves, and especially in others, and that they attempt to convey the impression that they never sought aggrandizement – it just befell them. Nor is there much reason to suppose that people have relaxed their mutual pressure and self-discipline concerning habits of punctuality, reliability, discretion, cleanliness, hygiene, dietary restrictions, precision, and accuracy, whereas their meticulousness in operating and maintaining all sorts of machinery and in participating in automobile traffic has necessarily increased (the sociologically interesting development is not the incidence of road accidents, but their relative rarity and the imposition of a deadly discipline in traffic). A small minority of Bohemians and academics may have abandoned some of these 'anal virtues' to a degree, and in so doing they have become highly visible to university professors commenting on the spirit of the epoch. But at the same time, and almost unnoticed, many millions have each year joined the rigidly timed and regimented life in schools, factories, large organizations, the world of traffic, and of taxes.

Undeniably, the management of affect is changing, but the widely held assumption that, all things considered, restrictions are loosening does not hold; not when it comes to the control of violence, nor with regard to the control of self-aggrandizement or of laxity. It does not even apply to the management of sexuality. As will become apparent from a second look at the development of sexual relations, these have become subject to different but certainly no less restrictive controls. Returning to the list of sexual manners that opened this section on changing morals, it appears to contain only those sexual activities involving no damage or degradation to others. (In the abortion debate, the issue is precisely whether another 'person' is involved.) Where a relaxation of restrictions occurs, it pertains to sexual relations between parties considered to be equal and responsible for their actions. The desires of the parties involved must receive equal consideration. Acceptance concerns intercourse between consenting adults. Less than before these relations are defined by canons of behaviour; wherever the negotiations between these relatively autonomous parties may lead them has become increasingly irrelevant, but these relations must be negotiated in mutual consideration and shaped by mutual consent, and they may not be imposed by unilateral compulsion or openly serve the self-aggrandizement of one of the parties. Rape, roughness, scorn, and degradation, so common and acceptable for employers to inflict upon servants and factory girls, or customers upon prostitutes only a few generations ago, have become more distasteful to the contemporary public. Self-aggrandizement and violence have become less acceptable and are increasingly subject to social compulsion, social compulsion to self-compulsion, and self-control, in that order. In sexual matters some canons of behaviour have relaxed or disappeared, but people now compel others and themselves to take into consideration more aspects of more people at more moments, to arrange their relations accordingly and to subordinate their emotional management to these considerations. In this process, many intimate relations have become less predictable for they no longer depend as much as before on the commands of social canons and personal conscience, but are shaped in a process of negotiation between relatively equal and autonomous parties. This requires new and different forms of self-control. It requires a degree of insistence and sincerity in voicing one's demands (now called 'assertiveness'), the surrender of means of physical or economic compulsion, and it requires a readiness to consider the desires of others and identify with them, along with a degree of patience and inventiveness to cope with them. At the very least, it requires the display of those qualities, for, in the history of morals, appearances are half the work.

Relations between people are increasingly managed through negotiation rather than through command. This applies to relations between the sexes, between parents and children, often to relations between people in adjacent ranks within organizational hierarchies, and sometimes to relations between local authorities and citizen groups. This makes for a larger variety of possible outcomes, but the process of arranging these relations imposes onerous restrictions upon the people involved. In a sense, this transition from management through command to management through negotiation represents an increase in freedom: freedom being taken to mean the possibility to do what one wishes in so far as it does not interfere with that possibility in others. But that is not very far: such a definition of freedom may fit the room for movement in allotment gardens, but it does not apply to most human relations. Desires and rights are almost always demands and claims upon other people and there exists no space which is not occupied also by the desires and rights of others. That is why this management through negotiation, even if it were to be thought of as freedom, is so rarely experienced as liberating. The shift from management through command to management through negotiation has tied people to one another even more intricately, in more and more subtle ways, in all phases of life, at all moments of the day, with regard to many more activities and desires. It compels each person, in turn, to scrutinize his own longings and to speak up for them and, at the same time, to be ready to abandon them if they clash with the claims of others. Now a couple may negotiate a promiscuous relationship, but they must control jealousy and the fear of desertion, deny anger and rivalry with the partner's partner, and force themselves to play the game according to the rules imposed upon them by their own mutual consent. Clearly, in the course of this process some people have gained a larger margin of movement, and others have lost. Municipal authorities have often lost a considerable amount of discretion to carry on business along lines of administrative efficiency; but neighbourhood groups have gained opportunities. Parents have lost the means to chide, chastise, and command children, but young people can afford greater freedom of movement, expression, and consumption. Organizational superiors find themselves forced to listen to their immediate subalterns, instead of running the department as they see fit, and the lower echelons can sometimes exact their demands. Men can afford less liberties towards women than they used to and women have gained in opportunities for physical and social movement. No wonder that many white, middle-aged males in high academic positions who produce the social criticism of the era show a keen eye for the increasing oppression in society and worry about the decay and decadence that others would call freedom.

The transition from management through command to management through negotiation is the result of various societal developments. The increasing and generalizing dependence of people upon one another and the resulting increase in equality between them is one such development. Another process consists in the consecutive tides of emancipatory movements: campaigns for universal suffrage, organized workers' struggle, movements for women's liberation, and the many ethnic, racial, and regional liberation movements. Each movement learned from a preceding one and each time inequalities that were considered natural until then were abolished, this instilled doubt about the inevitability of other types of discrimination. But a third, quite autonomous process may be detected in the emergence and development of large organizations. As such organizations became ever more complex and shifted from simple clerical and productive tasks to the management of increasingly subtle personal relations, clear, rectilinear lines of command proved inadequate. The officials in such organizations no longer performed well-defined routines but engaged in complicated interactions with colleagues, clients, or customers, using their personalities and judgemental capacities as occupational instruments. They could not be managed without a modicum of consent and they would not consent without their interests and desires being taken into consideration.[48] These organizations have had a twofold effect on contemporary family life. First, management through negotiation was carried over by these organizational middle-class workers, often women, from the sphere of work to the sphere of the family. And it is this organizational, 'professional-managerial'[49] middle class that has emerged and expanded in the course of this century and become the arbiter of contemporary life-styles and opinions. Second, a quickly increasing proportion of the population of modern capitalist (and state capitalist) countries has become the clients of such organizations, as pupils and students in schools, as patients in the health-care system, as claimants and clients of the social services. The modes of emotional and relational management of the organizational middle class have been transferred ('imposed,' says Lasch[50]) to these new clientele. Paramount in the innovation of modes of relational and emotional management is the profession of psychotherapy: the helping profession of the helping professions.[51] To a considerable degree, the transition of management through command to management through negotiation was eased by the external effects of the psychotherapy profession upon widening circles, first of related helping professions, then of clients, and then of the general public of potential clients: the process of proto-professionalization.

The argument has come full circle. People in this age define difficulties with one another in terms of psychic problems that refer to professional psychotherapeutic treatment. But these difficulties have changed as the relations between people have changed within a society undergoing global transformations. Increasing and generalized dependency corresponded to some increase in equality between people. Emancipatory movements helped to abolish many unequal relations. The development of complex arrangements of organizational care resulted within the organization in more egalitarian relations that spread from there to family relations. The psychotherapy profession, especially, provided concepts and stances for this transition from management through command to management through negotiation. All things considered, this development has not resulted in broadening margins of movement and expression for everyone, but it has made relations less predictable, because the outcome is not being structured by commands, but the process of relational and emotional management is being shaped by the requirements of mutual consideration and consent, and of the abstention from violence and self-aggrandizement.

The point has been reached where the limits of the argument must be indicated and the conclusions drawn from it. The relaxation of manners in the twentieth century affects only a limited range of activities. The restraint on violent behaviour has not lessened, the inhibition upon self-aggrandizement has probably increased, and the discipline in the handling of time, money, goods, and the body has grown. What has broadened are the margins of tolerance in sexual matters and in the expression of emotions and desires, especially in intimate circles. But even this relaxation is conditional upon the consideration of the wishes of others and upon their negotiated consent. Most aspects of human interaction are still ordered according to the canons of authority and the superego, managed through commands from without and within. But even where these orders have lost their sway, people do not abandon themselves to inconsiderate indulgence but negotiate some kind of arrangement with those close to them. This occurs in the family, between lovers, often among collaborators in organizations, and sometimes even in local politics. The burdens of poverty and tyranny may have lessened, but in other respects western society has lost little of its oppressive character, and in many respects discipline has increased. Yet, some limitations are not imposed, but rather incurred in relations managed through negotiation.

There is no guarantee whatsoever that such negotiations lead to dignified or fair arrangements: 'Authenticity replaced morality and sincerity replaced judgement.'[52] Worse, negotiators may even relinquish authenticity or sincerity, and mislead or manipulate one another. More important, management through negotiation paralyses rebellion: the dissidents agree themselves to deal, of their own free will, after ample consultation. Thus, the contract theory of citizenship and of economic man is extended to lovers, parents, and colleagues: one may take them or leave them. And this points to the basic flaw in any view of human relations as the outcome of negotiated consent: such negotiations always occur within a wider social context in which one party generally holds better alternative options than another. Within their marriage a man and women may be equal to each other, but outside it job opportunities or chances for remarriage are very different. Moreover, the scope of negotiations, of what is negotiable, are narrowly prescribed, not by the partners, but in the social context in which they find themselves. Thus, collaborators in an agency may bargain with one another – for example, over the distribution of caseloads – until all of them together are transferred by the board of trustees: then they may negotiate over who is to go first. The shift towards management through negotiation represents a change in the manner in which people control themselves and one another, especially in face-to-face relations. Seen within a larger social context such negotiations appear limited in scope, their outcome biased by the options that each party has in society at large, whereas the very occurrence of such negotiations legitimizes the social order in which such mutual consent is being achieved. Judged within its immediate context, management through negotiation seems to allow a greater variety of arrangements, better suited to the strivings of the partners that bring about the arrangement. But even in this context such a form of relational and emotional management forces people to take one another's demands into consideration and to relinquish some of their own. Some people forgo these options and steer clear of such threatening involvements, or avoid the negotiations and the ensuing engagements. They do not rebel but they reject, not with so many words, but tacitly, implicitly, with a strategy that denies itself, until it is expressed in a vocabulary of psychic problems, as depersonalization, as a pleasure-less promiscuity ('tertiary impotence'), or as phobia.

This allows us to see the behaviour of the agoraphobic in a new light. Agoraphobia must be understood as a particular manner of managing relational conflicts, both of the 'virtual' parental family and of the actual matrimonial family. It recreates, in fact, the semblance of the nineteenth-century bourgeois family, in its avoidance of the threatening and alluring erotic encounters on the street and in its one-sided erotic and economic dependency of the woman upon the husband for the sake of peacefulness and order in the family. But the agoraphobic couple succeeds in this task without the aid of social canons of behaviour; it has only a fantasy to work with, an inherited collective preoccupation, abandoned by most, but taken up again, elaborated upon, and repressed at the same time by the isolated couple. The couple succeeds in refusing negotiations with each other and with strangers, but it cannot adhere to commands that have long since lost their sway; instead, it creates an inexplicable anxiety to guide its actions and to protect its ways. Thus, global societal transformations have affected the modes of relational and emotional management in intimate networks, and this in turn has created difficulties which some people attempt to avoid through the formation of 'psychic problems' – namely, agoraphobia. The transition to management through negotiation is onerous and hazardous. Where no command can be heard from within or without, people may adopt fears and compulsions to help them refrain from what they are now allowed to do by others but what they find too difficult, too dangerous, and too lonely.

A POSTSCRIPT ON CIVILIZATION THEORY AND ON THE THEORETICAL CRITIQUE OF SOCIETY

It remains to link the present argument to the views of others who have commented upon the connections between societal transition and processes of emotional and relational management. The paramount question in this debate has been phrased by Wouters: has the civilizing process changed its course?[53] The question is whether broadening margins of conduct represent a decrease in the self-compulsion that constitutes the very essence of civilization, according to Norbert Elias and in the tradition of Freud and the classical sociologists. Wouters argues that many of these relaxations of restrictions constitute instances of a 'controlled decontrolling of emotional controls', borrowing a phrase from Elias. Such instances are noticeably different from the impulsive and overwhelming *Affekthaushalt* (emotional management) of earlier, less civilized human beings towards everyone they did not fear enough to curb their passions for. Wouters characterizes this contemporary mode of letting go in Elias' terms as a 'relaxation of manners' which is more equable, more automatic, and takes more into consideration the effect of one's conduct upon others and upon one's own future.[54] The privatization of bodily functions and emotional conduct, 'hiding it in the wings', continues unabated. What goes on is a certain loosening of manners, a process of 'informalization'.[55] Most important in this argument is the insistence that self-control has not diminished and that emotional and relational management continue to become more equable, flexible, and considerate of others and the future, even while people sometimes allow themselves a 'controlled decontrol'. Yet, a transition is taking place: the cues for this controlled decontrol are less and less taken from fixed canons of behaviour and strict superego demands, less from commands, and more and more from the claims people themselves bring forward and which are managed through negotiation. The outcome of these negotiations may be increasingly varied, but the process is bound by the remaining and increasingly compelling canons of sincerity, mutual consideration, and consent, and the abandonment of violence and self-aggrandizement.

The argument now may be related to the views of the Frankfurt critical theorists and those writers, mostly American, who have continued their tradition in widely divergent directions. All of them have taken a highly critical stance towards the societal development of their time as they saw it. They were convinced, and still are, that society, as it is taking shape, is increasingly oppressive and manipulative, even in the face of facts pointing to partial and gradual increases in equality and to the extension of the margins of emotional and relational management. And although these authors do not believe that people have become more free, surprisingly, they take all sorts of modern fashions at face value, accepting them as indications of a disintegration of restrictions. Their task is to demonstrate that this is nevertheless compatible with – and conducive to – increasing social oppression. However, they do not see the new and implicit canons that regulate the negotiations of otherwise autonomous parties, nor do they signal those aspects of emotional and relational management that have not relaxed, such as the control of violence and of self-aggrandizement, or the discipline in handling time, money goods, and the body. Instead, they accept the commonsense opinion that morals have grown laxer and then dismiss this development as the result of an improved manipulation by the ever-present means of commercial exploitation through the mass media and advertisements (Adorno), or by the omnipresent service bureaucracies

(Lasch). Advertisements and services are both considered merely instruments of oppression by the highly abstract capitalist state. The capacities of autonomous political judgement and the bonds that held the people together as kinsmen and friends have quietly been dissolved in this process. This development is both so subtle and so complete that every recent phenomenon may sternly be unmasked as one more contribution to this dismantlement of personal autonomy and of authentic bonds between people. These social critics share a rhetorical operation essential to their argument. All contemporary expressions and relational forms that come in for criticism are assigned to early developmental stages with the use of psychoanalytic terminology.

Adorno was one of the first to adopt this line of reasoning; the formula is reduced to its essentials in a later work:[56] 'that the liberation of sexuality in contemporary society is only apparent' constitutes the first position. He continues: 'turned off and on, steered, and exploited in countless forms by the material and cultural industry, sexuality, in tune with its manipulation, is being swallowed up by society, institutionalized, controlled. As it is bridled, it is accepted.'[57] This constitutes a second move: these apparent liberties only enable society to manipulate its members better. It still must be explained why these apparently spontaneous sexual relations are so easily manipulated and do not constitute an authentic and autonomous expression. Here psychoanalysis can help. 'Psychoanalysts have no difficulty demonstrating that in this total, monopolized, inspected and standardized sexual trade – forepleasure and vicarious pleasure have overshadowed pleasure itself.'[58] What is socially acceptable in sexuality has remained, but what is essential to it, *das eigentlich sexuelle Aroma*', remains forbidden: 'desexualization of sexuality.' But more and more sexual expressions have become socially acceptable, one might object, and does this not prove that none of them partakes of its essence? Something that is not accepted, then, must constitute essential sexuality. In the same article, however, Adorno argues strongly against the use of violence and social ascendancy in sexual relations. That certainly also is socially unacceptable. Yet, Adorno does not consider it the essence of sexuality. But what then does constitute 'real sexuality', or, for that matter, 'true autonomy'?

It remains for Marcuse to carry out the same intellectual hop-step-jump with a more brilliant show of terminology: 'sexuality is liberated (or rather liberalized) in socially constructive forms. This notion implies that there are repressive modes of desublimation.' Again psychoanalysis comes to the rescue, aided by dialectics: this repressive desublimation 'operated as the by-product of the social controls of technological reality, which extends liberty while intensifying domination'.[59] In fact the psychoanalyst Ernst Kris, in his study of the creative process, coined the phrase 'Regression in the service of the ego',[60] the way a person allows himself to act spontaneously, childishly, and impulsively in pursuit of some socially, morally, or intellectually acceptable activity such as the creation of a work of art or a psychoanalytic treatment. The concept is closely related to Elias' 'controlled decontrolling of emotional control'. In Marcuse's writings, this decontrol or desublimation is not a personal and autonomous action, but is rather the consequence of societal manipulation and stimulation. Philip Slater reproduces the same argument: 'the "relaxation" of restrictions on sexual material in all media is not a relaxation at all, but merely another intensification of the control release dialectic on which Western civilization is so unfortunately based.'[61] And the German author Reimuth Reihe elaborates on the theme of repressive desublimation in psychological terms, under the present social relations human beings do not achieve an adult, genital sexuality but remain 'immature' or 'regressive'. They never fully grew up in the first place.[62] A similar argument about regression instead of repression in the psychoanalytic sense may be found in Calogeras.[63]

Richard Sennett has exchanged desublimation and regression for a more contemporary psychoanalytic concept, 'narcissism', and he relates the emergence and prevalence of this personality type with the growth of the bureaucratic cadre that is hired and promoted not on the basis of its expertise, but because of its pliancy, co-operativeness, and companionability. This argument comes very close to the one developed in this chapter, except for Sennett's use of psychoanalytic concepts in a normative sense. Sennett, too, notes an increased awareness of the motives of others and a readiness to interpret the world in psychological terms, but this is entirely included under the new phenomenon of narcissism: 'The questioning of the motives of others similarly works to devaluate their actions, because what matters is not what they do, but what they feel when they do it.'[64] Narcissism is forced upon adults in contemporary society because that society is so structured 'that order and stability and reward appear only to the extent that people who work and act within its structure treat social situations as mirrors of self, and are deflected from examining them as forms which have a non-personality meaning'.[65] Clearly, the increased concern with one's own and others' desires or motivations may be perverted into an exclusive concern with one's own needs in the guise of concern for others and it may blind one for what Marxists would call 'the objective necessities' of societal development. It has already been pointed out that negotiations for mutual consent by no means guarantee a fair and decent outcome, that they do not imply equal opportunities outside the immediate setting and therefore neither within it.

In adopting their psychoanalytic terminology, these authors cannot help employing it with moralistic connotations. It is quite difficult to divest such terms of moralistic overtones in a purely clinical, psychoanalytic context – no one wants to be considered 'immature' – but such connotations become dominant when applied in social analyses for which they were never developed. Freud commented in 'The Future of an Illusion' upon his own reflections: 'These are only comparisons, with which we attempt to achieve an understanding of the social phenomenon, but individual pathology does not provide us with an adequate counterpart.'[66] Christopher Lasch, who is keenly aware of the danger 'merely to moralize under the cover of psychiatric jargon'[67] and devotes a good part of his book to a discussion of the term 'narcissism', nevertheless performs the same operation:

> The contemporary cult of sensuality implies a repudiation of sensuality in all but its most primitive forms . . . . A narcissistic withdrawal of interest from the external world underlies both the demand for immediate gratification – resoundingly endorsed by advertising, mass promotion, and the health industry – and the intolerable anxiety that continually frustrates this demand.[68]

The decline of external authority and of a relatively autonomous superego function only leads to a different, 'corrupt' form of social control. The importance that authors like Sennett and Lasch attach to the emergence of the professions and the service bureaucracies in shaping the structure of personality and of intimate interaction forms a point in common with the argument of this study. Lasch, however, considers these powers to be at once much more compelling and much more monolithic than appears justified. Granted all that is wrong with the mental health movement, the contemporary therapy cults, the helping professions, and the social security bureaucracies, most Europeans and Americans may still be suffering more from a lack of what these institutions have to offer than from an overdose. But since these arrangements are all evil to Lasch and his fellow critics, they do not seek to remedy what in their eyes deserves only abolition. They reject a tough individualism that would substitute benign neglect for social care, but the autonomous small communities of competence that they invoke instead appear so faint that in the end individualist capitalism seems to remain the only realistic alternative to the repressive bureaucratic Leviathan of capitalism in its final stage. Lasch concludes: 'The citizen's entire existence has now been subjected to social direction, increasingly unmediated by the family or other institutions to which the work of socialization was once confined.'[69]

But, of course, what the family and other institutions did in the way of socialization was precisely a form of 'social direction'. And what the maligned professions and service bureaucracies are at present engaged in is mediation between individuals and families on the one hand, and the state apparatus and capitalist enterprise on the other. They are essentially of a double nature, both helping *and* controlling institutions. Ignoring either aspect invalidates the analysis. Lasch and other critics of the contemporary welfare state picture it as a monolith: to speak in one breath of 'the extension and solidification of capitalist control through the agency of management, bureaucracy and professionalization'[70] as if they were all of a piece is to ignore the essential contradictions in contemporary society, between the state apparatus and the giant corporations, between the military conglomerate and the welfare bureaucracies, between the central regime and the service institutions, and to stress only the contradiction between the latter and the clientele. In this manner as little meaning adheres to the term 'corporate capitalism' as to that adolescent catchword of the sixties, 'the system'. By ignoring mediating institutions and their double character and by picturing all institutions, economic, military, and social, as one capitalist monolith, the use of psycho-analytic concepts has not become sociological, but still refers to individuals thrown back on themselves as *homines clausi*, whose narcissism almost appears warranted given the nature of the society in which they are alleged to exist. Paradoxically, this use of psychoanalytic qualifications to describe contemporary modes of emotional and relational management reinforces the monopoly of at least the psychoanalytic profession, since it now falls upon psychoanalytic cognoscenti, such as Lasch or Sennett, to distin-guish expertly between infantile regression and regression-in-service-of-the-ego, between narcissism and mature or autonomous self-indulgence, even between societies for mutual congratulation and communities of competence.

Social critics from Adorno to Lasch stand in a great tradition of moral protest. And, as moralists are prone to, when despairing of the impact of their words, they borrow terms that will convince their audience, in this instance the vocabulary of contemporary psychoanalysis. Yet, their analysis is essentially political and moral, and it would be better couched in the terms of that discourse. People have not yet been transformed into monads or zombies, they are very much dependent upon one another, very much involved in controlling one another and trying to make others gratify their strivings. They do so in the first place in networks of intimate relations, and they tend to do so increasingly by managing their emotions and relations through negotiations with one another. It is this mode of interaction in small circles that possibly makes for the appearance of narcissistic personalities, as it makes for the emergence of agoraphobics. This mode of emotional and relational management, also, mediates between individuals and the larger social entities they make up.

Chapter Eight

JEALOUSY AS A CLASS PHENOMENON: THE PETTY BOURGEOISIE AND SOCIAL SECURITY

Jealousy and envy are gut feelings, often acute and painful physical sensations, 'stings and pangs' with which the body reacts to others, and sometimes with such immediacy that it may appear as if it did so without the intervention of language, consciousness, or the self, working entirely on its own. In this respect, envy and jealousy belong in the same class as rage, lust, and fear. Among the emotions, this pair may well be the most venomous; it is certainly held lowest in regard.

Western languages tend to have at least two expressions conveying the displeasure at the advantages of others: the English pair 'jealousy' and 'envy' corresponds to *jalousie* and *envie* in French and similar pairs in Spanish and Italian. The Germans have *Missgunst* and *Neid,* and a third term (*Eifersucht*) which carries an element of rivalry; an analogous triad occurs in Dutch. The prevalence of different words, however, does not imply that they are being used with distinct meanings. In common usage their connotations blur into each other. Envy refers more specifically to the 'displeasure and ill-will at the superiority of (another person) in happiness, success, reputation or the possession of anything desirable' (*Oxford English Dictionary*). 'Jealous' seems to be the wider term, in everyday usage containing the meanings of 'envious', but also connoting '[4.] solicitous or vigilant in maintaining or guarding something' (*Random House Dictionary*). This meaning refers not so much to displeasure at the extra that others have or are, as to the anxious concern that someone else will obtain or achieve what one considers one's own. And, it may be added, even if one would not be the less for it (the eternal argument of the fickle lover – 'I love you no less for liking someone

168

else' – is therefore completely beside the emotional point of 'exclusive love').

Philosophers and psychologists have made many attempts at terminological clarification and tried to make a sharp distinction between the two emotions. Envy is clearly an 'upward' emotion, directed at those who have or are more; jealousy implies a concern with losing to someone else what one possesses already: here an element of legitimacy enters, which is absent in envy.[1] But what about the fear and anger at seeing others acquire or become what one has or is oneself, even if one will not be any the less for it? Just as it is part of the 'emotional work' to convince oneself that one's emotions are 'legitimate', it is characteristic of this kind of emotion that one can persuade oneself that one is the loser from someone else's gain. In other words, when dealing with the 'downward' emotion about others obtaining or achieving what one already has or is, the distinctions between jealousy and envy are blurred (if ever they were clear) and either term will do. Here the option is for 'downward jealousy'.

Schematically, this can be represented as follows: X resents Y being or having something which (s)he does not have; X's displeasure is envy in the strict sense, although in common usage it is often also called 'jealousy'. In this sociological context it will be called 'envy' (and sometimes 'upward envy').

X has or is something which (s)he does not want Y also to have or be (even if X would not have or be less for having because of it). This will be denoted as 'jealousy' (and sometimes 'downward jealousy').[2] It is this meaning of jealousy as the displeasure at others gaining advantages which one already possesses oneself which is of special interest in what follows.

Persons may be engaged in 'envious relations': one envying the other his or her advantages, the other jealously guarding them. Worse, the advantaged person may anticipate or, in Freud's terms, 'project' envy in the other party, suspecting the other to be as envious as he or she might have been in the other's place.[3] Worst of all, even while no one else is coming near, the jealous person cannot enjoy what he or she has obtained or achieved, for fear that someone else might share it – and therefore everybody else already constitutes a threat.

The main interest here is in group relations. The phenomenon of one group resenting the privileges and riches of another has been described quite often; it certainly is an example of 'upward envy' in a social sense. But sometimes a related phenomenon occurs in the opposite direction: one group resents another group's obtaining the privileges and resources that it already possesses (and need not lose). This may be called 'downward jealousy'.

JEALOUS GROUP RELATIONS

When jealousy, or envy, becomes a group feeling, it does so in a twofold sense: first, the emotion does not simply refer to individual persons but to a category in its entirety; and second, it requires sustained group work to provoke, articulate, and experience the feeling in this form. Very much as in the case of prejudice, there is 'social work' to be done. First, separate incidents or individual traits must be generalized into indicative symptoms and collective characteristics of an encompassing social category. Second, this categorization itself occurs as a group process, in gossip, and monitory tales, and so forth. The groups in their mutual relations are shaped by such definitional efforts.[4] A double collectivization of emotions occurs: the emotions are made to refer to a collectivity and are collectively articulated and experienced.

In general, excluding strangers and including one's own kind, defining relations of superiority and inferiority, or of distinction and emulation, is the kind of collective work in which groups are formed and maintained and their relations are shaped. When jealousy emerges as a group feeling, relations between groups tend to acquire an especially conflict-ridden quality. The advantages which one side believes to accrue to the other it perceives as losses to itself, regardless of whether it had to give up or forgo anything as a result or not. The advantages of others turn directly into its own disadvantage. Thus, where at first sight only indifference seems appropriate, since nothing is lost or gained (or where rosier expectations would lead one to expect pleasure at the well-being of others), bitterness at the sight of other people's good fortune appears. Such jealous group relations may occur in both directions, upward among the less well off who envy their luckier counterparts, and downward among the better-off who cannot bear for others to increase their well-being even if at no cost to themselves.

A social-psychological interpretation of group relations purely in terms of 'jealous relations' risks reducing real conflict of interests between the parties involved to mere psychological misperception on their part. It might tempt some to dismiss realistic claims as merely envious clamour, turning an insensitivity to the demands of others into a stance of moral superiority. Such psychologization is doubly dangerous, since it reduces both real interests and justifiable claims to infantile emotions – an operation that is itself both unrealistic and immoral. But this caveat, formidable in itself, does not rule out an analysis of the role of envy or jealousy in group relations.

Envy and jealousy as group feelings profoundly affect relations between groups in a formal respect: in terms of game theory, they transform 'variable-sum' situations into 'zero-sum' games. In other words, these emotions enormously increase the conflict potential of the situation, because the partners concerned perceive their interests as completely opposed, where an outsider might see mutually satisfying solutions if only jealousy had not changed the parties' evaluations. Thus, if there exists a feasible income distribution in which some may gain without others having to give up income, the latter might still refuse it since the others' gain would in itself provoke their jealousy and thus diminish their satisfaction with an income which nevertheless had remained the same.

The opposite, of course, would be 'generous group relations', under which people's satisfaction with their constant income grows, simply because the income of others increases. Such altruistic preferences are assumed by some welfare economists to account for philanthropy or the support for government income transfers to disadvantaged third parties.[5] Under these conditions, a more equal distribution of incomes may be Pareto optimal in the sense that those who have to give up part of their income for the sake of others nevertheless do not lose because their overall satisfaction increases as they see the poorest gaining in income.[6] Under generous group relations solutions exist in which some surrender advantages to others and yet all accept the outcome.

Clearly, jealous group relations greatly increase the conflict potential in society, even ruling out solutions that might improve one party's position without added cost to another, because the very improvement is resented as a loss by the other party.

171

These negative comparisons may sometimes perversely enter the evaluation of distributions; they are of the essence when social differentials themselves are at stake. The satisfaction of money need not be in having more of it than others, it may reside in having enough of it for oneself. But the satisfactions that go with social prestige are by their very nature bound up with being higher than others; they unavoidably involve comparisons, and negative comparisons at that. Prestige distributions necessarily involve jealous relations;[7] they are always competitive and conflict-ridden. A generalized non-aggression pact to end the struggle for prestige is inconceivable: no one would have the least bit more status than another and no one could raise themselves above the next person. Even the smallest differences would begin to count, and those would have to be abolished. This must end in total hypocrisy or total repression – or, as experience has shown, in both.

RELATIONS BETWEEN THE PETTY BOURGEOISIE AND THE WORKING CLASS

Our present disorders are especially worsened by the envious ambition of the small bourgeoisie and its blind contempt for the existence of the masses. When, under the combined pressure of circumstances and convictions, its morality will have been restored sufficiently, its head will blend with the patricians, and its mass among the proletarians in such a way as to dissolve the middle classes in the proper sense of the word.

(Auguste Comte)[8]

At this point the argument may be applied to the analysis of a historical episode: the emergence of compulsory social insurance for wage workers and the petty bourgeois opposition against such schemes.

In the astonishingly brief time-span of half a century, between 1880 and 1930, compulsory and collective nation-wide insurance against income loss from the vicissitudes of industrial working life was introduced in Europe and North America. Elsewhere I have argued that these arrangements were brought about by an activist political regime in coalition with either large employers or organized workers, or both.[9]

172

In general, the opposition against these innovations came not so much from large employers, but most of all from the petty bourgeoisie: from those people who saw themselves positioned 'between capital and labour', and who indeed both employed their own capital and applied their own labour as independent entrepreneurs.[10] Of course, they often also employed foreign capital and many among them did hire workers, but they themselves worked along with their employees and privately owned the means of production. This definition covers groups as diverse as small and medium farmers, shopkeepers, artisans, traders, manufacturers, and independently established professionals, such as lawyers and doctors. These categories tend to shade into other social strata, when the enterprise grows so large that the owner no longer works alongside his employees, or when it becomes so small that it hardly involves any capital at all and comes to resemble casual or 'put-out' labour. Hatzfeld has documented the resistance against social insurance by the petty bourgeoisie in France and demonstrated how it functioned as 'the brake' on the drive for national insurance.[11] Hay has provided some indications of the opposition by small employers in England.[12] Francis Castles has identified the opposition to social legislation with 'the right' and shown how its unity and strength determined the scope and timing of social legislation.[13] Castles, however, hardly distinguishes between small entrepreneurs on the one hand and, on the other, large employers who often did support social insurance.

Because the petty bourgeoisie was such a motley category and rarely united behind exclusive political organizations of its own, party positions on issues of social legislation cannot be identified unambiguously with the opinions of small entrepreneurs on the issues. More generally, it should be noted that in the present approach, a class, or any other social category, need not be treated as a unitary agent, unanimous in its animosity. On the contrary; the relations of exclusion and inclusion, superiority and inferiority, generosity and jealousy are part of the process of class formation. They are part of the social work to be done by human beings in more or less similar positions in order to distance themselves from those below them, to constitute social formations of their own, and try to approach those above them.[14]

Much empirical research remains to be done, and in anticipation of its results some conjecture is unavoidable. But one runs no

great risk in saying that by and large small independent entrepreneurs opposed workers' insurance, and often quite vehemently
at that.

Why they did so is by no means obvious. In so far as they were
employers, they feared having to pay insurance taxes, and some
schemes indeed imposed such fees, while many economically
marginal enterprises could hardly afford the added costs.[15] But
some plans excluded enterprises with a small number of
employees and all excluded those in which only family members
worked. Such proposals were opposed, nevertheless.[16] If the
insurance taxes were not financed from payroll taxes but from the
general tax fund, small entrepreneurs might still resist it for
increasing the overall tax burden and their share in it. But those
plans that entailed no contribution from general taxes still met
with objections from small entrepreneurs. Moreover, had they
perceived the entire issue strictly in terms of financial costs and
benefits, the small employers might also have appreciated the
savings on the disbursements they made privately or through
commercial insurance to their incapacitated and aged workers.
Support of needy or elderly employees was not usually a legal
obligation, but a moral one of widely varying stringency. To some
small employers it may have been a heavy burden indeed, and
others might have neglected it or not even considered it their
responsibility. Yet, by and large, employers did object to the
replacement of moral commitment by legal compulsion, a theme
often played upon by philanthropists and mutual associations also.
It is sometimes difficult to understand what privilege was lost
thereby other than the freedom not to fulfil one's moral
obligations. An informed and materialist guess would be that
voluntariness allows benefactors and employers to adjust their
hand-outs to the changing proceeds of risky enterprise. This might
well be economic rationale behind the theological insistence that
charity should come out of the 'fullness of one's heart', leaving it
to be determined by the fullness of one's purse.

What employers, small and large, did resent was bureaucratic
interference with their entrepreneurial autonomy. Especially the
small masters, unaccustomed to any kind of administration, hated
the paper shuffling. The small, independent middle class quickly
sensed that with social insurance it was up against another, major
addition to big government which it feared and hated as much as

174

it did big business, the large companies, the department stores and the chain stores, or the consumer co-operatives.[17]

In many cases, the autonomy of the small entrepreneur may have been mostly a myth, but it was an essential myth. Wage earners were dependent on the whim of their employers, tenants on the caprice of their landlords, but the petty bourgeois were boss in their own shop and their own house. That made them superior to working people, both in their own eyes and in those of the workers. In so far as they were indeed independent, their autonomy rested solely on the ownership of the means of production they worked with (and on the ownership of the major durable means of consumption, their own house, partly workshop, partly family dwelling).

The basis of relative autonomy was private property. Property served a twofold function as working capital and insurance against adversity. This property was to be accumulated by assiduous individual saving. Social insurance, on the other hand, represented an alternative to private property in its providential functions. It entailed the collective and compulsory accumulation of transfer capital to be disbursed in times of need. It thus relieved wage workers from the continuous self-compulsion to save for the future which was so essential and oppressive a feature of middle-class life. Workers would no longer be expected to save for their own future; their providential capital was being saved for them, collectively and compulsorily, under tutelage of the state. With social insurance, workers, too, would be secure in times of disease and disablement, during old age, and often even during periods of unemployment. This was what caused jealousy among the petty bourgeoisie and made them oppose the insurance plans.

In the course of the second half of the nineteenth century, the small independent entrepreneurs increasingly lost the field to large enterprise. At the same time, workers gained more income and security, while their social prestige also rose. A salaried position increasingly became an alternative for members of the small bourgeoisie. In other words, workers and petty bourgeois increasingly became involved in a competition for status, which was intensified because they often lived closely together in the same neighbourhoods, shared a common urban neighbourhood culture, and met as shopkeepers and customers, or worked together as craftsmen on the shop floor. Shop-owners gave credit to their working-class customers, a form of clientele formation which was acknowledged with customer loyalty and sometimes betrayed by shopping in the co-operatives and department stores. Workers who had succeeded in putting away some savings often established themselves in independent business, and businessmen many times had to hire themselves out as employees or saw their children accept salaried employment.

As class boundaries were vague, changing, and precarious, it seemed all the more pressing to maintain the small differences in status between the independent entrepreneur and the wage-dependent worker: 'It is likely that fears of proletarianization led many craftsmen and shopkeepers to exaggerate the remaining "small differences" – home-owning, the absence of unemployment (although not under-employment), or outward badges of respectability.'[18] The regularly employed workers, on their part, were equally eager to distance themselves from casual workers, vagrants, and paupers whom they in turn considered their social inferiors.[19] The *embourgeoisement* which had characterized so much of working-class culture in the unions, housing societies, and friendly societies since the late nineteenth century served as much to demarcate a boundary between these decent and steadily employed workers and the others, the dregs of society. The same emulation of middle-class forms of life acted as a pressure from below upon the independent middle class, which in turn sought to maintain its lower boundary by adhering even more strictly to the ways of the propertied classes.[20]

During the first half of the nineteenth century factory labour was generally considered a novelty, an anomaly which would disappear of itself as increasing numbers of workers succeeded in putting aside a small working capital to establish themselves in independent business. And many workers shared those illusions. They had themselves been craftsmen or peasants before; in rural areas they often still kept a few animals and worked a small plot of land on the side. In the cities, factory work alternated with casual jobs and 'putting out' production at home, while wives or children often also worked in the factory or operated a tiny shop of their own. The boundaries between wage dependency and independent enterprise had not been drawn sharply or once and for all. The ideal for almost all working people was to own a small business or a piece of land, and a house of one's own to live in: private property remained the ideal, and it was to be realized through individual saving. This private property was not considered as a source of income without labour; such expectations lay far beyond the horizon of working-class life. Property was considered as venture capital in the first place, for the owner to work with himself; even a privately owned house was first of all a shop or a farm to work in and next, as a matter of course, a dwelling space for the family. The second function of private property was to provide financial security. This may seem less obvious now, after traumatic episodes of hyper-inflation, and when small enterprise is associated with risk taking. But at the time, wage dependency was considered to be an even riskier form of existence. And in fact it was, given the vicissitudes of economic booms and slumps in early industrial capitalism and the complete absence of any form of protection against the hazards of factory work and of the labour market. Whoever could not work was condemned to the dole: 'too much to die and too little to live on', in the words of the Dutch singer Speenhoff.

A fundamental equation of nineteenth-century society runs: individual savings = private property = economic independence = financial security. In this light, the ever-vexing question was why the workers did not save to acquire the blessings of propertied existence. The simplest answer is also the best: they did not earn enough to save. But even when they could afford to put aside a small sum they often spent it anyway. An entire literature of reflections on the moral character of the working class has been devoted to this consumption pattern.[21] Yet there exists a simple materialist explanation: in a social environment of dire poverty, whoever has some unused resources at his or her disposal is under constant and intense pressure from less fortunate kin, neighbours, and fellow workers to lend or give them in their pressing need. Refusing such requests means either refusing help to those who once helped oneself, or destroying long-standing solidarities which might well be a vital necessity some day in the future and thus a source of security in themselves. In other words, poor people do not save because their peers demand that they spend their surplus on them and there is more security in heeding that request than in keeping one's surplus to oneself (and this – with the fear of the tax man – also explains the traditional secretiveness of hoarding peasants in rural societies).[22]

177

In other words, the formula savings = property = independence = security did not apply to the working class. For the small middle-class, however, it increasingly became a moral precept. Private accumulation was also considered proof of moral and social rectitude and earned one the esteem of one's fellow citizens. On the other hand, the poor, who did not save, were thought of as improvident spendthrifts, who had gambled away their claims to sympathy. This, of course, is a most comfortable view of social inequality, but it was not just hypocrisy. Small middle-class families must have made great sacrifices and forgone many satisfactions for the sake of private accumulation. And as the century proceeded, in many cases this self-denial produced ever more niggardly results. Economic independence often did not lead to a secure existence, but on the contrary to ever-increasing dependency on banks, large suppliers, and big industrial customers. Craftsmen found themselves driven out of business by factory production and shopkeepers by department stores and co-operatives. Small enterprises often proved to be the most vulnerable to the risks of economic recession, while inflation ate away fastest at small holdings which could not easily be invested elsewhere.[23]

In many respects, the petty bourgeoisie was the worst victim of its own moral preachings. If individual saving, and with it private property and independent enterprise, were indeed the tenets of moral superiority, then they had to be continued even after it had become quite clear that they were insufficient to maintain autonomy and undermined rather than guaranteed individual security.

The middle-class ideal was still to leave one's sons a 'nice business' and marry one's daughters to a propertied suitor. 'The problem of suitable marriages for daughters could prove even more awkward for those with sufficient property to fear the threat to its security that was implied by a bad marriage.'[24] As these goals proved increasingly difficult to realize, small entrepreneurs also began to invest in education for their children, ensuring them a position in the cadre of a large organization, be it a corporation or a government bureaucracy.[25] 'In this manner the second generation did not so much climb or step down on the social ladder, it rather made a step aside, crab-wise', into the hierarchy of the new salariat.[26]

In the last quarter of the nineteenth century, the conditions of the industrial proletariat began to improve. Urban sanitation spread. A beginning was made with working-class housing. The worst abuse of industrial labour was contained by factory legislation. And factory work was no longer considered a deplorable but transitional phenomenon that would go away of itself once general wealth had sufficiently increased, or as an unhappy interlude in the existence of those who had not yet succeeded in establishing themselves as independent shopkeepers or craftsmen. On the contrary, industrial workers increasingly were being considered as the backbone of the nation, and factory production as the true source of national wealth. New ways were being sought to make the existence of wage workers more secure. And if individual workers did not manage to save enough to provide against adversity, then maybe they might succeed collectively in accumulating funds: the recipe of the friendly savings associations. These mutual funds were an important transitional institution on the road to compulsory collective insurance on a national scale.

In outline, the foregoing presents the classical image of the rising working class and the waning petty bourgeoisie. But what matters in this context is that through their collective and compulsory schemes for the accumulation of capital – through social insurance, that is – workers succeeded in obtaining a functional alternative for the providential aspects of private property. Social insurance provided them with as good a protection, if not a better one, against the adversities of working life, as private property bestowed upon the small independent entrepreneur.

> Other small businessmen in Britain protest about the job security given to workers in recent pieces of legislation. Again they complain about the curtailment of their rights as property holders. . .but all make substantially the same point: that what is at issue is not just, not principally, an economic hurt – it is a moral hurt of which they complain . . . . They are responding to the growth in the political and economic strength of organised labour which in most of these societies has at least won some form of welfare provision to cushion the worst aspects of exploitation.[27]

Wage earners, protected by social legislation and covered by national insurance, were no longer a prey to misery at the first

179

stroke of adversity. And this eliminated an important, maybe the cardinal, difference between the petty bourgeoisie and the working class, certainly one which was at the core of the status distinction. And so it was experienced by small entrepreneurs – for example, by Frank Bulen, as his *Confessions of a Tradesman* of 1908 testifies:[28]

> The doctrines I heard preached by the socialists in the open air simply filled me with dismay. For it was nothing else but the unfit and incurably idle, the morally degenerate, at the expense of the fit, the hard-working, and the striving classes.

And:

> It makes me positively ill to hear the blatant cant that is talked about the working man, meaning journeymen and labourers only. The small London shopkeeper toils far harder than any of them, is preyed upon by them to an extent which must be incredible to those who don't know.

It is this ill will at the possible advantages of another group in society which colours the resistance of the petty bourgeoisie against the social insurance schemes for industrial workers. Jealously certainly goes far in explaining the petulant, unreasonable, and stubborn quality of so much middle-class opposition to social legislation.

The high ideological tone of many political interventions may have served to convey emotionality while avoiding the articulation of the underlying emotions. In this sense also, ideology may function as false consciousness, as a rationalization, not so much of class interests as of group feelings. Small entrepreneurs did raise objections to the increasing role of the state – except when it served middle-class interests by imposing store closing hours or limiting the expansion of department stores and co-operatives. They did object to the undermining of individual responsibility – but much less so when it came to legislating on sexual or marital conduct. Their rejection of government intervention and of the limitation of personal responsibility can therefore not be explained by political principles alone, nor can it be completely understood on the sole basis of economic interest. Behind middle-class protests there may well have been 'a vigilance in maintaining and guarding something': jealousy of a working class that stood to gain the security which once had been the sole privilege of the propertied classes. It is not easy to document this group feeling adequately. It was often hidden behind more elaborate ideological stances, if it was expressed at all. And it may be uncovered only by studying private sources, such as personal correspondence, diaries, and maybe letters to the local press.

The assumption may also serve as a guideline in interpreting more recent group feelings; for example, the downward jealousy of social security and welfare recipients among low-paid wage-earners. In countries such as the Netherlands where minimum wage incomes are not much above maximum benefits, a downward jealousy can be sensed: what workers earn by hard work, others receive without effort or merit.[29] Here too, the small financial difference masks a crucial status distinction. And again these jealous relations are ambivalent, since the employed workers are well aware that they may be next to go on the dole. And again, these feelings remain mostly private. Trade unions, speaking on behalf of organized workers, tend to resist such jealous comparisons between workers and claimants as much as they can. Unions represent the collective interests of the workers couched in rational terms and they control the public expression of the workers' point of view; the articulation of downward jealousy as a group feeling remains restricted to more intimate settings – until, of course, such jealousies find an appropriate, high ideological tone for their covert representation in public.

INTIMATE RELATIONS AND DOMESTIC ARRANGEMENTS: NOTES ON THE SOCIOGENESIS OF INTIMACY

Sigmund Freud held that the primal scene (*Urszene*), the child's confrontation with the parents' sexual act, was a crucial event in the early development of neurotic patients, almost inevitably part of their childhood history.[1] The primal scene, of course, entails first of all a breach of intimacy, but by an equally intimate intruder. Parental intercourse must have occurred before, certainly at least once, if only to produce the uninvited spectator. But more likely, it was a regular occurrence in this procreative phase of family life. And by the time the parents were caught in the act, the event may well have occurred dozens, if not hundreds of times.

The intriguing aspect of Freud's notion is that he assumed the event to have remained hidden from the child's perception for many years at a stretch, and yet, at some point, the parents' secretiveness was bound to be infringed upon by the child, at least by those children who later in life were to turn into neurotics. This was, indeed, a precariously balanced privacy, well-protected yet bound to break down at least once in the time-span from, say, the third to the eighth year of the infant's existence.

It may have been that parents neglected to take precautions, believing that the child would not understand anyway and that the scene might not affect the child: 'Nor is it only in proletarian families that it is perfectly possible for a child, while not yet credited with possessing an understanding or a memory, to be a witness of the sexual act between his parents or other grown-up people.'[2] Here, a sudden social realism pops up in the argument: in proletarian families, children might quite likely be witness to their parents' intercourse, and, one may infer, much less so in the middle-class circles which supplied almost all of Freud's patients.

This prompts the question whether it affected working-class children as much as it did bourgeois youngsters. And it goes to show that proletarian parents either did not bother to hide their sexual activities, or that they were in no position to do so, while a bourgeois couple apparently could protect its intimacy if only it cared enough to do so.

But while Freud immersed himself in a reconstruction of the impact of the primal scene, he took its domestic setting almost completely for granted.[3] Yet, in this and many other traumatic episodes, one particular kind of domesticity forms the indispensable framework of events, the necessary condition for the traumatizing drama to develop.

For the primal scene to appear as a traumatizing event it must be unique and unanticipated. In other words, Freud assumed apparently that the infant did not usually sleep in one room with his parents and certainly not in the same bed.[4] The little child had to stumble upon the scene, a sleepwalker astray and barging in upon the unalerted lovers, waking up from a bad dream to witness a frightful reality, or sound asleep and awakened to the drama by unaccustomed noises.

What matters here is the particular domestic setting which on the one hand allows protection of parental passions against infantile intrusion and on the other hand permits a confrontation to occur, albeit as a very rare exception. What kind of household combines such a high degree of seclusion of its members with an equally intense proximity, while yet at times producing a dramatic interruption? As Freud himself already tacitly suggested: bourgeois domesticity.

It is this particular arrangement of spaces, objects, and persons into a family household which constitutes the material base of intimacy. The confrontation with the primal scene exploded parental intimacy and once and for all destroyed the child's illusion of complete and equal intimacy with its parents. But the primal scene took its dramatic character from the very precariousness of this balance of intimate relations in the bourgeois household – a form which since then has become the general mould of modern family life.

Intimate relations may be explored by studying the development of their material context. Intimacy must be enacted within a particular spatial arrangement which permits the hiding of some things to most people, and the revelation of other things to some. The preconditions of intimacy are embodied in the physical structure of the family home, both a stage on which to perform domestic roles and a shield to protect family life from outside intrusion. Intimacy consists of both intensely inclusive relations within a restricted circle, and sharply exclusive relations with the outer world. The development of housing created the facilities and the constraints for the creation and maintenance of intimate relations.

In order to define the situation more clearly, the family setting which Freud had in mind may be contrasted with two other settings. In one situation, the confrontation with the primal scene was well-nigh impossible, in the other it must have been so common as to rule out much drama or trauma.

Among aristocratic and grand bourgeois families at the close of the eighteenth century small children were effectively segregated from their parents' life, both in terms of space and time. And even the spouses lived quite separate lives with distinct quarters for each of them. Here Norbert Elias's description of the aristocratic *hôtels* in Parisian court circles is especially instructive.[5] The master and the mistress of the house each lived in a separate wing of the mansion, with bedrooms, antichambers, and boudoirs of their own, waited upon by their own servants. The children had a nursery and later rooms of their own, there were nurses and governesses attending them. They made their carefully managed appearances at appointed moments of the day in rooms arranged for the purpose. Moreover, in many cases, infants spent their first years away from home, in the care of a wet nurse, and quite often they would again leave home for a boarding school during their years of puberty.

Relations between spouses, and between parents and children in these aristocratic circles, were remarkably formal, although they may have been quite affectionate in individual cases. The mode of address and comportment was often no different from the style adopted between acquaintances of identical rank. Formal status rather than family ties seemed to determine the quality of relations, at least in those situations that were considered fit for observations and descriptions that have survived the ages.

If relations between family members strike us as quite aloof and devoid of a special inclusiveness, they were also less exclusive than contemporary family relationships. Paradigmatic in this respect are the rituals around the king's *levée* whose morning routines of dressing were the occasion for assembly of the courtiers and display of royal favour. Clearly, the king was the state incorporated, and his bodily health and humours symbolized the state of the body politic. But even in much later times and among lesser mortals, the great and not so great families of the realm, the royal court remained exemplary.[6] Even in the wealthier bourgeois families, servants were not excluded from situations which by succeeding generations would be considered highly intimate. 'No man is great in the eyes of his servant' may at one time have meant that no man – or woman, for that matter – needed to keep up appearances for his valet or maid: social distance was so vast and seemed so secure that the servants' glance did not count, their opinions or feelings needed no consideration; in a word, a servant was a non-person. That explains why the master or the mistress of the house felt no embarrassment in appearing nude in front of servants and allowed them to wash, dry, and dress them without misgivings.[7] This extreme confidence in the solidity and vastness of social distance, the complete indifference towards social inferiors disappeared almost entirely in the course of the nineteenth century.

At the other end of the social gamut, matters were almost completely the opposite. The vast mass of rural and poor urban families continued to live until the end of the nineteenth century and beyond in dwellings where all domestic activities had to be carried out in one and the same room – where the fire was burning. Around this hearth food was stored, prepared, and eaten; close to it people slept on straw sacks, mattresses, or in wooden beds if there were any.[8] Parents and little children shared a sleeping place, without partition or at most secluded by curtains from the older children, who slept two or more to a mattress. A room of one's own brought little comfort, since it was bound to be cold, and often dark, damp, and filthy also.[9] Indoors, there was no way to escape the surveillance of parents or siblings:[10] 'Chacun est sous le regard de l'autre.'[11] If seclusion could be found at all, it had to be outdoors, in the woods and the fields of the countryside or in the alleys and courtyards of the city. Only there could boys and girls make acquaintance without interference and would lovers find a somewhat precarious privacy. Only when the twentieth century was well under way did cars allow both mobility and seclusion for increasing numbers of young people who could prise away father's keys.

The dwellings of common people, both in the city and the countryside, allowed their inhabitants no seclusion from one another. Eating, sleeping, grooming, loving, fighting went on in front of all: shared activities, passively or actively, willingly or unwillingly. But in another respect rural and urban industrial life differed: peasant families in their more or less isolated homes had to lodge their labourers and often distant kin, but at least they could exclude outsiders, landlords excepted, from the domestic circle. But urban industrial workers and paupers found themselves constantly confronted with family scenes next door and could not shield their own domestic setting from the scenes, sights, smells, and sounds of the neighbours. Thus, in rural homes the domestic circle was relatively closed but included servants and relatives beyond parents and their offspring, while in the city the domestic circle might include father, mother, and children only, but was penetrable by outsiders, neighbours, landlords, and, increasingly, city inspectors.[12]

The history of housing may be rewritten in embryological terms. In the dark beginnings there was only a single walled space around the hearth, the '*salle*', '*Stube*', '*hall*', where all dwellers came together to carry out almost all their business. Later and in wealthier dwellings a closed room was added to this hall, for the master and his wife to sleep and keep their more precious belongings. In a next phase and again among the better off, a third cell appeared – the *studiolo*, *cabinet*, or *closet* – another closed room, where the lord of the house would withdraw and keep his records, correspondence, books, and treasures.[13] As time went on and depending on the wealth of the inhabitant, more and more cells formed around this nucleus, each one specializing in a specific function, separating a particular activity from others and shielding the person performing it from the rest. A nursery might be added for the younger children, bedrooms for the older ones. The lady of the house obtained a room of her own. A dining room was separated from the kitchen; foods were kept in a special pantry; after-dinner conversations were relegated to a library, while the women withdrew into yet another room. And so on. Spatial and social differentiation proceeded together, but all the while the edifice was intended for a single family only. This division, proliferation, specialization, and differentiation of the family home reached its height in the '*hôtels*' of eighteenth-century court society and the mansions of the very rich which since then have reproduced this pattern with more or less variation.

But in the course of the nineteenth century, the evolution of housing took another turn: the single family dwelling no longer consisted of either a sober single-cell structure with minor additions, or an increasingly extensive and differentiated multi-cellular conglomerate; rather, an intermediate form became more and more general – the middle-class home with a living room, a kitchen, two or three bedrooms, a bathroom-cum-WC, and maybe a small study, possibly a cellar and an attic, all connecting to a small hall or a staircase, and neatly closed by doors. A further spatial differentiation and specialization of activities proceeded, not at the level of the individual dwelling but on a higher level of integration, the neighbourhood, or the city: much food storage and processing was taken care of in factories and shops, clothes were made in workshops and sold in department stores, banquets and parties were given in restaurants and rented halls, games were played, entertainments enjoyed in specialized establishments, many males spent part or most of their leisure time in bars and clubs.[14] As has often been remarked, the family lost many of its economic functions, and the middle-class home became the scene of a more limited range of activities, a more exclusive pattern of relations, more strongly shielded against intrusion from outside.

During roughly the same period, the aristocratic ideal of strict spatial separation of different activities within the house, and of more distant and formal relations between close kin, were gradually abandoned – also among the emulating grand bourgeois – for a domestic ideal of family intimacy. Spouses were expected to share a bedroom and even a bed for the full extent of their marriage. And increasingly, they were expected to remain on close and affectionate terms and take an intense and enduring interest in their children.

Not much later, the close proximity and promiscuity in sleeping, dressing, undressing and grooming, cleaning, cooking, and eating gradually, only very slowly, began to disappear among the working classes as wealth increased and social housing policy began to have an impact – say, between 1880 and 1940, or, roughly during the period of Freud's adult existence.[15]

In the course of the twentieth century, almost all families have come to live their lives in a highly organized spatial setting: a standard dwelling in almost all modern countries comprises first of all a living room, to which all members of the family have unlimited access and where they engage in shared activities, most importantly the joint evening meal. Adjoining this room is a kitchen where the mother prepares the meals and where the other family members may enter, with her permission. To facilitate the mother's chores, kitchen and living room are usually next to each other. In many modern houses – now that electrical ventilators can prevent all smells – an 'open' kitchen again forms part of the dining room. In working class and most middle-class families other joint activities also take place in the dining room, which is therefore rightly called the 'living' room. It is in this room also, where some of the family's most cherished possessions are exhibited and the books displayed on their stacks, that guests are received. In these houses, the parental couple shares a bedroom which can be closed (and locked) and which is accessible to the children only with their parents' consent. What goes on there cannot be seen or heard – that is, as long as it remains within the limits of well-tempered emotional expression. The room is sometimes shown to friendly strangers on a tour of the house, almost invariably with the words 'don't mind the mess' to convey that it has not been arranged for the purpose of display to outsiders.[16]

There is a separate room for the younger children, and the older ones very often have a room entirely to themselves; adolescents of different sexes rarely share a bedroom, let alone a bed.

The spatial segregation of the house is not carried through all the way: apart from the common living room, there are other jointly used spaces, such as the bathroom. The bathroom often connects with the parental bedroom, but it is accessible to the children also. The use of this common space is, however, strictly regulated in time. Family members generally use the same facilities, but not at the same time, except for spouses, or for very small children and a parent. In English and American usage the term 'bathroom' is somewhat ambiguous, since it denotes a secluded space which may contain a bath (as the case may be with a WC) or it is used as a euphemism for a space which contains only a WC, and where one goes to 'wash one's hands'.

As far as bathing goes, rules of seclusion and access seem to be somewhat more relaxed, but when it comes to disposing of bodily waste they tend to be rather severe: the user is expected to lock the door from the inside and others are not supposed to demand access when somebody is in there.[17]

The home in its entirety is screened off from outsiders, and family life is protected from their view or hearing: the sights and sounds of family life can be shielded from the eyes and ears of passers-by (it would be considered highly impolite to stand still and peep or listen at the doors or windows of a strange house). Even with the curtains open, there are blinds or lace curtains to let in the light while protecting the indoor scene from strange eyes. Thus, the greater part of family life can be hidden from outsiders. And, conversely, it is up to the family to decide whom it will invite inside and thus allow to be a witness to some aspects of its domesticity. It depends very much on the closeness of the acquaintance how much is permitted to be seen, or rather what kind of family drama is being produced for the visitor's sake.

As time went on the family circle became more exclusive in its composition also: more distant kin, grandparents, cousins, spinster aunts gradually disappeared from the house and the nuclear family remained. Fewer were the servants who continued to live under the same roof as their employers. To have a maid or *bonne* (that is, *'une bonne à tout faire'*) still implied membership in the superior class of people who were being waited upon instead of doing the waiting.[18] Middle-class families, however, could less and less afford such help, while young, unskilled women could find other, more attractive employment. Moreover, in homes with a maid, it became more and more difficult to combine secluded domesticity with the presence of someone who was not admitted in its circle, and yet could not any longer be treated as a complete non-person. Less spacious dwellings no longer permitted the relegation of the maid to separate servants' quarters, and this too made her more intrusive. These bourgeois families, moreover, were not rich and powerful enough to guarantee permanent employment and a retirement pension in old age. As a consequence, they could never be sure of the lasting discretion and loyalty of their servants, who might after all terminate their job and seek another employer. The family thus had to take into account at least some of their objections, had to suffer their presence as witnesses to the scenes of family life and to fear their gossip to other servants, and worse, to other families of equal rank.

In other words, the creation and maintenance of intimate family relations was severely hampered by the omnipresence in relatively small dwellings of a live-in servant who was considered too low to be admitted into intimacy,[19] but not low enough to be ignored as a non-person whose knowledge and testimony of domestic matters were simply irrelevant. (This pernicious problem has by now reached even the very highest social circles as servants and secretaries sell their stories of royalty to the yellow press.) It goes without saying that the servant girl, on her part, lacked both the autonomy and the personal space to enact any kind of intimacy of her own: she was under the constant scrutiny of the mistress of the house who tried to prevent close encounters with the husband or the grown-up sons, and strove to control all outside contacts. In the years between the wars live-in servants became an exception and the number of domestic personnel dwindled (at least in the official statistics). In contemporary middle-class families a measure of decorum is maintained when the cleaning lady makes her occasional visits, and more often than not the same discretion is maintained in her presence as for close acquaintances (the home often being tidied up before she is scheduled to come in).

This quick tour of the modern family home permits the conclusion that its architectural layout is such that it permits the family as a unit to withdraw behind the wings ('*hinter den Kulissen*', as Elias expresses it) and stage an appropriate performance for those outsiders who are allowed in. Equally, each grown-up family member is allotted some 'backstage area' (this time the expression is Goffman's) where he or she may take care of bodily grooming, prepare for acting out a suitable part in the family proceedings, or join with someone else in some exclusive activity such as parental intercourse or teenage sociability.

Meals, television entertainment, and games are the most collective activities within the domestic circle, accessible to the entire family and its acknowledged guests. Separate bedrooms allow the family members to manage their sleep in relative seclusion. This facilitates the hiding of such revealing facts as snoring, false teeth, wigs, medication, and so on from others. Family members, especially the older ones, can if they wish protect their nudity from the eyes of others. All places where they dress and undress permit seclusion either in space or time. Parents can hide their sexual episodes from children (and older children theirs from their parents, unless they insist on entering rooms without warning).[20]

Disposing of bodily wastes, defecation and urination, may also proceed in complete isolation (although the other family members do notice when, how often, and for how long someone absents him- or herself). If carefully managed, most of the smells of defecation may be spared the next user, one sanitary innovation which has profoundly affected the presentation of self in the course of a few generations.[21]

In other words, the family home as a living arrangement allows its members a relatively large degree of privacy, certainly if compared with the great mass of human beings in earlier periods in history. This seclusion operates for the family in its entirety with respect to all outsiders and for each family member. If family members do to get to see or hear more of one another, this is increasingly because the others allow it, not because circumstances force such confrontations upon them. This voluntary character of family exposure will provide us with one of the keys to modern practices of intimacy.

Intimacy as a characteristic of relations between people implies first of all the inclusion of insiders, the sharing of information, feelings, activities, places; next, it also implies the exclusion of outsiders from this sharing relationship. And, except for very small children, the sharing that goes with intimacy is voluntary. Intimate relations are usually restricted to very few people – a couple, parents and children, or three or four friends at the most. Intimacy thus means internal participation and external seclusion.

Although it would be unusual, one might speak of 'intimate financial relations' as characterizing the common management of household income in families. And no doubt, this material base of family life is a condition for maintaining the inclusive–exclusive character of intimacy in all other respects. 'What is mine is yours, what is yours is mine, what is ours is nobody else's.' That is the grammar of intimacy. And, one might add: 'What belongs to everyone is no concern of ours.' The last proposition transforms intimacy into 'amoral familism', as Banfield has called it.[22] It is this aspect which has provoked much resistance among socially minded critics of the nuclear family.

191

Intimate relations involve sharing desires, fantasies, opinions, preferences, biographical facts, which are kept hidden from practically everyone else. A partner to intimacy is not only allowed to hear these secrets, but also to see and touch the other person in ways which are barred to outsiders. It is the exclusive character of this privileged access which provides it with its intimate, 'special' character. To expose an ankle was a sign of intimacy for as long as the lower leg remained covered by the hem of a dress in all other situations; only then was it a favour, a sign of election, offered in trust and to be reciprocated accordingly. Once near-nudity became commonplace in vacation resorts and saunas, and promiscuity an accepted transitional phase in adolescence, exposure of almost the entire body lost this exclusive character and with it its intimate quality. It may be that at present self-exposure through confessions of jealous anxiety, erotic preferences, or fears of desertion and sexual inadequacy constitutes a first bid for the establishment of an exclusive–inclusive intimate relation.

What matters from a sociological point of view is first of all that the nature of intimate relations changes with the transformations in collective and public modes of behaviour, almost in complementary fashion. And equally important is the fact that intimacy implies a necessity for people to manage several appearances at once: one for public use, one for private purposes. Moreover, people presumably have the capacity to do so; they have at their disposal the material means to manage their appearances and to control the setting in which they present themselves, for example, the layout of their homes. And finally, people are apparently more or less free to choose their partners in intimacy.

These assumptions certainly do not apply to the *condition humaine* in general, as conditions that transcend the distinctions of time, place, and class. On the contrary, they are rather particular, and maybe even exceptional, as characteristics of contemporary bourgeois society. Only very recently, in the course of the last hundred years, have these conditions been extended to the vast majority of citizens of western capitalist democracies.

Intimacy is the civilized compromise between external and internal repression. It presupposes at the same time that a person will control many of his or her emotional impulses, hiding them from the outside world, and that these affects are still consciously accessible to this person so that they may be articulated in a particular setting with specific partners in a specified manner. Creating and sustaining intimacy is artful work. It implies that there is something to be kept away from most others and to be shared with only one or very few partners. Impulses must be controlled, affects managed until the right occasion and the right company presents itself. The process which both necessitated and facilitated this particular form of affect management has been called, by Norbert Elias, the civilizing process.

Elias has argued that the emerging court society provided the first setting for a more systematic and sustained dissimulation of affect, coupled with its more controlled and measured expression. Whether indeed the management of affect which constitutes the heart of the civilizing process was always so closely tied up with pacification, state formation, and the emergence of courtly society first and bourgeois society later remains a matter of sociological and anthropological investigation. But Elias's argument is certainly persuasive for the civilizing process in Europe and America.

Intimacy thus presupposes a distinction between behaviour in public and in private, and it requires the necessity, the 'Fremdzwang', as well as the capacity, the 'Selbstzwang', to shift easily from the one to the other. Both the necessity and the capacity developed as an aspect of the civilizing process.[23] The pressures of civilization have imposed the need for a constant self-monitoring upon human beings. It is this permanent control of one's own impulses which constitutes the major discontent of civilization (Freud's 'Unbehagen in der Kultur'), while creating the subjective state of being a 'homo clausus' (Elias), a closed personality, a person within, tightly guarded from appearing before others, its tongue locked behind the fence of its teeth. Intimacy arises in the carefully protected small circle of kin or friends, where a person may show at least part of a 'real' or 'inner' personality. The family then indeed becomes 'haven in a heartless world', but Christopher Lasch who chose this expression as the title of a book tends to overlook that the lack of heart is both a characteristic of the 'outside world' and of the person's self-presentation to those outsiders.

The external and internal pressures for this specific form of affect management require material conditions for their actual realization. If strong emotional expression and a range of bodily functions are to disappear 'hinter den Kulissen', as Elias has it, then the domestic setting must provide the actors with such protective scenery for the *mise-en-scène* of their bourgeois domesticity. The family home, the hard shell of domestic life, represents a major material precondition – a preceding and a necessary condition – for the enactment of intimacy, in permitting a controlled revelation of personal characteristics to others of one's own choosing.[24] The walls that surround people and the doors that connect them have helped to shape their personalities and their relations with others.

Chapter Ten

THE SURVIVORS' SYNDROME: PRIVATE PROBLEMS AND SOCIAL REPRESSION

'One man will always be left alive to tell the story.'

(H. Arendt)[1]

Almost half a century after the war, the survivors of the Nazi terror still suffer from what happened to them in those years. In the meantime, their pain has been labelled and referred to a specialist sphere of competence, made the object of appropriate treatment. With denominators such as 'KZ-syndrome', 'post-concentration camp syndrome', or 'survivors' syndrome' it has become a psychiatric category. Many survivors of the German annihilation camps recognize themselves as suffering from the syndrome and come to seek treatment in the psychotherapist's consulting room or the psychiatric clinic.[2] In expert circles, the scientific debate centres on the diagnosis (should the victims of terrorism and disaster be classed in the same category?); the causes (what is the role of preceding disorders in the emergence of the syndrome?); the correct organization of care (psychiatrists only, or also psychologists, social workers, volunteers?); the most effective form of treatment (individually or in groups? ambulatory or clinical?). What is of interest here is not the content of the discussion, but rather its form and locus.

In the expert debate, the political history of the annihilation of the Jews in Europe is broken up into a discussion of separate case histories, while in the presentation for a mass audience it is fragmented into personal memories and confessions by individual victims in memoirs, documentaries, diaries, and television plays.

The discussion of the fate of those whom the Nazis tried but failed to murder occurs as a discourse among experts, couched in scientific terms and carried on in academic and clinical settings. As in many other domains, the emergence of professional practices and vocabularies as a means to define and to treat human troubles has served to lift these out of a strictly private context without, however, allowing them to enter the sphere of public discussion. They may be discussed, but behind the closed doors of the clinic and consulting room; they are described, but in professional journals and confidential reports.

How citizens as a nation, how colleagues in a work setting, friends in an intimate circle, fellow believers in a church, associates as a club, or relatives as a family should cope with the survivors in their midst is a question that hardly arises, and when it does it is phrased as a question to be submitted to a professional, to an expert helper. This is not the result of purposeful action by expanding professional circles; rather, it is the outcome of an unintentional relegation of all kinds of difficulties of everyday life, of experience and interaction, to professionally qualified specialists. Such processes of medicalization, juridization, psychologization – or, generally, of 'proto-professionalization' – have been repeatedly described. The treatment of war survivors provides an example of this development. Those who are engaged in helping them have often signalled the development and sometimes bemoaned or criticized it.[3]

However, even more than in the case of other ills experienced and expressed individually, the question of the social implications of the survivors' troubles must be raised, for two reasons. First, in a more poignant sense than in other cases, the survivors survived a 'man-made disaster', or more precisely, a crime, a murder campaign waged for many years by a modern state apparatus with an extensive police force, a fully equipped and adequately organized army, supported or abetted by the vast majority of the nation, tolerated by the citizens of many other countries. If ever there was a 'social ill', this was it. And, second, the survivors are confronted with the question how this could ever have come about, what they could have done to escape it, what they should have done to prevent and avoid it, whether they can come to terms with what they saw others do and what they learned about themselves. These are not questions men can answer for themselves alone; they are matters to be discussed over and over again, until one has found a few others whose judgement can be trusted and until one has found some way of assimilating these experiences to those of others and to the realities of the society one now lives in. In the end, some may come to terms with their wartime experiences. But that is what many survivors find impossible:

> They are convinced that their environment cannot understand them. Many patients have repeatedly told their doctors: 'You cannot understand it if you have not gone through it yourself.' In language, feeling and communication these victims of cruelty feel misunderstood.[4]

Yet this misunderstanding cannot be the survivors' problem alone. It is equally the failure of others – whose turn had not yet come during the war – to cope with what the survivors might have told them.

Stated in the simplest terms, the persistent psychic problems of the survivors arise out of the impossibility of telling others in a meaningful way what they have witnessed. Sometimes the story cannot be told at all, or it cannot even be remembered; sometimes part of it must be told again and again, relived, dreamed, repeated to close relatives and friends, but in these cases, too, some things are left out that must go the rounds of endless repetition.

The unspoken experiences return in disguise, as symptoms, as uncomprehended behaviour, or physical disorders. And all the time there is a story that cannot be told.

When a tale cannot be told, the fault is both with the teller and with the listener. If the one cannot talk, then the other cannot listen. But the stories of the survivors are hard to hear and what the survivors have to tell is unbearable; what they say about the world we live in may be intolerable. It all happened during their lifetime, not far away, not long ago, in a world that was essentially the same as this one. No one really understands how it could have happened and no one knows if it can happen again and how to prevent it. But the survivors have lived through it; they are the witnesses. And they may as yet be silenced, with a few comfortable clichés:[5] the war is over; it is so long ago; it is all so far away. And why did they not resist; why did they go as sheep to the slaughter? How come they did not escape? Why did they not see it coming? What did they do anyway in order to survive? They must also be guilty; of course anyone in their case would have done the same, but they did it, or didn't they?[6] And why did they cling so tenaciously to their faith, their folkways, their neighbourhoods? Did not their kinsmen betray them? So, it is a tragedy, of course, a horrible drama, but what business is it of ours? Maybe it never happened at all.

Thus, silence falls between people and within them: repression public and private.

Several authors have recently pointed out that both in Germany and in the invaded countries there was a strong inclination after the war to forget about the past and to concentrate all energy upon political and economic restoration. Those survivors who could muster the effort joined in this active society. Those who could not, fell by the wayside, at best they became patients and clients of professional helpers, social workers, and psychiatrists. If their incapacity could not be legitimated by evident somatic symptoms, their sufferings required new labels, and psychiatrists began to provide those, so that their patients' intimates might respectfully accept their condition, if not out of empathy, at least out of awe for a scientific diagnosis; and so that the state would support the survivors when they could still use its aid, if not out of a political loyalty to those it could after all not protect when they needed it, then at least out of social concern for the disabled.

But the helping professionals did more than just provide impressive labels; they also listened, and they tried to understand. In this manner the testimony from the political history of murder was transformed into a succession of complaints in the consulting room.

In this manner the circle of professional helpers constitutes a buffer zone between the private troubles of individual survivors and the society of their contemporaries, between the private and the public domain. The professional circle protects the individual against bluntness or stupidity, and the community against too perturbing expressions of individual emotions.

Doctors, lawyers, and social workers have fulfilled similar functions in many sectors of society and provided adequate solutions in doing so. But the private difficulties of the survivors of the annihilation camps cannot be understood as individual problems alone, they also are separate versions of the political history of the assassination of the Jews in Europe. That history cannot be dealt with only in the consulting room; as a historical and political problem it must be coped with in public discussion.

It may appear as if this public coping process has been in full swing for years: one after the other the testimonies on the annihilation camps appear. Almost everybody now is aware of what human beings did there to other human beings. But it seems as if it refers to a different world, populated with a different species, as if it were of no consequence for this society.

Alexander and Margarete Mitscherlich have written a book about the social process of coping with the wartime past, titled *The Inability to Mourn*.[7] They discussed German society in a stage of massive repression of the Nazi past, a 'social amnesia' which since has been mostly overcome. Yet, the case of Germany, as the inheritor of the Nazi *Reich*, is very different from that of the invaded and the victorious nations.

Some years ago the American psychiatrist Bruno Bettelheim published a collection of his essays under the title *Surviving*.[8] In 1938 Bettelheim spent twelve months in Dachau and Buchenwald. Almost uniquely he was released and escaped to the United States. There, he wrote a report on the German camps which to this day forms the point of departure for all sociological and psychological literature on the inmates' experience. In a preface to this reprinted essay, Bettelheim describes how for years he had to insist on having his account published. His version of the horrors was not believed, or was considered too shocking for an American audience.

This is a most uncompromising, and at times harsh, book. The one insistent message is a protest against every attempt to minimize, vulgarize, beautify, or routinize the Nazi murders. The history of the extermination must first stand as a bare fact. It must not be explained away, moralized over. The very term 'Holocaust' Bettelheim finds objectionable.

> To call this vile mass murder 'the holocaust' is not to give it a special name emphasizing its uniqueness which would permit, over time, the word becoming invested with feelings germane to the event it refers to. The correct definition of 'holocaust' is 'burnt offering' . . . . By using the term 'holocaust', entirely false associations are established through conscious and unconscious connotations between the most vicious of mass murders and ancient rituals of a deeply religious nature. (p. 92)

Equally, 'By calling the victims of the Nazis "martyrs" we falsify their fate.' They did not undergo their fate voluntarily. Neither can the victims and survivors of Nazi persecution collectively be called heroes, no matter how brave many of them proved to be in those years. What defines the victims is not what fate they chose, but that a modern state tried and almost wholly succeeded in exterminating them, and what defines the survivors is not how courageously each of them behaved, but that they escaped the campaign to kill them.[9]

The extermination of the Jews cannot be assimilated to contemporary culture without completely changing that very culture, or maybe even abandoning it. In Adorno's outcry: 'The idea that after this war life could proceed normally, even that the culture could be reconstructed – as if the reconstruction of culture were not its negation – is idiotic. Millions of Jews have been murdered, and that should be an intermezzo and not the catastrophe itself. What is this culture really still waiting for?'[10]

In Bettelheim's essays there is a grim insistence upon recognizing the facts as they occurred, upon calling them by their true names. As to the survivors: 'Survival in the camps – this cannot be stressed enough – depended foremost on luck: to be able to survive, one had to escape being killed by the SS' (p. 108). In order to use one's opportunities, one had to maintain a sense of autonomy, of self-respect, and of realism. And Bettelheim then stresses how desperately the victims clung to any trace of sympathy and solidarity from the outside world: 'One cannot meet catastrophic events, and survive when deprived of the feeling that somebody cares' (p. 102). But no such messages of concern reached the Jewish communities in occupied Europe: 'What happened to them impressed on them that nobody cared whether they lived or died, and that the rest of the world, including foreign countries, had no concern for their fate' (ibid.). Bettelheim believes that this indifference weakened their ability to cope with their condition. 'Had the Jews felt that important voices in the rest of the world were raised in their behalf, that people in the free world cared and truly wanted them to live, they would not have needed to engage in the defense of massive denial, but could have realized what was going on, and reacted differently to it' (p. 102).[11]

This brings us back to the main point, that the survivors' testimony is unbearable for their contemporaries. It is not lost upon anyone living in these times, in these countries, that not yet fifty years ago the European nations let millions of Jews from among their ranks go to their destruction. On the rare occasions when the question is raised, it is turned into a moral issue. But first of all it is a fact. This obstinate fact may provide a clue to interpret the difficulty which the contemporaries have in listening to the survivors, for example in the Netherlands.

The Netherlands is a small country, much greater in industry and commerce than its size would suggest, greater also than its inhabitants often realize in matters of culture, letters, and sciences. But in the dangerous traffic among states it has had for centuries no other choice than precarious neutrality or docile loyalty to a great power. In the course of almost three centuries it attempted to avoid wars, won a few colonial and neighbourly battles, and lost the confrontation with French and German expansionism. It took the German armies five days to crush the Dutch defences, and after five years of subjugation liberation came through foreign arms. In the aftermath of the Second World War, the Dutch, after losing some overseas campaigns, finally realized that they had already lost an empire.

For the Dutch the lesson from the history of the last forty years is one of powerlessness. They could not hold an empire together, they could not prevent the occupation of their territory, they could not even protect their own citizens from extermination by an invading criminal state. In an age where even superpowers have become incapable of protecting their inhabitants against nuclear destruction and in which human helplessness against equally human destructiveness has become universal, this is a timely lesson to learn. But this sense of insecurity and helplessness, no matter how realistic and adequate, is hardly a suitable theme for official discussion or for public education.

Until now the problem of the survivors was implicitly also a problem of the people around them who knew and did not want to know and remained deaf. But already the majority of the population has been born after the war, does not know, and believes it wants to listen. Again, Bettelheim deals with the issues most lucidly. Young people today are brought up in a pacified society, in surroundings almost entirely devoid of violence and intimidation. While parental tolerance for sexual desires is extending, toilet training and feeding regimes are becoming less rigid, discipline at school and at home is relaxing somewhat, the acceptance of violence is actually diminishing.[12] In this pacified context even minor outbursts of violence (minor compared to what is at issue here) such as street crimes and terrorist acts become highly disturbing and elicit strong reactions. 'These outbursts are conspicuous: by their spectacular nature, they even give the impression that ours is an age of violence. So we clamor for still greater suppression of even small eruptions of violence that could act as safety valves, draining off small amounts and leaving a balance that the individual could assimilate' (p. 190).

As the facts of violence are hidden from children and as their own violent impulses are strongly repressed, they are ill prepared to live in this world. First of all, 'This attitude prevents children from forming a clear understanding about the world of difference that separates violent fantasy from acting violently in reality' (p. 188). And also, 'Particularly in matters of violence, there is no protection in ignorance.' Bettelheim directly connects this observation to the naïvety of those threatened by the Nazis.

Even though most people live their lives in pacified surroundings, strongly repressing violent impulses in themselves and others, this is a very violent and dangerous world in which domestic peace is maintained only by strong individual and social repression. That truth is difficult to convey to children, and even adults, without creating an impairing sense of anxiety.

The Dutch as a nation did not save the Jews among them from destruction; they were equally powerless to save the lives of their countrymen in Indonesia. Had the Dutch seriously tried to protect the Jews from their murderers, it would have required a transformation of their society for which they were not at all prepared. It would have presupposed large-scale disobedience to the Dutch and German occupation authorities, massive civil resistance, systematic dissimulation, fraudulence and sabotage at every level, and a concerted protest against the German extermination programme. But instead the vast majority of the Dutch tried for a way of life under the Germans that would be just bearable and just honourable and part of the price of this accommodation was the surrender of the Dutch Jews for deportation. Other European nations have similar histories to forget, some on balance a bit more glorious, some a bit more shameful. So, the Dutch, as other nations, let their Jews be deported to a not-so-uncertain destination. Quite understandably as a nation they prefer to remain silent about it, and quite understandably they indignantly deny either this silence, or else the very facts.

But in fact, although this history does not reveal much about individual Dutchmen or about the characteristics of the Dutch nation, it is, however, revealing for Dutch society as for other modern societies: apparently, without disturbing public order, a well-organized and well-armed state apparatus can deport and kill citizens by the millions.

It is this fact that cannot be coped with in public opinion, implying as it does that the Dutch state is unable to protect its citizens against massive terror and violence. Entitled to the vote and to their social benefits, obliged to pay taxes and fulfil their military service, the citizens find in their own state no warrant against the threat from state violence. Even their own state might turn against them as a terror apparatus.

Many Jews have conceived of the Nazi terror as a chapter in the destiny of the Jewish nation, as a fate that had to befall the Jews. Some of them found comfort in the idea. But the thought is mostly reassuring to non-Jews who might believe that such a fate could befall no other humans than the Jews. Yet, human beings have been exterminated by the millions in other countries too, by their own or foreign governments. The progress of technology has made mass destruction more feasible and more difficult to avoid.

When the survivors cannot tell their story, sometimes not even to themselves, or when they cannot stop repeating it, it is also because their contemporaries have turned a deaf ear, when it happened, and once it was over.[15] Because the story had to be repressed, the witnesses were silenced. And as human beings together form the nation that forms them, the witnesses silenced themselves as they were muted. Their political history is written by academic historians, their individual complaints are treated by professional helpers. And, as Bettelheim has so stridently shown, their most intimate experience is often robbed from them and exploited in contemporary works of popular art, religion, and philosophy, continually abused in political debate and propaganda to embarrass opponents whatever side they are on.

It is quite difficult to imagine a different course of events. The awareness and memory of the nation's history is not produced at any specific location, the Dutch hesitate to institutionalize official celebrations and commemorations, prefer not to prescribe courses in civil consciousness, and keep the political education of students and recruits at a low key. The idea of public celebrations for the survivors of the Nazi extermination is embarrassing at best. On the whole, public authorities, church leaders, and the mass media have taken great pains to appear sensitive about the issues and to avoid offending anyone. On some occasions, such as on the adoption of the law granting payments and provisions to those persecuted during the war, or the recurrent announcements of the release of the Nazi criminals held at Breda Prison (until 1989), there have been large-scale public discussions in which many of the issues were articulated. At least, the outbursts and confrontations on those occasions may be recognized as wholesome and necessary.

It is only realistic to concede that a modern society such as that of the Netherlands does have a few institutions in which private troubles can be expressed and understood as public issues. At every point social developments are reduced to individual problems, problems to be dealt with in specialized institutions such as hospitals, courts, prisons, or schools, by qualified professional experts such as doctors, lawyers, parole officers, and educators. Society is divided up into categories of individuals, each with its own diagnostic label, its own helping institutions, and its own supporting profession. Somehow, those citizens whom the state could not protect from deportation and almost certain murder by a foreign invader became one of these categories.

The survivors' message can find no public expression, no collective, official articulation.[14] It would require a public monument of failure, an official commemoration of loss and default denying the very reasons of existence to the states that should have protected them. The survivors are left to their own devices and to the loyalty of those who dare to listen and share the anxiety.

NOTES

INTRODUCTION

1 On this remarkable episode, see Sjaak van der Geest, 'Censorship and medical sociology in the Netherlands', *Social Science and Medicine* 28. 12 (1989) pp. 1339–41.

2 Chaps 1, 2, 3, 4, 7, and 10 were included in a Dutch collection of my essays, *De Mens is de Mens een Zorge*, Amsterdam: Meulenhoff, 1982 (1986). Chapters 5 and 6 appeared originally in Dutch as part of A. de Swaan, R. van Geldem, and V. Kense, *Sociologie van de Psychotherapie (I)*. *Het Spreekuur als Opgave*, Utrecht/Antwerp: Aula/Het Spectrum, 1979. Chapter 3 appeared earlier in *Social Science and Medicine* 28, 11 (1989) pp. 1165–70.

Chapter 4, 'On the sociogenesis of the psychoanalytic situation', appeared earlier in *Psychoanalysis and Contemporary Thought* 3 (3) (Dec. 1980): 381–414 and in *Human Figurations: Essays for Norbert Elias*, Amsterdam: Amsterdams Sociologisch Tijdschrift, 1977, pp. 381–413.

Chapter 7, 'The politics of agoraphobia; on changes in emotional and relational management', was published in *Theory and Society* 10 (1981): 337–58, followed by comments by John Alt and Alvin Gouldner and with a rejoinder by the author.

Chapter 8 appeared in Dutch as 'Jaloezie als Klasseverschijnsel', *De Gids* 151 (1) (1988): 39–49. It was originally presented as 'Jealousy as a class phenomenon', a paper for the British Sociological Association Theory Group, Conference on 'The Body and Sociology', Stoke-on-Trent, 17–18 Sept. 1987, and appeared in the *International Journal of Sociology* 4. 3, September 1989.

Chapter 9 was originally presented in German translation at the Conference on Intimacy of the 9. Jahrestagung der Deutschen Arbeitsgemeinschaft für Familientherapie, Göttingen, 25–7 Feb. 1988.

Chapter 10 was published in English as 'The survivors' syndrome: private problems and social repression', *Israel–Netherlands Symposium on the Impact of Persecution* I, Dalfsen/Amsterdam, 14–18 April 1980, Ministry of Cultural Affairs, Recreation and Social Welfare, Rijswijk, 1981: 85–94.

CHAPTER 1: DISEASE AND DEPENDENCY

1 See, for example, Norbert Elias, *What is Sociology?*, London: Hutchinson, 1978.
2 Cf. C. P. M. Knipscheer, *Oude Mensen en Hun Sociale Omgeving; een Studie van het Primaire Sociale Netwerk* (Dissertation, University of Tilburg, 1980: 137); Chris Phillipson, Miriam Bernard, and Patricia Strong (eds) *Dependency and Interdependency in Old Age: Theoretical Perspectives and Policy Alternatives*, London: Croom Helm, 1986.
3 Robert Dingwall, *Aspects of Illness*, London: Robertson, 1976: 94.
4 Talcott Parsons, *The Social System*, London: Routledge & Kegan Paul, 1951, especially chap. 10.
5 Cf. Chapter 6.
6 The term 'residual deviance' was coined by Thomas Scheff, *Being Mentally Ill: a Sociological Theory*, Chicago: Aldine, 1966, especially chap. 2.
7 Andrew C. Twaddle, 'Illness and deviance', *Social Science and Medicine* 7 (1973): 751–62, p. 753.
8 For a recent attempt to develop 'sociological types of chronic illness' next to a medical terminology, cf. Peter Conrad, 'The experience of illness: recent and new directions', in Julius A. Roth and Peter Conrad (eds) *Research in the Sociology of Health Care: a Research Annual*, vol. 6: *The Experience and Management of Chronic Illness*, Greenwich, CT/London: JAI Press, 1987: 1–31. The author distinguishes among other types 'lived-with illness', 'mortal illness', and 'at risk illness'.
9 E.g. Julius A. Roth, *Timetables: Structuring the Passage of Time in Hospital and Other Careers*, Indianapolis: Bobbs-Merrill, 1963, especially chap. 3; Gerald V. Stimson and Barbara Webb, *Going to See the Doctor: the Consultation Process in General Practice*, London: Routledge & Kegan Paul, 1975.
10 Talcott Parsons has asked why doctors generally treat their patients decently (*The Social System*, London: Routledge & Kegan Paul, 1951, p. 457) and concludes that it is the strict separation of professional activity from other spheres of life that warrants this 'functional specificity' and 'affective neutrality' (p. 458). This describes a function of professional separation, but does not explain its emergence and continuity. Strong adds that mutual competition compels doctors to display 'good bedside manners', but finds that in England this 'medical gentility' continues towards National Health patients in the absence of any competition among doctors; 'because the financial position, prestige and degree of self-control of the profession as a whole are under direct political management and are themselves a political issue, it pays doctors to be polite to the great mass of their patients'. And: 'In other words, polite medical service can be the product of a trade-off between organized labour and capital and may be bought through political as well as financial muscle.' But this rather original assumption does not explain why individual doctors might not misbehave if this would only harm the profession as a

whole, unless of course a disciplinary agency might punish them for their rudeness. Cf. P. M. Strong, *The Ceremonial Order of the Clinic: Parents, Doctors, and Medical Bureaucracies*, London: Routledge & Kegan Paul, 1979: 215.

11 'The dependency measures usually used in service policy planning concentrate on physical or mental dependency. There is a tendency to play down emotional, structural, political and economic dependency, despite the fact that all these aspects may interact with physical dependency', G. Clare Wenger, 'What do dependency measures measure? Challenging assumptions', in Chris Phillipson, Miriam Bernard, and Patricia Strong (eds) *Dependency and Interdependency in Old Age: Theoretical Perspectives and Policy Alternatives*, London: Croom Helm, 1986, pp. 69–84, p. 70.

12 Robert Dingwall, *Aspects of Illness*, London: Robertson, 1976, p. 39, notes that a concept such as 'network' – for example, 'lay referral network' – is a construction *ex post* and that the contacts had to be sought, established, and described by those concerned. D. M. Boswell, 'Personal crises and the mobilization of the social network', in Clyde Mitchell (ed.) *Social Networks in an Urban Situation: Analysis of Personal Relationships in Central African Towns*, Manchester: Manchester University Press, 1969, pp. 254, 288, points out that kin relations, for example, may remain dormant for a long time only to be mobilized in a critical phase of life. Thus, during a period of network contraction due to disease or old age, next to the medical nexus a family nexus may be intensified: an adult daughter as the caretaker of a sick parent, for example.

13 Cf. Lisa F. Berkman, 'Physical health and the social environment: a social epidemiological perspective', in L. Eisenberg and A. Kleinman (eds) *The Relevance of Social Science for Medicine*, Dordrecht: Reidel, 1981: 63. Cf. also Maria Evandrou, 'Who cares for the elderly: family care, provision and receipt of statutory service', in Chris Phillipson, Miriam Bernard, and Patricia Strong (eds) *Dependency and Interdependency in Old Age: Theoretical Perspectives and Policy Alternatives*, London: Croom Helm, 1986, pp. 150–66: 'spouses are the main source of help for elderly people living with elderly or non-elderly spouses' (p. 158); and 'The daughters and daughters-in-law constitute the largest group of carers of elderly people' (p. 150); and, finally: 'Community care is a euphemism for family care, and more specifically women' (p. 164). In the eighties official interest in the patient's social network increased considerably when budget-cutting governments discovered it as an alternative to professional care in their visions of a 'responsible' or a 'caring' society.

14 John B. McKinlay, 'Social network influences on morbid episodes and the career of help-seeking', in L. Eisenberg and A. Kleinman (eds) *The Relevance of Social Science for Medicine*, Dordrecht: Reidel, 1981; Jean K. Langlie, 'Social networks, health beliefs, and preventive health behavior', in *Journal of Health and Social Behavior* 18 (1977): 244–60.

15 Mark S. Granovetter, 'The strength of weak ties', *American Journal of*

Sociology 78 (4) (1973): 1365–80. Cf. also Angela Finlayson, 'Social networks as coping resources: lay help and consultation patterns used by women in husbands' post-infarction career', *Social Science and Medicine* 10 (1976): 97–103.

16 Cf. Marijke Mootz, *De Patient en zijn Naasten*, Dissertation, University of Limburg, 1981.

17 A. P. N. Nauta, *Contact en Controle tussen Buren*, Alphen aan de Rijn: Samsom (1973): 187 finds that precisely those people who needed help and contact rarely appealed to their neighbours because they were unable to do something in return.

CHAPTER 2: AFFECT MANAGEMENT IN A CANCER WARD

1 In rewriting the original research report (cf. Introduction, n. 2), I used material gathered from foreign and Dutch observers of hospitals for the chronically ill. I have not quoted all Dutch sources in this translation, but I owe much information to the reports and publications of B. Brouwer; C. van Brederode-Ritten and Miriam Floor; Jos Evenhuis, Willy Klos, and Bert van Lingen; F.S.A.M. van Dam; Jan Derksen, Max Boute, and Paul de Lange; Kitty Geneuglijk; H. Ten Have; M. Herngreen and L. Francis-Schram; Th. Indewey Gerlings-Huurdeman; Veralien Kragt; Jan Matse; F.L. Meijler; M. Notenboom; Louis Sinner; and A. Thiadens. Full references may be found in the Dutch version of this chapter in *De Mens is de Mens een Zorg*, Amsterdam: Meulenhoff, 1982 (1989). The original report was based on observations by the members of the research team and A. Van Dantzig.

2 This fragmentation and shortening of the perspective on the future has been described for tuberculosis patients by Julius A. Roth, *Timetables: Structuring the Passage of Time in Hospital Treatment and Other Careers*, New York/Indianapolis: Bobbs-Merrill, 1963; for poliomyelitis patients, by Fred Davis, 'Definitions of time and recovery in paralytic polio reconvalescence', *American Journal of Sociology* 61 (May 1956): 582–7; for cancer patients, by Barney G. Glaser and Anselm L. Strauss, *Time for Dying*, Chicago: Aldine, 1986.

3 This approach agrees with Isabel E. P. Menzies, 'A case-study of social systems as a defence against anxiety: a report on a study of a general hospital', *Human Relations* 13 (1960): 95–121.

4 Richard M. Titmuss, *Social Policy: an Introduction*, London: Allen & Unwin, 1974: 150.

5 Cf. Robert Pinker, *Social Theory and Social Policy*, London: Heinemann, 1971: 153.

6 This uncertainty plays a central role in Talcott Parsons' theoretical discussion of the role of the sick and the functions of the medical profession (*The Social System*, London: Routledge & Kegan Paul, 1951, 'The case of modern medical practice'). Fred Davis distinguishes 'real' or 'clinical' from 'functional uncertainty', which doctors tend to

keep alive even after they have reached clinical certainty (*Illness, Interaction, and the Self*, Belmont, CA: Wadsworth, 1972).

7 Robert Pinker, *Social Theory and Social Policy*, London: Heinemann, 1971.

8 Cf. Barney G. Glaser and Anselm L. Strauss, *Anguish: the Case History of a Dying Trajectory*, San Francisco: Sociology Press, 1970.

9 Julius A. Roth, 'Some contingencies of the moral evaluation and control of the clientele: the case of the hospital emergency service', *American Journal of Sociology* 77 (5) (1972): 839–56.

10 Cf. Norbert Elias, *The Civilizing Process* (1939), vol. 1: *The History of Manners*, Oxford/New York: Blackwell/Urizen, 1978: 150; Johan Goudsblom, 'Public health and the civilizing process', *Milbank Quarterly* 64 (2) (1986): 161–88; similar conclusions were reached in their M.A. theses (Dept. of Sociology, University of Amsterdam, 1981) by Hennie Oosterbaan on the development in the codes of behaviour in the Old and New Hospice at Delft and by Veralien Kragt on handbooks for nurses' training in patient care.

11 A somewhat similar approach to the division of labour in the hospital is adopted by Anselm Strauss, Shizuko Fagerhaugh, Barbara Suczek, and Carolyn Wiener, *Social Organization of Medical Work*, Chicago and London: University of Chicago Press, 1985. The authors distinguish various types of 'work', such as 'comfort work' and 'sentimental work', 'composure work', 'identity', 'awareness context', and even 'rectification', 'articulation', and 'information work'.

12 Cf. Isabel E. Menzies, 'A case-study of social systems as a defence against anxiety: a report on a study of a general hospital', *Human Relations* 13 (1960): 103.

13 Cas Wouters and Herman ten Kroode, 'Informalisering in het Rouwen en in de Omgang met Doden op de Snijzaal', *De Gids* 143 (7) (1980): 492 (a study of medical students in the dissecting room). Cf. Renate Maintz, 'The nature and genesis of impersonality: some results of a study on the doctor–patient relationship', *Social Research* 37 (3) (1970): 443: 'Only one item [in the questionnaire – AdS] was in fact accepted by a sizable majority, namely the statement that a doctor should not feel disgusted with or abhorrence of anything he has to look at or to do while practicing.'

14 Barney G. Glaser and Anselm L. Strauss, *Chronic Illness and the Quality of Life*, St Louis, MO: Mosby, 1975, p. 55.

15 Norbert Elias, *The Loneliness of the Dying*, Oxford: Blackwell, 1985, p. 23.

16 Cf. P. M. Strong, *The Ceremonial Order of the Clinic: Parents, Doctors and Medical Bureaucracies*, London: Routledge & Kegan Paul, 1979, pp. 150ff.

17 C. Wouters and H. ten Kroode, 'Informaliserung in het Rouwen en in de Omgang met Doden op de Snijzaal', *De Gids* 143 (7) (1980): 489.

18 'We laugh a lot . . . , They are silly things, like someone almost got dropped out of the Hoyer lift.' Carol P. Hanley Germain, *The Cancer Unit: an Ethnography*, Wakefield, MA: Nursing Resources, 1979, p. 168.

19 Rose Laub Coser, 'Some social functions of laughter', in J. K. Skipper and R. C. Leonards (eds) *Social Interaction and Patient Care*, Philadelphia/Toronto: Lippincott, 1965, p. 303.
20 Cf. Edwin A. Weinstein and Robert L. Kahn, *Denial of Illness: Symbolic and Physiological Aspects*, Springfield, IL: Thomas, 1955, p. 31.
21 Ibid., p. 129.
22 The hospital is, of course, a 'total institution'. This allusion to the ideas of Erving Goffman presents an occasion for mentioning how much his perspective has influenced the preceding discussion: cf. *Asylums: Essays on the Social Situation of Mental Patients and Other Inmates*, Harmondsworth: Pelican, 1968; and *Stigma: Notes on the Management of Spoiled Identity*, Harmondsworth: Pelican, 1968.
23 For an attack from the 'right' upon established medicine, especially oncology, cf. James T. Patterson, *The Dread Disease, Cancer and Modern American Culture*, Cambridge, MA/London: Harvard University Press, on the 'Cancer counter culture' (p. 166) versus 'official optimism about the imminent discovery of a cure' (p. 296).

CHAPTER 3: EXPANSION AND LIMITATION OF THE MEDICAL REGIME

1 A. de Froe, 'Alle Mensen Zijn Altijd ziek', *De Gids* 136 (9–10) (1973): 583.
2 Throughout the nineteenth century doctors' interventions in everyday life for the sake of health were aimed especially at women; cf. Barbara Ehrenreich and Deirdre English, *For Her Own Good: 150 Years of Experts' Advice to Women*, Garden City, NY: Anchor/Doubleday, 1979. Cf. also Ann Oakley, *Women Confined: Towards a Sociology of Childbirth*, Oxford: Martin Robertson, 1980, who demonstrates how medical criteria regarding the place of delivery and the forms of intervention increasingly replaced the women's personal choices.
3 Cf. Hans Jürgen Teuteberg, 'Die Ernährung als psychosoziales Phänomen; Uberlegungen zu einem verhaltenstheoretischen Bezugsrahmen', *Hamburger Jahrbuch für Wirtschaft und Gesellschaftspolitik* 24 (1979): 262–82, especially p. 272.
4 Christiaan van Weel, *Anticiperende Geneeskunde in de Praktijk*, Dissertation, Erasmus University, Rotterdam, 1981.
5 Ibid., p. 44.
6 Ibid., p. 47.
7 Gregory Bateson, 'Double bind', in *Steps Toward an Ecology of Mind: Collected Essays in Anthropology, Psychiatry, Evolution and Epistemology*, San Francisco: Chandler Publishing Co., 1972.
8 See Chapter 5.
9 Jürgen Habermas, *Technik und Wissenschaft als 'Ideologie'*, Frankfurt am Main: Suhrkamp, 1968.
10 Michel Foucault, *The Birth of the Clinic: an Archaeology of Medical Perception*, New York: Pantheon, 1975.

11 Vicente Navarro, *Medicine under Capitalism*, New York: Prodist, 1976.
12 Eliot Freidson, *Profession of Medicine: a Study of the Sociology of Applied Knowledge*, New York: Dodd, Mead, 1970.
13 Cf. Leon Eisenberg and Arthur Kleinman, 'Clinical social science', in L. Eisenberg and A. Kleinman (eds) *The Relevance of Social Science for Medicine*, Dordrecht: Reidel, 1981, pp. 1–26.
14 Cf. H. Jamous and B. Peloille, 'Professions or self-perpetuating systems? Changes in the French university-hospital system', in J. A. Jackson (ed.) *Professions and Professionalization*, Cambridge: Cambridge University Press, 1970.
15 See Chapter 5.
16 Cf. Gerhard Nijhof, *Individualisering en Uitstoting; Van Maatschappelijk Probleem naar Psychische Stoornis; een Perspectief voor een Psychiatrische Sociologie*, Nijmegen: Link, 1978.
17 Cf. David Wilsford, 'The cohesion and fragmentation of organized medicine in France and the United States', *Journal of Health Politics, Policy and Law* 12 (3) (Fall 1987): 481–503, who argues the crucial value of unity and cohesion in the ranks of organized medicine. The AMA's cautious strategy to maintain internal consensus is illustrated with the example of the birth control issue in the 1930s (p. 499).
18 Cf. Leon Eisenberg and Arthur Kleinman, 'Clinical social science', in L. Eisenberg and A. Kleinman (eds) *The Relevance of Social Science for Medicine*, Dordrecht: Reidel, 1981, p. 17: 'If sociologists have done the public and the profession a service by criticizing the unwarranted extension of the biomedical model beyond its domain of applicability, they themselves, by arguing for a "social model", advocate a position which implies the involvement of health experts (albeit nonmedical ones: sociologists, in fact) in the management of an even wider range of everyday activities.'

CHAPTER 4: ON THE SOCIOGENESIS OF THE PSYCHOANALYTIC SITUATION

1 S. Freud, 'Recommendations to Physicians Practising Psycho-Analysis', (1912), *Standard Edition*, 12:111–20, Hogarth Press, London, 1958; 'On Beginning the Treatment (Further Recommendations on the Technique of Psycho-Analysis I)', (1913a), *Standard Edition*, 12:123–44, London: Hogarth Press, 1958; 'Remembering, Repeating and Working-Through (Further Recommendations on the Technique of Psycho-Analysis II)', (1914b), *Standard Edition*, 12:147–56, Hogarth Press, London, 1958; 'Observations on Transference-Love (Further Recommendations on the Technique of Psycho-Analysis III)', (1915), *Standard Edition*, 12:159–71, London: Hogarth Press, 1958.
2 See the surveys of the literature in W. La Barre, 'Influence of Freud on American Anthropology', *American Imago* 15 (3), Fall 1958, pp.275–328; W. Muensterberger, and A.H. Esman, *The Psychoanalytic*

Study of Society, International University Press, New York, 1972; R.A. Jones, 'Freud and American Sociology, 1909-1949', *Journal of the History of the Behavioral Sciences* 10 (1), January 1974, pp.21-39; R. Jacoby, 'Negative Psychoanalyse und Marxismus; Ueberlegungen zu einer objektiven Theorie der Subjektivität', *Psyche* 29 (11), November 1975.

3 See T.W. Adorno, *The Authoritarian Personality*, Harper & Row, New York, 1950; various articles by Talcott Parsons (see R.A. Jones [1974] for a bibliography); F. Weinstein and G. Platt, *Psychoanalytic Sociology; an essay on the interpretation of historical data and the phenomena of collective behavior*, Baltimore, 1973.

4 N. Elias, *Ueber den Prozess der Zivilisation; Soziogenetische und psychogenetische Untersuchungen*, Bern and München: Franke Verlag, (1936), 1969, part I, p.302.

5 G. Devereux, *From anxiety to method in the behavioral sciences*, The Hague/Paris: Mouton, 1967, makes a first attempt at a psychoanalytic understanding of social research activity.

6 P.L. Berger, 'Towards a Sociological Understanding of Psychoanalysis', *Social Research* 32 (1), Spring 1965, pp.26-41; and E. Heller, 'Psychoanalysis and Literature', *Salmagundi* (A Quarterly of the Humanities and the Social Sciences: published by Skidmore College; 10th Anniversary Issue), Fall 1975-Winter 1976, no.31-2, pp. 17-28, have written very perceptive essays on the pervasive presence of psychoanalytic ideas in contemporary American culture.

7 An early study, although somewhat marred by hostility, is that of K. Mittenzwey, 'Zur soziologie der Psychoanalytische Erkenntnis', in Scheler (ed.), *Versuch zu einer Soziologie des Wissens*, München 1924, pp. 365-75. See also S. Moscovici, *La psychanalyse, son image et son public; étude sur la représentation sociale de la psychanalyse*, Presses Universitaires de France, Paris 1961; J.C. Burnham, *Psychoanalysis and American medicine: 1894-1918; Medicine, science and culture* (Psychological Issues V (4), New York: International Universities Press, 1967; N.G. Hale Jr., *Freud and the Americans. The beginnings of psychoanalysis in the United States, 1876-1917*, New York: Oxford University Press, 1971.

8 The most perceptive study of this kind for the US is that of C. Kadushin, *Why People Go to Psychiatrists*, Chicago: Atherton. For an elaboration of Kadushin's argument and an application to the Netherlands, see A. De Swaan, R. van Gelderen, and V.W. Kense, *The Initial Interview as a Task*, presented at 11th International Congress of Psychotherapy, Amsterdam, August 27-31, and also Chapter 5.

9 For a recent survey of the literature see the 'Bibliographical Essay' in P. Gay, 1988, p.741-80.

10 Silas Weir Mitchell, an American neurologist, poet, and author, proposed in his *Fat and Blood* (1872), 'a form of treatment which consists in absolute rest of body and mind, administration of highly nutritious and easily digestible food in large quantities, and massage to take the place of muscular exercise' (W.R.R. Thomson, *Black's Medical Dictionary*, 29th ed., Black, London, 1971). Various methods of

electrotherapy were in use: faradization consisted in the application of alternating electrical currents of low frequency to parts of the body afflicted by hysterical paralysis; galvanization consisted in a similar application of direct current *(Oosthoek's Encyclopedie,* Utrecht: Oosthoek, 1968-1973).

11 See J. Breuer and S. Freud, 'Studies on Hysteria', *Standard Edition,* 2, London: Hogarth Press, 1955.

12 This was specifically a problem with electrotherapy. Only in the middle of this century did less bulky, more easily transportable equipment become available. The advent of the transistor solved the problem by the time the treatment itself began to be abandoned.

13 Quoted by I. Vieler, *Die Deutsche Artzpraxis im 19. Jahrhundert,* Inaugural Dissertation Gutenberg U. Mainz, 1958, p.4. *(my translation).*

14 Quoted by Vieler, *ibid.*

15 Quoted by Vieler, *op.cit.,* p.12 *(my translation).*

16 E. Heischkel-Artelt, 'Die Welt des praktischen Arztes im 19. Jahrhundert', in W. Artelt and W. Rüegg (eds), *Der Arzt und der Kranke in der Gesellschaft des 19. Jahrhunderts,* Frankfurt a. M., Stuttgart: Enke, 1967, p.10.

17 See S. Bernfeld and S.C. Bernfeld, 'Freud's First Year in Practice, 1886–1887', in *Bulletin of the Menninger Clinic* 16 (2), March 1952, p.37; E. Jones, *The Life and Work of Sigmund Freud. Vol. 1: The Formative Years and The Great Discoveries, 1856-1900,* New York: Basic Books, 1953, p.157.

18 E.H. Erikson, 'Freud's "The Origins of Psychoanalysis"', *International Journal of Psycho-analysis* 36 (1), 1955, p.4.

19 The controversy turns on the question of whether Freud's opinions were received with as much hostility as he himself reports in 'An Autobiographical Study', (1925), *Standard Edition,* 20: 7–74, London: Hogarth Press, 1959. See S. Bernfeld and S.C. Bernfeld, *op. cit.;* E. Jones, *op. cit.,* 1953, p.229–32; K. Sablik, 'Sigmund Freud und die Gesellschaft der Ärzte in Wien', *Wiener Klin. Wochenschr.,* 80:107–110; and H.F. Ellenberger, *The Discovery of the Unconscious: The History and Evolution of Dynamic Psychiatry,* New York: Basic Books, 1970, p.437–42. More recently controversy has also raged about Freud's alleged repeal of his 'seduction theory' and the nature of his relations with his sister-in-law, Minnie Bernays. See for a summary Peter Gay, 1988, pp. 75, 90–6.

20 'in a district near the new university, which since the sixties had become one of the most fashionable residential areas of the city. The house was dignified, the rooms were large and beautiful'. S. Bernfeld and S.C. Bernfeld, *op.cit,* p.38.

21 S. Breton, *Les Pas perdu (Interview du Professeur Freud),* (1920), Paris: Gallimard, 1969.

22 Ellenberger, *op.cit.,* p.465

23 H. Sachs, *Freud, master and friend,* Harvard University Press, Cambridge (Mass.), 1945, p.51. This too has become the subject of polemics.

Ellenberger attempts to establish a sociological point: 'Freud could also be understood if seen as a typical representative of the Viennese professional world of the end of the nineteenth century. It was not unusual in Vienna, an ethnic and social melting pot, that a gifted man from the lower middle class could climb the social ladder and reach, by middle life, a fairly high social and financial status, provided that he had gone to secondary school and a university', *op.cit.*, p.463. E. Federn, 'Einige Bemerkungen über die Schwierigkeiten, eine Geschichte der Psychoanalyse zu schreiben', *Jahr. Psychoanal.*, 7:9–22, p.16, reproaches Ellenberger for insinuating that Freud lived as a grand bourgeois (Grossbürger), in comparison with Adler's modest life style, a comparison 'at Freud's expense'.

24 Cf. S. Pankejeff, 'The Memoirs of the Wolf-Man', in: M. Gardiner, (ed.), *The Wolf-Man and Sigmund Freud*, Penguin, Harmondsworth, 1973; Jones, *op.cit.*, I, 1953, p.361, II, p.424–5; Sachs, H., *op.cit.*, p.51.

25 Jones, *op.cit.*, I, 1953, p.142.

26 S. Freud, *The Letters of Sigmund Freud*, (1873-1939), ed. E.L. Freud, New York: Basic Books, 1975, p.217.

27 L. Chertok, and R. de Saussure, *Naissance du psychoanalyse, de Messmer à Freud*, Paris: Payot, 1973, p.188–192.

28 J. Breuer and S. Freud, *op.cit.*, p.106.

29 J. Breuer and S. Freud, *op.cit.*, p.171.

30 J. Breuer and S. Freud, *op.cit*, p.155.

31 S. Freud, *Aus den Anfängen der Psychoanalyse, Briefe an Wilhelm Fliess, Abhandlungen und Notizen aus den Jahren 1887-1902*, London: Imago, 1950, p.63.

32 S. Freud, 'Freud's Psycho-Analytic Procedure', (1904), *Standard Edition*, 7:249–54, London: Hogarth Press, 1953, p.250.

33 S. Freud, (1913a), 1958, *op.cit.*, p.131.

34 *ibid.*

35 *ibid.*

36 L. Chertok, and R. de Saussure, *op.cit.*, p. 65 (note).

37 D.W.G. Ploucquet, *Der Arzt: oder über die Ausbildung, die Studien, Pflichten und Sitten, und die Klugheit des Arztes*, Tübingen, 1797, p.201, *(my translation)*.

38 The medical customs of the time are reconstructed here from indications found in various guides to the practice of medicine, following the pioneering example of Norbert Elias, who used manuals of courtly etiquette in his study of the civilizing process *(op.cit.*, 1939). With some modification, his arguments for the validity of this procedure (p.61) also apply in this instance. The medical guides quoted here are of course the products of individual authors, yet these doctors did attempt to convey what was generally considered 'good practice' or 'proper manners' in their professional circle.

39 B. Liehrsch, *(Bilder des ärtzlichen Lebens oder) Die wahre Lebenspolitik des Arztes für alle Verhältnisse*, Berlin, 1842, p.186, *(my translation)*.

40 B. Liehrsch, *op.cit.*, p.187, *(my translation)*.

41 B. Liehrsch, *op.cit.*, p.189, *(my translation)*.

42 S. Freud 'New Introductory Lectures on Psycho-Analysis', (1933), *Standard Edition*, 22:5–182, London: Hogarth Press, 1964.

43 van W.F. Leeuwen, 'Aard en gebruik van psychoanalytische hypothesen', in: *Inval* (1/2), 1971, p.259–276; from the same author, 'Het psychoanalytisch minimum', in: H.P. Cassee, P.E. Boeke and J.T. Barendregt (eds.), *Klinische Psychologie in Nederland*, part I, Van Loghum, Deventer 1973, p.56–79.

44 B. Liehrsch, *op.cit.*, p.186, *(my translation)*.

45 B. Liehrsch, *op.cit.*, p.188, *(my translation)*.

46 W. Hooker, *Physician and Patient; or a practical view of the mutual duties, relations and interests of the medical profession and the community*, (E. Bentley, ed.), London, 1850, p.289.

47 In moral masochism, early anxieties about genital integrity are transposed, at a later age, into similar anxieties with respect to prestige and status. The moral masochist fears being 'belittled' and at the same time refrains from insisting on prompt and equitable tribute, while harbouring fantasies of moral greatness. 'The patient feels himself to be a *unique, exalted person*, an exception superior to his fellow men, a martyr... his original ideas of being powerful and grand- *grand in martyrdom* (J. Lampl-de Groot, *The Development of the Mind: Psychoanalytic Papers on Clinical and Theoretical Problems*, New York: International Universities Press, 1965, p.354). It must be emphasized, however, that this argument does not mean that nineteenth-century doctors were moral masochists in the clinical sense of the term. They found themselves in a social configuration that entailed certain contradictions concerning status and payment. When acting in their professional role they found that a prevalent resolution of these contradictions consisted in a moral masochistic manoeuvre. How individual doctors resolved the many other contradictions in their lives is an entirely different question.

48 S. Wolin, *Politics and vision; continuity and innovation in western political thought*, Boston: Little, Brown & Co., 1960, p.346.

49 N. Elias, *op.cit.*, 140ff.

50 To what extent anti-Semitism in Austria hampered Freud's professional opportunities has become a matter of controversy. J. Gicklhorn and R. Gicklhorn, *Sigmund Freuds akademische Laufbahn im Lichte der Dokumente*, Urban, Vienna/Innsbruck, 1960, have tried to show that Freud was in no way discriminated against in his appointment as a professor. Their study has been vehemently attacked by K.R. Eissler, *Sigmund Freud und die Wiener Universität. Über die Pseudo-Wissenschaftlichkeit der jüngsten Freud-Biographik*, Bern/Stuttgart/Vienna: Huber, 1966.

51 E. Jones, 1953, I, *op.cit.*, p.142.

52 E. Jones, 1953, I, *op.cit.*, p.142–3.

53 For example, S. Freud, (1873-1939), *op.cit.*, p.209, 216; (1887-1902), 1950, *op.cit.*, p.136–7.

54 S. Freud, (1913a), 1958, *op.cit.*, p.131–2.

55 S. Freud, (1913a), 1958, *op.cit.*, p.132.

56 *ibid.*

57 M. Gardiner, *op.cit.*, p.160.

58 S. Freud, (1873-1939), 1975, *op.cit.*, p.235.

59 It is important to distinguish between the technical rules as laid down by Freud in the *Recommendations* and his own actual practice, as it may be gleaned from his case histories, personal notes, correspondence and from patients' memoirs. S.D. Lipton, 'The Advantages of Freud's Technique as Shown in His Analysis of the Rat Man', *International Journal of Psycho-Analysis* (58), p.225–73, has stressed that Freud did not always adhere too strictly to these rules, which have come to be known as 'the classical technique'. My discussion centres on the social figuration within which Freud developed the rules for his practice. How strictly these rules were in fact adhered to by and how closely contemporary psychoanalysts should follow them is a different matter, admirably dealt with by Lipton.

60 S. Freud, (1913a), 1958, *op.cit.*, p.126.

61 *ibid.*

62 B. Liehrsch, *op.cit.*, p.132, *(my translation).*

63 S. Freud, (1913a), 1958, *op.cit.*, p.126–30.

64 Quoted by J. Wortis, *Fragments of an Analysis with Freud*, New York: Simon & Schuster, 1954, p.8.

65 H. Sachs, *op.cit.*, p.89; see also F. Wittels, *Sigmund Freud: His Personality, His Teachings and His School*, New York: Dodd, Mead, 1924, p.35.

66 D. Riesman, 'The Themes of Work and Play in the Structure of Freud's Thought', in: *Individualism Reconsidered and Other Essays*, Glencoe: Free Press, 1954, ascribes to Freud a 'Puritan attitude towards work in general', assuming that he went much further in the direction of 'asceticism' than did most of the members of his class or culture, even if they, too, ascribed to the ideal.

67 B. Liehrsch, *op.cit.*, p.96–7, *(my translation).*

68 S. Freud, 'An Outline of Psycho-Analysis', (1940), *Standard Edition*, 23:144–207, London: Hogarth Press, 1964, p.174.

69 J. Breuer, and S. Freud, *op.cit.*, p.127.

70 *ibid.*, p.160.

71 D.W.G. Ploucquet, *op.cit.*, p.80.

72 B. Liehrsch, *op.cit.*, p.99.

73 L. Chertok and R. de Saussure, *op.cit.*

74 J. Breuer, and S. Freud, *op.cit.*

75 E. Jones, *The Life and Work of Sigmund Freud. Vol. 2: Years of Maturity, 1901-1919*, New York: Basic Books, 1955, mentions many of these unavoidable exceptions to the rule, and P. Roazen *(Brother Animal: The Story of Freud and Tausk*, Harmondsworth: Penguin Books, 1973, p.194), adds a few, among them Anna Freud's analysis with her father. L. Stone, *The Psychoanalytic Situation: An Examination of Its Development and Essential Nature*, New York: International Universities Press, 1961, p.122, speculates that Freud was also 'already groping for a solution' to the problem of terminating the transference when he invited a patient to supper during the final stage of the analysis (as Freud

mentions in a letter to Fliess).

76 S. Freud, (1913a), 1958, *op.cit.*

77 *ibid.*, p.125

78 H.A. van der Sterren, 'Zur Psychoanalytischen Technik', *Jahr. Psychoanal.*, 3:153–173, p.166, comments that conversations with others about the analysis should not be prohibited, but after analysis of the countertransference (e.g., envy toward the third party), such activities by the patient are to be interpreted in the context of the transference (e.g., as attempts to arouse envy in the analyst).

79 E. Jones, 1955, *op.cit.*, p.235.

80 S. Freud, (1912), 1958, *op.cit.*, p.120.

81 S. Freud, (1912), 'The Interpretation of Dreams', (1900), *Standard Edition*, 4 & 5, London: Hogarth Press, 1953, p.100–1.

82 M. Fain, 'De Grondregel', in: *Inval* I (1), Fall 1968, p.24, *(my translation)*.

83 S. Freud, (1912), 1958, *op.cit.*, p.107.

84 L. Stone, *op.cit.*, p.33.

85 R. Schafer, *A new language for psychoanalysis*, New Haven and London: Yale University Press, 1976, p.149.

86 J. Wortis, *op.cit.*

87 S. Freud, (1915), 1958, *op.cit.*, p.165 (in this paper on 'transference-love' the patient is taken to be female).

88 S. Freud, 'Lines of Advance in Psycho-Analytic Therapy', (1919), *Standard Edition*, 17:159–168, London: Hogarth Press, 1955, p.162.

89 S. Freud, (1914b), 1958, *op.cit.*, p.153.

90 H.A. van der Sterren, 'Life Decisions during Analysis', in: *International Journal of Psychoanalysis* 47 (2–3), 1966, p.297.

91 S. Freud, (1914b), 1958, *op.cit.*, p.153.

92 S. Freud, (1915), 1958, *op.cit.*, p.160–8.

93 *ibid.* p.164.

94 *ibid.*, p.166.

95 S. Freud, 'Introductory Lectures on Psycho-analysis', (1916-1917), *Standard Edition*, 15 & 16, London: Hogarth Press, 1963, p.439.

96 S. Freud, (1913a), 1958, *op.cit.*, p.139.

97 J. Habermas, *Erkenntnis und Interesse*, Frankfurt A. M.: Suhrkamp, 1968, 1973, p.284, *(my translation)*.

CHAPTER 5: FROM TROUBLES TO PROBLEMS

1 Cf. my *In Care of the State: Health Care, Education and Welfare in Europe and the USA in the Modern Era*, Oxford/New York: Polity Press/Oxford University Press, 1988, especially chap. 7.

2 Unfortunately, the term has been usurped almost entirely by its connotations 'beyond the physical world'. It is here used in its first meaning, 'of the psyche, or mind', whenever 'mental' seems too bland.

3 Irving K. Zola, 'Healthism and disabling medicalization', in I. Illich

(ed.) *Disabling Professions*, London: Marion Boyars, 1977, pp. 41–68.

4 J. Caplan, 'Lawyers and litigants: a cult reviewed', in I. Illich, *Disabling Professions*, London: Marion Boyas, 1977, pp. 93–110.

5 T. R. Dewar, 'Professionalization of the client', *Social Policy* 8 (4) (1978): 4–9.

6 Cf. Terrence J. Johnson, *Professions and Power*, London: Macmillan, 1972; Eliot Freidson, *Professional Powers: a Study in the Institutionalization of Formal Knowledge*, Chicago and London: University of Chicago Press, 1986.

7 Harold L. Wilensky, 'The professionalization of everyone?' *American Journal of Sociology* 70 (2) (1964): 137–58.

8 Cf. William J. Goode, 'Encroachment, charlatanism, and the emerging profession: psychology, sociology and medicine', *American Sociological Review* 25 (1960): 902–14.

9 Norbert Elias, 'Studies in the genesis of the naval profession', *British Journal of Sociology* 1 (1950): 291–309, p. 292.

10 William E. Henry, John H. Sims, and S. Lee Spray, *The Fifth Profession*, San Francisco: Jossey Bass, 1971.

11 Anselm L. Strauss (ed.) *Psychiatric Ideologies and Institution*, New York: Free Press, 1964, p. 3 (italics).

12 Cees J. Schuyt, K. Groenendijk, and Ben Sloot, *De Weg naar het Recht; een Rechtssociologisch Onderzoek naar de Samenhangen tussen Maatschappelijke Ongelijkheid en Juridische Hulpverlening*, Deventer: Kluwer, 1976.

13 Charles Kadushin, *Why People Go to Psychiatrists*, New York: Atherton, 1969.

CHAPTER 6: THE INITIAL INTERVIEW AS A TASK

1 This study is based on the transcripts of thirty initial interviews which were held in July and August 1975 at the Institute for Multidisciplinary Psychotherapy (IMP) in Amsterdam, Holland. The interviews each took between twenty and sixty minutes and were conducted by seven different interviewing doctors. Office consultations by four general practitioners in Amsterdam and a dozen preliminary interviews conducted by four therapists at an Amsterdam regional institute for ambulatory mental health care, the Dercksen Centre, served as material for comparison and, sometimes, as illustrations. The project was carried out with the assistance of Christien Brinkgreve, Regina van Gelderen, Victor Kense, and Jan Onland.

2 Charles Kadushin, *Why People Go to Psychiatrists*, New York: Atherton, 1969.

3 The letters 'T' and 'C' refer to 'Therapist' and 'Client' respectively; 'D' stands for 'Medical Doctor', 'P' for 'Patient'. The sign '—' indicates that something has been omitted from the original recording, '[ ]' that something has been altered or added; ' . . . ' denotes a pause.

4 Alfred Lorenzer, *Die Wahrheit des Psychoanalytischen Erkenntnis: ein*

historisch-materialistischer Entwurf, Frankfurt am Main: Suhrkamp, 1974, p. 107. (This and following citations from works in languages other than English have been translated by this author.)

5 Herman Argelander, *Das Erstinterview in der Psychotherapie*, Darmstadt: Wissenschaftliches Buchgesellschaft, 1970, p. 18.

6 Sigmund Freud, 'Fragments of an analysis of a case of hysteria' [Dora] (1901, 1905), in: *Standard Edition of the Complete Psychological Works of Sigmund Freud*, vol. 7, London: Hogarth Press, 1951, pp. 7–122, 16–17.

7 The sociolinguistic analysis of conversations has become a vast academic field; a survey of recent developments in the study of therapeutic discourse may be found in Robert L. Russell (ed.) *Language in Psychotherapy: Strategies of Discovery*, New York and London: Plenum, 1987. For an approach that is in some respects similar to the present one, see Kathy Davis, 'The process of problem (re)formulation in psychotherapy', *Sociology of Health and Illness* 8 (1) (March 1986): 44–74.

8 Thomas J. Scheff, 'Negotiating reality: notes on power in the assessment of responsibility', *Social Problems* 16 (1) (1968): 13.

9 C. Th. van Schaik, 'Over het Initiële Interview', *Inval, Tijdschrift voor Psychoanalytici* 1 (1968): 12–13.

10 Eric Heller, 'Psychoanalysis and literature', *Salmagundi* 31 (1975–6): 20.

11 Roy Schafer, *A New Language for Psychoanalysis*, New Haven, CT: Yale University Press, 1976, p. 8.

12 Jacques Lacan, 'Le séminaire sur "La Lettre volée"', *Écrits*, Paris: Éditions du Seuil, 1966, p. 11.

13 The terms have been borrowed from the Dutch novelist Harry Mulisch, *De Verteller Verteld, Kommentaar, Katalogus, Kuriosa en een Katastrofestuk*, Amsterdam: De Bezige Bij, 1971.

14 Ralph R. Greenson, *The Technique and Practice of Psychoanalysis*, vol. I, New York: International Universities Press, 1967, p. 193.

15 The terms are borrowed from Norbert Elias, *What is Sociology?* London: Hutchinson, 1978.

16 Cf. Herman Argelander, *Das Erstinterview in der Psychotherapie*, Darmstadt: Wissenschaftliches Buchgesellschaft, 1970, pp. 55–60, 100.

17 Aaron V. Cicourel, *Cognitive Sociology: Language and Meaning in Social Interaction*, Harmondsworth: Penguin, 1973, p. 59.

18 Ibid., p. 61.

19 Erving Goffman, *Frame Analysis: an Essay on the Organization of Experience*, Cambridge, MA: Harvard University Press, 1974, p. 386.

20 Erving Goffman, 'Alienation from interaction', in J. Laver and S. Hutcheson (eds) *Communication in Face to Face Interaction*, Harmondsworth: Penguin, 1972, p. 348; appeared originally in *Human Relations* 10 (1957).

21 Edwin Thoman, Norman Poulansky, and Jacob Kounin, 'The expected behavior of a potentially helpful person', *Human Relations* 8 (1955): 170.

22 Peter McHugh, *Defining the Situation: the Organization of Meaning in*

Social Interaction, Indianapolis: Bobbs-Merrill, 1968.

23 Cf. Harold Garfinkel, *Studies in Ethnomethodology*, Englewood Cliffs, NJ: Prentice-Hall, 1967; E.T. Hall, 'Silent assumptions in social communication', in J. Laver and S. Hutcheson (eds) *Communication in Face to Face Interaction*, Harmondsworth: Penguin, 1972.

CHAPTER 7: THE POLITICS OF AGORAPHOBIA

1 E. Durkheim, *Le Suicide*, Paris: Presses Universitaires de France, 1930, p. 283.

2 K. Marx and F. Engels, *Manifest der Kommunistischen Partei*, Leipzig: Verlag Philipp Reclam, 1965, p. 37.

3 Cf. J. A. Weijel, *De Mensen Hebben Geen leven (It's No Life for People)*, Haarlem: De Erven Bohn, 1971.

4 Cf. R. Sennett, *The Fall of Public Man: On the Social Psychology of Capitalism*, New York: Vintage, 1978, p. 130.

5 Lyn H. Lofland, *A World of Strangers: Order and Action in Urban Public Space*, New York: Basic Books, 1973, pp. 61–5.

6 J. and A. Romein, *De Lage Landen bij de Zee (The Low Countries by the Sea)*, Utrecht: De Haan, 1940, p. 595.

7 Such as the first woman doctor in the Netherlands, Aletta Jacobs: A. Jacobs, *Herinneringen (Memoirs)*, Nijmegen: SUN, 1924, 1978, p. 73.

8 L. Stratenus, *De Opvoeding der Vrouw: Kleine Handleiding voor Gegoede Standen Bewerkt (The Education of Woman)*, Amsterdam, 1891, p. 82 (my translation).

9 Ibid., p. 84.

10 D. H. Engelberts, *De Goede Toon (The Bon-Ton)*, De Rijp: Van Raven, 1895, p. 287.

11 Cf. C. Amory, *The Proper Bostonians*, New York: Dutton, 1947, pp. 123–30 for nineteenth-century Boston; D. Crow, *The Victorian Woman*, London: Allen & Unwin, 1971, p. 64 for Victorian London.

12 E. Zaretsky, *Capitalism, the Family, and Personal Life*, New York: Harper & Row, 1976, pp. 51ff.

13 Cf. Amory, *The Proper Bostonians*, p. 70; E. C. van de Mandele, *Het Wetboek van Mevrouw Etiquette in 24 Atikelen (The Code of Manners of Madam Etiquette)*, Utrecht, 1897, p. 133, for descriptions of incidents in which policemen decided that the lady in question had brought a degrading exchange upon herself simply by being there.

14 Sennett, *The Fall of Public Man*, p. 217.

15 Stratenus, *De Opvoeding der Vrouw*, pp. 94–5.

16 C. Smith-Rosenberg, 'The hysterical woman: sex roles and role conflict in 19th century America', *Social Research* (1972): 652–78; J. S. and R. M. Haller, *The Physician and Sexuality in America*, University of Illinois Press, 1974; R. Statow, 'Where has all the hysteria gone?', *Psychoanalytic Review* (Winter 1979/80): 463–77.

17 Cf. N. Elias and J. L. Scotson, *The Established and the Outsiders*, London: Cass, 1965; and Elias' theoretical introduction to the Dutch edition,

De Gevestigden en de Buitenstaanders, Utrecht: Aula/Spectrum, 1976.

18 Cf. H. A. Rappard, *Goede Manieren: Wat men Doen en Laten Moet in het Dagelijks Leven (Good Manners)*, Haarlem, 1920, p. 110.

19 E.g., A. Querido, 'Gedachten over de Evolutie van het Ziekenhuis' ('Reflections on the Evolution of the Hospital'), *De Gids* 136 (1973): 619–28.

20 C. Wouters, 'Onderhandelen met De Swaan', *De Gids* 142 (1979): 510–21. Unpublished English version, 'Negotiating with De Swaan', paper presented at British Sociological Association, Conference on 'The Civilizing Process and Figurational Sociology', Oxford, 5–6 Jan. 1980.

21 G. H. Jansen, *De Eeuwige Kroeg: Hoofdstukken uit de Geschiedenis van het Openbaar Lokaal (The Perpetual Pub: Chapters from the History of the Public House)*, Meppel Boom, 1976; J. M. Fuchs and W. J. Simons, *De Reizendehens: Openbaar Vervoer in Grootmoeders Tijd (Travelling man: Public Transport in Grandmother's Time)*, Amsterdam: Ruys, 1968; F. Rauers, *Kulturgeschichte der Gaststätte*, vol. 2, Berlin, 1941, p. 1367; Jacobs, *Herinneringen*, p. 72; J. Kloos-Reyneke von Stuwe, *Gevoelsbeschaving: Handboek voor Huis en Gezelschapsleven (Sense of Manners)*, Rotterdam, 1927, p. 125.

22 C. Westphal, 'Die Agoraphobie: Eine neuropathische Erscheinung', *Archiv für Psychiatrie und Nervenkrankheiten* 3 (1872): 138–61; E. Weiss, *Agoraphobia in the Light of Ego Psychology*, New York: Grune and Stratton, 1964.

23 Westphal, 'Die Agoraphobie', pp. 139, 143–4, 147.

24 Ibid., p. 141.

25 Ibid., p. 160, my translation.

26 B. Brun, *De l'Agoraphobie: Ses Rapports avec les Lésions Auriculaires*, Lyon, 1899, my translation.

27 *Handbuch der Psychologie*, vol. 3 1. Halbband, Göttingen, 1977, p. 349, my translation. Cf. A. M. Nicholi, *The Harvard Guide to Modern Psychiatry*, Belknap/Harvard University Press, 1978, p. 186.

28 *Handbuch*, p. 351.

29 Figures quoted by O. van Maanen and C. Starren, *Inventarisatie van Test-Materiaal en van een Aantal Sociale Kenmerken van Fobische Patiënten (Inventory of Test Material and Some Social Characteristics of Phobical Patients)*, Amsterdam: University of Amsterdam, Psychology Laboratory, 1976.

30 Cf. also T. Tuinier, 'Vermijding als Modelgedrag. Over de Kulturele Kontekst van Fobieën' ('Avoidance as a Model of Behaviour'), *Bulletin Persoonlijkheidsleer*, 7 (1979): 64–104.

31 S. Freud, 'Inhibition, Symptom and Anxiety', *Standard Edition*, vol. 20, London: Hogarth Press, p. 109

32 Ibid., p. 128.

33 H. Deutsch, 'The genesis of agoraphobia', *International Journal of Psycho-Analysis* 10 (1929): 51–69.

34 Westphal, 'Die Agoraphobie', p. 160. Cf. the descriptions of Manzoni's panic at losing his wife in the crowd and his subsequent

agoraphobia (1810, 1815) in Weiss, *Agoraphobia*, pp. 98ff.

35 J. T. Barendregt and A. A. M. Bleeker, 'Een Geval van Agorafobie bij een Esoforie' ('A Case of Agoraphobia with Esophoria'), *De Psycholoog* 8 (1973): 48, my translation.

36 W. F. Fry, 'The marital context of an anxiety syndrome', *Family Process* 1 (1962): 251.

37 R. Moulton, 'Sexual conflicts of contemporary woman', in E. G. Witenberg (ed.) *Interpersonal Explorations in Psychoanalysis*, New York: Basic Books, 1973, p. 196.

38 C. Wouters, 'Informalisation and the civilizing process', in *Human Figurations: Essays for Norbert Elias*, Amsterdam: Amsterdams Sociologisch Tijdschrift, 1977, pp. 437-55.

39 N. Elias, *Uber den Prozess der Zivilisation* (1939), 2 vols, Bern: Francke Verlag, 1969. Cf.Wouters, 'Informalisation', for an English discussion of Elias' views on the subject.

40 Ibid., II, p. 312.

41 J. C. Chesnais, *Les Morts violents en France depuis 1826: comparaisons internationales*, Paris: Presses Universitaires de France, 1976, pp. 210, 298.

42 *Zeventig jaren Statistiek in Tijdreeksen 1899-1969 (Statistical Timeseries)*, Centraal Bureau voor de Statistiek, 's-Gravenhage: Staatsuitgeverij, 1970, p. 160; *Sociale Atlas van de Vrouw (Social Atlas of Women)*, J. L. Meyer, Sociaal en Cultureel Plan-bureau, S. C. P.-cahier, 11, 's-Gravenhage: Staatsuitgeverij, 1977, 200; *Statistisch Zakboek (Statistical Vademecum)*, Centraal Bureau voor de Statistiek, 's-Gravenhage: Staatsuitgeverij, 1978; J. P. S. Fiselier, 'Omvang en Beweging van de Geweldscriminaliteit', in *Geweld in Onze Samenleving (Violence in Our Society)*, 's-Gravenhage: Staatsuitgeverij, 1978, pp. 25-44.

43 J. Selosse, 'Statistical aspects of violent crime', in *Violence in Society (Collected Studies in Criminological Research*, Vol. XI), Strasburg: Council of Europe, 1974, pp. 23, 28.

44 L. Lenke, 'Criminal policy and public opinions towards crimes of violence', ibid., pp. 60-124; see also Fiselier, *Violence in our Society*, 1978.

45 L. Chertok and R. Saussure, *Naissance du Psychanalyste*, Paris: Payot, 1973, p. 128.

46 M. Herr, *Dispatches*, New York: Knopf, 1977.

47 Riesman's 'antagonistic cooperation': D. Riesman (with N. Glazer and R. Denney), *The Lonely Crowd*, New Haven, CT: Yale University Press, 1963, p. 81.

48 J. A. A. van Doorn calls this the transition to the late-organizational stage: *Sociologie van de Organisatie (Sociology of the Organization)*, Leiden: Stenfert Kroese, 1956, pp. 197ff.

49 B and J. Ehrenreich, 'The professional-managerial class', *Radical America* 2 (1977): 7-31.

50 C. Lasch, *Haven in a Heartless World: the Family Besieged*, New York: Basic Books, 1977.

51 Cf. Chapter 5.

52 L. D. Nachman, 'The solitude of the heart: personality and democratic culture', part of 'A symposium: Christopher Lasch and *The Culture of Narcissism*', *Salmagundi* (Fall 1979): 180.
53 Wouters, 'Informalisation'.
54 Elias, vol. II, p. 418.
55 Wouters, 'Informalisation'.
56 T. W. Adorno, *Eingriffe: Neun Kritische Modelle*, Frankfurt am Main: Suhrkamp Verlag, 1963, p. 100, my translation.
57 Ibid., p. 101.
58 Ibid.
59 H. Marcuse, *One-dimensional Man: Studies in the Ideology of Advanced Industrial Society*, Boston: Beacon, 1968, p. 264.
60 E. Kris, *Selected Papers of Ernst Kris*, New Haven, CT: Yale University Press, 1975, p. 264.
61 P. R. Slater, *The Pursuit of Loneliness: American Culture at the Breaking Point*, Boston: Beacon, 1970, p. 92.
62 R. Reihe, *Seksualiteit en Klassenstrijd (Sexuality and Class Struggle)*, Amsterdam: Meulenhoff, 1969, p. 86.
63 R. C. Calogeras and F. X. Schupper, 'Shifts in defence and certain consequences for analytic technique', *American Imago* 28 (1971): 53ff.
64 Sennett, *The Fall of Public Man*, p. 325.
65 Ibid., pp. 326–7.
66 S. Freud, 'The Future of an Illusion', *Standard Edition*, vol. 21, London: Hogarth Press, 1927, p. 43.
67 C. Lasch, *The Culture of Narcissism: American Life in an Age of Diminishing Expectations*, New York: Norton, 1978, p. 25.
68 Lasch, *Haven*, p. 183.
69 Ibid., p. 189.
70 Ibid., p. xvi.

Acknowledgements

The contributions of Yvonne van der Doelen, research assistant, are gratefully acknowledged, as are the suggestions by the members of the 'Postdoctural Colloquium over de Sociologie van de Psychotherapie' and of the 'Psychoanalytisch Dispuut'.

Earlier publication of this essay provoked some intense polemics. The reader is referred to John Alt, 'Authority, reason, and the civilizing process: a polemic against de Swaan', pp. 387–405; my 'A rejoinder to Mr Alt's critique', pp. 407–11, and Alvin W. Gouldner, 'Doubts about the uselessness of men and the meaning of the civilizing process', pp. 413–18. All essays appeared in *Theory and Society* 9 (3) (May 1981).

CHAPTER 8: JEALOUSY AS A CLASS PHENOMENON

1 The most complete review of the literature is Helmut Schoeck, *Envy: a Theory of Social Behaviour*, New York: Harcourt, Brace & World, 1966.

Shoeck makes much of the distinction between 'envy' and 'jealousy', although he admits that it hardly operates in English usage. Crucial to him is Simmel's argument that 'the expression "jealousy" should be restricted to an asset upon which there is a legitimate claim' (p. 95). But this is very awkward in psychology (or sociology, for that matter), since legitimating emotions, i.e. 'rationalizing' them, is an aspect of being emotional, one in which the envious may succeed as well as the jealous. It is like trying to distinguish empirically between 'legitimate' and 'unreasonable' rage.

2 Thus, in common usage, 'jealousy' denotes meanings which 'envy' does not: if envy could be envious it would envy jealousy its additional connotations, whereas jealousy might jealously guard its connotations from envy usurping them.

3 'Whoever possesses something that is at once valuable and fragile is afraid of other people's envy, in so far as he projects on to them the envy he would have felt in their place.' Sigmund Freud, 'The "Uncanny"' (1919), in *Standard Edition of the Complete Psychological Works of Sigmund Freud*, vol. 17, London: Hogarth Press, 1955, pp. 219–56, p. 240.

4 Cf. N. Elias and J. L. Scotson, *The Established and the Outsiders: a Sociological Inquiry into Community Problems*, London: Cass & Co., 1965; especially chap. 7, 'Observations on gossip'.

5 Cf. for example P. Hennipman, 'De Verdeling in de Paretiaanse Welvaartstheorie', in P. J. Eijgelshoven and L.J. van Gemerden (eds) *Inkomensverdeling en Openbare Financiën: Opstellen voor Jan Pen*, Utrecht/Antwerp: Het Spectrum, 1981, pp. 128–70. Although such 'utility interdependencies' are an important addition to economic theory, the *ad hoc* assumption of altruistic preferences seems to be too sudden a departure from the gist of economic doctrine to provide a satisfactory account of either philanthropy or egalitarian income transfers. The motivation of the richer in accepting more equal distributions must not be sought in their sympathy with the poor, but rather in their desire to ward off the dangers of discontent among them. Cf. my 'Armenzorg als Collectieve Actie; Naar een Sociogenetisch Paradigma van het Collectiviseringsproces', in P. K. Keizer and J. Soeters, *Economie, Sociologie en Psychologie: Visies op Integratie*, Assen/Maastricht: Van Gorcum, 1987, pp. 103–21; cf. also the discussion of poor relief at the parish level (chap. 2.3) in my *In Care of the State: State Formation and Collectivization of Health Care, Education and Welfare in Europe and America in the Modern Era*, New York/Cambridge: Oxford University Press/Polity Press, 1988.

6 Similar preferences have been observed, e.g. by Adam Szirmai, 'Equality Observed: a Study of Attitudes Towards Income Inequality', Dissertation, University of Groningen, 1986, pp. 212, 347. Respondents frequently showed 'downward generosity': they appeared to support more egalitarian income distributions under which they themselves would be worse off. However, they not only produced the 'socially desirable' response, but often they also

underestimated their position in the distribution and erroneously believed that they would profit from the re-distribution.

Albert O. Hirschman has observed similar altruistic evaluations, this time as 'upward generosity', when people in developing countries seem to rejoice in the newly acquired wealth of others, as long as they take it as a sign of more prosperous times to come for themselves also: the 'tunnel effect'. Cf. 'The changing tolerance for income inequality in the course of economic development', in Hirschman, *Essays in Trespassing*, Cambridge: Cambridge University Press, 1982.

7 Some economic goods also can be enjoyed only on condition that others have less or none of them. Fred Hirsch (*Social Limits to Growth*, Cambridge, Mass.: Harvard University Press, 1976) mentions as an example of such 'positional' goods, country houses in an urban society. Other products are so designed that their pleasure resides not in their performance *per se* but in their ostentatious superiority over the products others employ. Theoretically, everyone could have a sports car or a mink coat, but when such total saturation is achieved these goods lose their prime attraction: they are essentially not positive but comparative and superlative products.

8 Auguste Comte, *Cathéchisme Positiviste*, 10th dialogue, Paris: Garnier, p. 310; quoted by Henri Hatzfeld, *Du Paupérisme à la Sécurité Sociale, 1850–1940*, Paris: Colin, 1971, p. 314 (transl. AdS).

9 Cf. chap. 6 of my *In Care of the State*, New York/Cambridge: Oxford University Press/Polity Press, 1988, especially chap. 6.

10 Cf. Crossick in Geoffrey Crossick and Heinz-Gerhard Haupt (eds) *Shopkeepers and Master Artisans in Nineteenth-Century Europe*, London: Methuen, 1984, p. 9: 'We find the unique feature of the petite bourgeoisie in the fact that its livelihood is derived both from its capital and its own labour . . . it is the former that sets it apart from the proletariat, the latter from the bourgeoisie . . . any labour it hires is on a very limited scale.'

11 Hatzfeld, *Du Paupérisme à la Sécurité Sociale, 1850–1940*, Paris: Colin, 1971.

12 R. Hay, 'The British business community, social insurance and the German example', in W. J. Mommsen (ed.) *The Emergence of the Welfare State in Britain and Germany*, London: Croom Helm, 1981, pp. 109–32.

13 Cf. Francis G. Castles, *The Working Class and Welfare; Reflections on the Political Development of the Welfare State in Australia and New Zealand*, London: Allen & Unwin, 1985.

14 E.g.: 'In these circumstances the finely struck balance of envy and resentment not only separated some petits bourgeois from others; it could co-exist within one individual. It is evidence of this kind which has led some to talk of the self-hate of the petite bourgeoisie.' D. Blackbourn, 'Between resignation and volatility: the German petite bourgeoisie in the nineteenth century', in G. Crossick and H-G. Haupt, (eds) *Shopkeepers and Master Artisans in Nineteenth-Century Europe*, London: Methuen, 1984, p. 47.

15 Payroll taxes were sometimes paid by workers, sometimes by

employers, most often by both; sometimes the state added its part. In practice, the formal division of shares between employers and workers did not make all that much difference, since each party would try to make the other pay for it by adjusting wages, and since the parties together would try to compensate for insurance fees by increasing prices. The payroll tax functioned in fact as a frozen component of wages, earmarked for compulsory, collective saving and to be disbursed at times of income loss.

16 E.g., the English unemployment insurance of 1911 initially covered only heavy industry and the building trades; the French 'insurance sociale' of 1930 excluded agrarian workers; the Dutch Workmen's Compensation Act of 1901 excluded agrarian workers (cf. my *In Care of the State*, New York/Cambridge: Oxford University Press/Polity Press, 1988, chap. 6).

17 Cf. especially the contributions by Crossick in G. Crossick and H-G. Haupt (eds) *Shopkeepers and Master Artisans in Nineteenth-Century Europe*, London: Methuen, 1984.

18 Blackbourn in G. Crossick and H-G. Haupt (eds) *Shopkeepers and Master Artisans in Nineteenth-Century Europe*, London: Methuen, 1984, p. 48.

19 Cf. Ali de Regt, *Arbeidersgezinnen en Beschavingsarbeid*, Amsterdam: Arbeiderspers, 1984.

20 Cf. Norbert Elias, *The Civilizing Process*, vol. 2: *Power and Civility* (1939, 1969), Oxford/New York: Blackwell/Pantheon, 1982.

21 Cf. Peter Gay, 'On the bourgeoisie: a psychological interpretation', in John Merriman (ed.) *Consciousness and Class Experience in Nineteenth-Century Europe*, New York/London: Holmes & Meyer, 1979, pp. 187–203: 'nineteenth century public debate, letters to the newspapers abound in such self-serving reproaches: it is the intemperance of the poor that keeps them poor, not the harshness and the acquisitiveness of their masters' (p. 199).

22 Cf. Samuel H. Popkin, *The Rational Peasant: the Political Economy of Rural Society in Vietnam*, Berkeley, CA: University of California Press, 1979.

23 On the consequences of inflation and economic crisis on the political attitudes of the small bourgeoisie in Europe see Charles S. Maier, *Recasting Bourgeois Europe: Stabilization in France, Germany, and Italy in the Decade after World War I*, Princeton, NJ: Princeton University Press, 1975.

24 Crossick in G. Crossick and H-G. Haupt (eds) *Shopkeepers and Master Artisans in Nineteenth-Century Europe*, London: Methuen, 1984, p. 79.

25 Cf. Crossick, in ibid., p. 21.

26 Blackbourn in ibid., p. 44.

27 Frank Bechhofer and Brian Elliott, 'Petty property: the survival of a moral economy', in Frank Bechhofer and Brian Elliott (eds) *The Petite Bourgeoisie*, New York: St Martin's Press, 1981, pp. 182–200, p. 197.

28 Quoted by Crossick in G. Crossick and H-G. Haupt (eds) *Shopkeepers and Master Artisans in Nineteenth-Century Europe*, London: Methuen,

1984, p. 263.
29 Cf. Emma Verhey and Gerard van Westerloo, 'De Pont van Kwart over Zeven', in *Ons Soort Mensen*, Amsterdam: Raamgracht, 1984.

CHAPTER 9: INTIMATE RELATIONS AND DOMESTIC ARRANGEMENTS

1 'Among the occurrences which recur again and again in the youthful history of neurotics – which are scarcely ever absent – there are a few of particular importance, which also deserve on that account, I think, to be brought in greater prominence than the rest. As specimens of this class I will enumerate these: observation of parental intercourse, seduction by an adult and threat of being castrated.' Sigmund Freud, '23 Lecture: The Path to the Formation of Symptoms', *The Complete Introductory Lectures on Psychoanalysis*, New York: Norton, 1966, pp. 368–9.
2 Ibid. Freud is aware that without much foreknowledge the scene remains entirely unintelligible, as the lovers' bodies protect their private parts from sight. The cited sentence continues: 'and the possibility cannot be rejected that he will be able to understand and react to the impression *in retrospect*', ibid., p. 369.
3 As a matter of fact, Freud appears to have had his first glimpse of his mother's nakedness in the crammed environment of a train compartment at the age of four; cf. Sigmund Freud, *The Origins of Psycho-Analysis: Letters to Wilhelm Fliess, Drafts and Notes: 1887–1902*, New York: Basic Books, 1954, p. 219. See also Peter Gray's comments on this key episode, *The Bourgeois Experience: Victoria to Freud*, Oxford: Oxford University Press, 1984, pp. 10–16.
4 Ibid., pp. 267–8.
5 Cf. Norbert Elias, *The Court Society*, Oxford/New York: Blackwell/Pantheon, 1983, pp. 41–65.
6 'This family way, both in public and in private, is the object of a *mise en scène* with more or less precise rules. Among a bourgeoisie haunted by the memory of the court, these are pushed to the extremes' (transl. AdS). This refers to France during the July monarchy. Michelle Perrot, 'La vie de famille', in: Philippe Ariès and Georges Duby (eds) *Histoire de la vie privée;* vol. IV: *De la Révolution à la Grande Guerre*, Paris: Editions du Seuil, 1987.
7 Cf. Michelle Perrot, 'Figures et rôles', in Philippe Ariès and Georges Duby, ibid., pp. 182–3.
8 Cf. Jean-Louis Flandrin, *Familles, Parenté, Maison, Sexualité dans l'Ancienne Société*, Paris: Editions du Seuil, 1976, p. 97.
9 Cf. Allain Collomp, 'Familles, habitations et cohabitations', in Philippe Ariès and Georges Duby (eds) *Histoire de la Vie Privée;* vol. III: *De la Renaissance aux Lumières*, Paris: Seuil, 1987, pp. 501–41.
10 Cf. Heidi Rosenbaum, *Formen der Familie: Untersuchungen zum Zusammenhang von Familienverhältnissen, Sozialstruktur und Sozialem*

Wandel in der deutschen Gesellschaft des 19. Jahrhunderts, Frankfurt am
Main: Suhrkamp: 1982, p. 110.
11 'Each one is under the glance of the other.' Michelle Perrot,
'Manières d'Habiter' in Philippe Ariès and Georges Duby (eds)
Histoire de la Vie Privée, vol. IV: *De la Révolution à la Grande Guerre,* Paris:
Editions du Seuil, pp. 307–22.
12 For a more extensive discussion of the lack of domestic privacy among
the nineteenth-century urban poor and of the mutual vexation this
caused among middle-class families who lived among them, cf. my *In
Care of the State,* op. cit. 1988, chap. 4, especially pp. 118–28, which also
contain references to the literature on the subject.
13 Cf. Ornest Ranum, 'Les Refugés de l'intimité', in Philippe Ariès and
Georges Duby (eds) *Histoire de la Vie Privée,* vol. IV, pp. 211–65.
14 Cf. Donald J. Olsen, *The City as a Work of Art: London, Paris, Vienna,* New
Haven, CT: Yale University Press, 1986.
15 Cf. Rémy Butler and Patrice Noisette, *De la Cité Ouvrière au Grand
Ensemble: La Politique Capitaliste du Logement Social 1815–1975,* Paris:
Maspéro, 1977; John Burnett, *A Social History of Housing 1815–1970,*
Newton Abbot: David & Charles, 1978.
16 Cf. Gleichmann on bedrooms and sleeping.
17 Cf. Peter R. Gleichmann, 'Die Verhaüslichung Körperlicher
Verrichtungen', in P. R. Gleichmann, J. Goudsblom, and H. Korte
(eds) *Materialien zur Norbert Elias' Zivilisationstheorie,* Frankfurt:
Suhrkamp, 1976, pp. 254–78; also Peter R. Gleichmann, 'Städte
Reinigen und Geruchlos Machen, Menschliche Körperentleerungen,
ihre Geräte und ihre Verhaüslichung', in Hermann Sturm (ed.)
Ästhetik und Umwelt, Tübingen: Gunter Narr, 1979; Roy Palmer, *The
Water Closet: a New History,* Newton Abbot: David & Charles, 1973;
Lawrence Wright, *Clean and Decent: the History of the Bathroom and the
Water Closet,* London: Routledge & Kegan Paul, 1960.
18 Michelle Perrot, 'Figures et rôles', in Philippe Ariès and G. Duby,
Histoire de la Vie Privée, vol. 4: *De la Révolution à la Grande Guerre,* pp.
121–91, p. 178. Cf. also Anne Martin-Fugier, *Les Bonnes.*
19 Not too low, of course, to be implied in intimate affairs with the lord
or the sons of the house.
20 The impermeability of the older children's 'backstage areas' to
parental scrutiny continues to be a major area of domestic conflict.
One day the history of masturbation and teenage petting must be
rewritten in terms of doors and door locks, and subsequently of cars,
car keys, and parking lots. It might just be that the great late
nineteenth-century masturbation scare occurred when an increasing
number of boys in puberty no longer slept in the same room as their
parents, or under supervision in school dormitories, but were 'out of
control' in their own bedroom.
21 'Excretion obsesses the urban imagination,' writes Corbin, about the
nineteenth-century bourgeoisie, noting a lowering of the 'threshold
of olfactory tolerance' in terms much reminiscent of Elias' description
of the general, long-term decrease of the 'threshold of embarrass-

ment', which he considers to be one aspect of the civilizing process. Cf. Alain Corbin, *Le Miasme et la Jonquille; l'Odorat et l'Imaginaire Social, 18e–19e siècles*, Paris: Aubier, 1982, p. 169.

22 Edward C. Banfield, *The Moral Basis of a Backward Society*, New York: Free Press, 1958.

23 The most explicit and succinct discussion of the theory may be found in Norbert Elias, *The Civilizing Process*, vol. 2, *State Formation and Civilization* (1939, 1969), Oxford: Blackwell, 1982 (also published with the subtitle: *Power and Civility*, New York: Pantheon, 1982), Part 2: 'Synopsis/Toward a Theory of the Civilizing Process', pp. 229–336.

24 Equally, the secluded layout of the consulting room and the sequence of separate office hours provide the material preconditions for the achievement of intimacy between doctor and patient, especially in psychotherapy.

CHAPTER 10: THE SURVIVORS' SYNDROME

1 Hannah Arendt, *Eichmann in Jerusalem*, New York: Viking, 1962.

2 J.P. van Praag, 'Background, problems and possibilities of treatment in cases of extreme stress', and N. Boeken, 'Psycho-social care of victims of persecution in the Netherlands', both in *Israel-Netherlands Symposium on the Impact of Persecution* (Jerusalem, 16–24 Oct. 1977), Rijswijk, 1979. See also the bibliography prepared by the Werk-en Adviescollege, *Interim-rapport*, Vol. IV, Feb. 1977; and Martin S. Bergmann and Milton E. Jucovy (eds) *Generations of the Holocaust*, New York: Basic Books, 1982.

3 E.g. Van Praag, ibid., p. 12.

4 J. Bastiaans, 'Control of aggression and psycho-therapy', in *Israel-Netherlands Symposium*, ibid., p. 31. Bastiaans concludes his doctoral dissertation with a note of warning to professionally trained listeners, medical doctors: 'Nowhere more than in this field, where the significance of emotogenic factors is realized on the psychic and somatic plane, there exists the danger of denial, repression, underestimation and over-estimation of the central problems by the investigators themselves. Because of the aforementioned, medical judgment of these problems may remain incomplete or be falsely influenced.' J. Bastiaans, *Psychosomatische Gevolgen van Onderdrukking en Verzet*, Amsterdam: Noord-Hollandsche Uitgeversmaatschappij, 1957, p. 472.

5 About these 'myths', ensuring the survivors' silence, cf. the excellent study by Yael Danieli, 'The treatment and prevention of long-term effects and intergenerational transmission of victimization: a lesson from Holocaust survivors and their children', in Charles R. Figley, *Trauma and its Wake: the Study and Treatment of Post-traumatic Stress Disorder*, New York: Brunner/Mazel, 1985, p. 298.

6 This is the delicate question adopted as the core of psychotherapeutic attention in the treatment of survivors of concentration camps by J.

Spanjaard, 'De Rol van het Zelfgevoel bij Concentratiekamp-gevoigen', *Tijdschrift voor Psychotherapie,* 5(6), 1979.

7 Alexander and Margarete Mitscherlich, *The Inability to Mourn: Principles of Collective Behavior,* New York: Grove Press, 1975.

8 Bruno Bettelheim, *Surviving and Other Essays,* London: Thames & Hudson (Knopf), 1979.

9 Terms used to denote the victims and the survivors both reflect and shape the attitudes and demeanour of their contemporaries. Sometimes, in religious ceremonies and public commemorations, words such as 'martyrs' and 'heroes' were used but they did not gain wide acceptance, although in later years the term 'holocaust' did, especially in the United States. More striking is it to note how public spokesmen are at a loss for words to denote the victims without alienating any of the survivors or dependants.

10 Theodor W. Adorno, *Minima Moralia: Reflections from a Damaged Life,* London and New York: Schocken, 1978, p. 55.

11 E. A. Cohen, 'Het Post-Concentratiekamp Syndroom: een "Disaster"-Syndroom', *Nederlands Tijdschrift voor Geneeskuncie* 116 (38) (16 Sept. 1972), quotes evidence on the fact that among concentration camp inmates from Norway who did receive Red Cross parcels mortality was 8%, as compared to 45% among those who did not.

On the attitudes of the various European nations from where Jews were deported and on the effects of these attitudes upon the execution of Nazi extermination policy, cf. Hannah Arendt, ibid.

12 'Violence: a Neglected Mode of Behavior', in Bettelheim, ibid.

13 Keilson, after an extensive statistical and clinical investigation into 2,000 cases of Jewish war orphans in the Netherlands, concludes that children with a relatively favourable 'traumatic sequence' during the war years, but an unfavourable-sequence during the immediate post-war years (difficulties with foster-parents, contested guardianship), showed a less favourable development than the children whose wartime experience had been especially unfavourable, but whose experiences immediately after the war were relatively less traumatic. Hans Keilson, *Sequentielle Traumatisierung bei Kindern. Deskriptiv-klinische und quantifizierend-statistische follow-up Untersuchung zum Schicksal der jüdischen Kriegswaisen in den Niederländen* (with Herman R. Sarphatie), Stuttgart: F. Enke, 1979, p. 444.

14 Martin S. Bergman, 'Reflections on the psychological and social functions of remembering the Holocaust', *Psychoanalytic Inquiry,* 5 (1) (1985): 9–20, uses the term 'collective sublimation'.

INDEX